The quest for a radical profession

Social service careers and political ideology

David Wagner

Introduction by Richard Cloward and Frances Fox Piven

UNIVERSITY
PRESS OF
AMERICA

Lanham • New York • London

Copyright © 1990 by
University Press of America®, Inc.
4720 Boston Way
Lanham, Maryland 20706

3 Henrietta Street
London WC2E 8LU England

Library of Congress Cataloging-in-Publication Data

Wagner, David.
The quest for a radical profession : social service careers and
political ideology / David Wagner.
p.   cm.
Includes bibliographical references.
1. Social workers—United States.   2. Radicalism—United States.
I. Title.
HV40.8.U6W34   1990   361.3'2'02373—dc20   90–11978 CIP
7/3/7
ISBN 0–8191–7750–4 (alk. paper)
ISBN 0–8191–7751–2 (pbk. : alk. paper)

 The paper used in this publication meets the minimum requirements of
American National Standard for Information Sciences—Permanence
of Paper for Printed Library Materials, ANSI Z39.48–1984.

To Marcia

without whose help and support,
this book would not have been possible.

ACKNOWLEDGEMENTS

Like most books, this work would not have been possible without the help of many people. However, not liking the style of thanking the whole world and losing the most critical in the process, I will keep my acknowledgements brief.

First, and most importantly, this study would not have been possible without the enthusiastic participation and cooperation of the unnamed subjects, who not only gave extensively of their time, but were willing to risk exposure of their personal and political lives at a time of political conservatism. I thank them for their trust and hope the material in the study accurately reflects on their lives and advances the principles for which they stand.

This book began as a doctoral dissertation, and I was blessed to work with three people who were intellectually stimulating, creative, and emotionally supportive, a rare occurrence for a doctoral committee. Michael Brown helped me conceptualize this study, supported me strongly in pursuing a controversial subject, and was the strongest advocate for my turning my work into a book. I owe tremendous intellectual debts to Irwin Epstein who years before had pursued a similar line of inquiry to mine. He encouraged a new approach to the question of radicalism and professionalism and continually helped me ground my work in the theoretical literature. Paul Montagna provided me with a great deal of my initial interest in the sociology of work and the professions, beginning with a seminar I took with him in the Fall of 1984. Paul, like Irwin, provided intellectual guidance and a strong supportive climate.

Marcia B. Cohen lived through the events of this book as a participant in the events described, as the person with whom ideas, interpretations, and written drafts were always shared, and as the person who lived through the ups and downs of writing and publishing a book.

A number of people were extremely helpful to me

over the years in reading my manuscript, advising me as to style and content, and helping me with the world of publishing. I want to thank in particular Mimi Abramovitz, Paul Betz, Joel Blau, Richard Cloward, Evelyn Ehrlich, David Forbes, Don Matson, and Ivan Syzelani. Finally, the University of Southern Maine provided me with a summer fellowship to help revise this book, and the editors and reviewers of *Social Work* and *Social Service Review* provided me with helpful comments in publishing articles from this study.

CONTENTS

INTRODUCTION
by

Richard A. Cloward
Columbia University

and

Frances Fox Piven
City University of New York

In this fascinating account of the surge and decline of radical thought and activities by social workers since the 1960s, David Wagner has contributed greatly to our understanding of the impact of large-scale cycles of protest in American society on the profession of social work. Two implications of his work struck us in particular.

One is the essential isolation in which radical social workers have found themselves as these cycles of protest ebb. The cycles begin with mass unrest and the outbreak of protest movements. The 1930s gave rise to the greatest movement of the unemployed in American history, together with the greatest industrial strike wave. And the postwar black movement, by the 1960s, had generated a tidal wave of direct action campaigns and urban rioting. At these moments, professional idealism flowers, expectations for progressive change spiral, and some fraction of social workers, especially entrants to the profession, think they see a certain identity and linkage between the profession itself and the mass movements of the period, thus suggesting that the occupation of social work can be an important vehicle for social change. Indeed, a kind of radical millenarism takes hold in sectors of the profession. But millennial hopes are always disappointed, as the inevitable ebbing of mass unrest confirms.

Still, there is something about the end of protest cycles in the American experience that has

ix

been uniquely awful for the left, and David Wagner's research highlights the source. It is the condition of extreme marginality experienced by the left. This sense of isolation pervades the interviews reported in this book. Once mass movements subsided, radical social workers felt stranded, thrown back on their own resources, compelled one-by-one to make individual decisions as how best to survive in a professional and political climate grown inhospitable to their values and aspirations. One mode of adaptation -- a major focus of this book -- has been to band together in radical groupings of one kind or another, seeking solace and support, and a sense that there are others ready to stand fast despite broad reactionary trends.

There is no other western industrial democracy in which the political left has been so isolated. There have been similar cycles of protest elsewhere, to be sure, and similar periods of political reaction. But there have been political party vehicles that provided continued linkages between left intellectuals and professionals, and mass working-class constituencies. Here, by contrast, those linkages only develop when mass movements erupt. And since mass movements are always episodic, it is marginality that has made up the larger part of the radical social worker's political fate.

Why it was, on the eve of industrialization, that the United States followed a course of political development so different than elsewhere in the industrialized West is a question constantly debated. For our part, we think it would be hard to overestimate the impact on party formation of the broad disenfranchising movement that overtook the American democracy in the latter decades of the 19th century and early decades of the 20th. Using literacy tests, longterm residence requirements, poll taxes, and a cumbersome system of periodic personal voter registration requirements, southern plantation elites succeeded in driving turnout down from an average of 67% in the presidential elections during that latter half of the 19th century to a mere 19% in 1924, which meant that only upper-stratum whites had access to the ballot. And by largely similar measures, northern industrialists drove turnout down from an average of 83% to 55%, with the industrial immigrant working-class the most deterred from voting. Thus did southern planters and northern industrialists shield themselves from threats posed by populist dirt farmers, blacks, and insurgent industrial workers.

The broad electoral realignment and the rise of mass protest movements -- especially in interaction, since movements politicize voters and voting numbers protect movements -- ought to have produced a class-based party system in the 1930s. In some measure, the party of the New Deal did represent the working class. But it fell far short of being a labor party. Voting restrictions kept northern working-class voting levels lower than they would otherwise have been, and restrictions in the South continued to keep blacks and most poor whites from voting at all. Consequently, the northern working class was outnumbered and outflanked. Southern Democrats joined with Northern Republicans in a conservative congressional coalition to thwart the full development of social welfare state programs, and to cut back other working-class gains -- especially the newly-won rights of organized labor -- in the postwar period. A further consequence was that the Democratic Party, unlike the labor-based parties of Europe, never became a vehicle of vigorous class socialization, which accounts in part for weaker class identification in this country. Indeed, the southern wing of the party was a vehicle for racist socialization.

The weaknesses in the Democratic Party have worsened in the years since. Given the history of racist socialization in the South, the postwar black struggle turned many southern whites toward the Republican Party, helping to produce a sectional realignment. The globalization of the world economy has empowered business by facilitating capital flight, leaving labor increasingly on the defensive. Moreover, the power of organized labor in the councils of the Democratic Party is diminishing in proportion as the manufacturing sector shrinks. And as the Democratic Party delivers less and less to working people, their allegiance to it falters. In short, the success of the business offensive against labor and the welfare state that took form fully with the election of 1980 reflected these weaknesses in the Democratic Party, and ultimately help explain our current political marginalization.

The rapidly enlarging service sector represents a new possibility for progressive politics, and therefore for overcoming our isolation from mass constituencies. The new service proletariat, composed largely of women and minorities, is not doing well in the market, where real wages are falling and benefits are meager, at least for many. Their needs can only be met through expanded social welfare programs in health, housing, income-maintenance, and day care. Meanwhile, there are also signs that the business offensive may have run its course, undermined by its failure to sustain real living standards, and by its corruption of the tax system, of the defense and housing programs, and of the banking system. And business is also being deprived of the "cold war" as a rallying cry to mobilize conservative forces. The opinion polls already show that Americans are once more moving to support a more interventionist stance by government to solve social and economic problems which have been neglected or worsened under a business-dominated administration.

There is some hope, then, for a new cycle of protest. If so, it is women and minorities in the new service sector who will provide its crucial social base. This could spell a real difference in our relationship to insurgency, for we, after all, are part of that new service sector. The welfare state may thus be the basis for a natural alliance between women, minorities, and the field of social work, and the basis for overcoming our isolation. Whether a new cycle of protest will have the more enduring consequence of reorganizing the party system along class and gender lines is difficult to predict. However, tendencies in that direction will certainly be aborted, as they were in the 1930s, if current efforts at voter registration reform fail, since it is among the new service sector workers that registration levels are lowest.

So much for marginalization. We said there were two implications of David Wagner's book. The other concerns expectations. Cycles of protest inflate them, so that they rise too high and then fall too low. We may not have achieved what we hoped in the 1960s, but we achieved a good deal. The issue of client rights was politicized, for the first time in our memory, and a literature criticizing the violations of client

xii

rights embedded in much public policy gained a wide readership. Advocacy and professional participation in client protest gained a certain acceptability. And mass advocacy and collective protest, together with litigation, changed public policy in ways that have partially endured. The point is that it takes a lot of pushing and shoving to gain even modest reform.

The struggle by radical social work activists to cope with disappointment generated by unbridled expectations is vividly conveyed in the interviews which comprise the empirical foundation of this book. Still, the book suggests many radical activists survived their disappointments and went on to do decent and useful work as progressive social workers. When the cycle turns, and more is again possible, they will be ready to contribute to a larger movement. That is the message of David Wagner's valuable book.

New York, New York
November 1989

A RADICAL PROFESSIONALISM?

A "Big Chill" in the 1980s?

One of the features of the conservative 1980s has been a critical, at times hostile, view of professionals. Beginning in the 1984 election campaign, the term "yuppie" arose as a vague, but popular, appellation for young professionals who were now presumably interested only in personal consumption and comfort rather than in radical politics or activism. Phrases such as the movie title "The Big Chill" were seized upon by the media and others to ascribe to the 1960s generation a new de-politicized mobility and complacency.

Yet only two decades ago, many social theorists sought to locate the source of rebellion and turmoil in American society among its youthful, affluent baby boom generation. Critics of radicalism[1] sought to locate in a "new class" of alienated young intelligentsia the total responsibility for the social unrest of the 1960s. Many radicals themselves hailed the rise of a "new professionalism" among anti-Establishment professionals[2] or saw revolutionary potential for youthful professionals (for example, the 'new working class' theories of Gorz, Mallet, and Touraine[3]).

What, then, has happened to the middle class radicals of recent times? The current hostility towards young professionals and the media's frequent disparagement of the 1960s social movements obscures the fact that a large number of baby boomers did not become business executives, bankers or investment brokers. Many activists of the 1960s consciously avoided positions of high social status and income in a kind of "Great Refusal"[4] of the privileges of middle class or upper class society. Many radicals from the 1960s or 1970s, like many of their peers, work in farms, factories or small businesses, eking out a living, and many participate in social movements ranging from the anti-nuclear and environmental issues to anti-intervention movements in Central America.

In even greater numbers, many people influenced by the social movements of the 1960s and 1970s (the antiwar movement, the New Left, the civil rights movement, the women's movement) sought to carry on their ideals through professions which "served the people" such as medicine, social work, urban planning, law, and teaching. Between 1965 and 1975, hundreds of radical collectives, caucuses, and journals were formed among radical professors, social workers, lawyers, doctors and health care workers. Most of these collectives and critical journals started out by challenging their professions to oppose the Vietnam War or institutional racism; but most of them came by the 1970s to challenge the very existence of professional power and authority represented by such groups as the American Medical Association and the American Bar Association. Even though these groups have declined in numbers and impact, thousands of academics, social workers, planners, and lawyers continue to view their work as a way to advance social change.

This book will explore what happened to one group of activists: those idealistic students and young professionals who tried to carry forward their ideals through work with people in the social service professions. Have these professionals now become conservatized as they embarked on what German student leader Rudi Dutschke called the "long march through the institutions," which he warned held the constant danger of careerism and conservatism? Indeed, radicals of the New Left were acutely aware that by accepting positions in the "Establishment," they were in danger of "co-optation," of being absorbed in the very bureaucratic institutions that they had so criticized. On the other hand, many critics of the more liberal professions, such as social work or university teaching, often charge that these professions are dominated by people far to the left of the mainstream of American politics. Are these professionals then a subversive underbelly in the 'system'? And perhaps this explains why some early studies of 1960s radicals found professions such as teaching and social work helped sustain radical sentiments[5].

Up until this time, few empirical studies have been done on groups of self conscious radicals who attempted to influence a profession. Is there a radical professionalism? Can established professions and institutions accommodate revolutionary ideas? What happens to those with radical and militant views after their many years of professional training when they begin to practice? And what happens to them when they move into positions of responsibility within the institutions of our society? And what happens to the social movements of radical professionals? Have they become "de-radicalized" as the popular culture implies or do they remain radical or revolutionary over the years?

Professionalism as Conservative or Radical?

Sociological theory about the professions has generally stressed professionalism's system maintaining features and professionalization as a middle class social movement aimed at upward mobility. Early sociologists[6] saw upward mobility into the high status of a "professional" along with the growing professional monopoly over knowledge and power as a bulwark against revolution and control by the masses. Recent historical work on the professions generally supports these views, noting the efforts of physicians, lawyers, and others to develop a "skill claim" which deprives ordinary people of authority and buttresses their own social power as an elite[7]. Over the last century, the major professional organizations, often functioning as protective guilds, became frequent targets of hostility among reformers of many different stripes.

Not surprisingly, in the 1960s and 1970s when widespread unrest among students, consumers, and clients occurred (for example, agitation by parents for community control over their schools, by welfare clients for rights to due process, by students for control over the universities, and by patients for the right to understand or even terminate their treatment) professionalism and professionals came under even further attack. Theorists attacked the professions as "hidden hierarchies"[8], stressing the exclusiveness, elitism, and social closure endemic to professionalism and professionalization[9]. Radicals influenced by the New Left in particular were, by the end of the 1960s, calling for an abandonment of professional privilege. In their view, people's needs could only be met through an end to profit over the misery of others and an end to social power derived from their suffering. As the journal *The Radical Therapist* stated:

> ...We must collectivize emotional support and help, and end the mercenary nature of professionalism..."Radical Therapists" should raise high the motto:*We want to put ourselves out of business!*[10]

Since the professions as organized collectivities were primarily interested in their own power and in excluding their clients/consumers from power, early organizers of the New Left who began to see radical students growing up and entering the people-serving professions such as medicine, social work, and teaching, advised a guerilla strategy. Radical professionals could attract followers, raise anti-war, anti-racist or other political issues, but only if they were clear that they were in hostile territory:

> The first principle of orientation for a radical who chooses to work in a profession is that he (sic) is different. He (sic) must reject and separate himself(sic) psychologically from the commonly held social definition of his (sic) work. He (sic) must substitute an agenda of his(sic) own...A radical cannot have an orientation toward professional 'success.' If we function as radicals, high status and respect and rewards in the professional establishment are foreclosed. We must expect job instability, the likelihood of getting fired periodically, the danger of increasing difficulty in finding jobs...[11]

The danger of subordinating radical politics to professional goals and the fear of co-optation by high status or institutional loyalty was highlighted by

A Radical Professionalism?

Students for a Democratic Society's (S.D.S.) "Radicals-in-the-Professions Project" which began in 1966:

> ...A radical cannot see his (sic) loyalty as being to the profession or institution in which he (sic) works. Our loyalty is to our political comrades and to the political aims for which we are organizing. Obviously this presents a moral difficulty because others will assume we have traditional loyalties; and we will, in fact, be playing a two-faced game, knowing that we will 'betray' them when difficult issues arise. But then, that is what being a radical is about and the question is whether you betray your professional colleagues or your political comrades...[12] (author's emphasis)

While criticism and suspicion of professional status and professional privilege is well established in the popular consciousness, within sociological theory and the radical left literature, there is an interesting contradiction between the presumed conservatism of professionals and professionalism and the fact that some professions, such as social work, often attract large numbers of radicals. At its extreme, the sociological analysis of professionalization tends toward "over-determination" in that it would suggest that *all* professionals become conservative. As Irwin Epstein noted after reviewing the literature on social service professionalization, the critique of professionalism fails to account for the very social actors who so often attack professionalism. As he pointed out, "those critical of social-worker conservatism...(are) social workers who, by standards of education, expertise, professional participation, and prominence, are (themselves) highly professionalized."[13]

In fact, since the days of Jane Addams, there has been a strong normative commitment in the social work profession to social activism and social justice. Many writings and texts in social work[14] and the professional code of ethics in social work[15] mandate such values and commitments as part of being a professional. There is evidence that many social work professionals hold political views that would be considered radical by the standards of American

5

society. Some studies indicate, in fact, that this is true cross nationally[16]. Many students enter the profession of social work for political and idealistic reasons, so that selection of a profession itself may indicate a form of ideological self-selection.

At various points in the history of the social work profession, leftists have assumed a prominent position. In the 1930s, a radical social work movement called the Rank and File Movement gained many adherents and came to dominate newly formed social service unions. The Rank and File Movement also found an influential place in theory development in social work, within the ranks of academia, and within social service administration. Like many other radical social workers, Bertha Reynolds, the most prominent Marxist thinker in social work, viewed the rise of radical social work as *consistent* with the ethics and values of the profession. She argued that to be a good social worker, one had to be a radical[17]. In her autobiography, Reynolds asserts that the 1930s-1940s radical movement in social work "was (only) putting into practice (principles which) were not new to social work. It was only a new thing to take them seriously."[18]

Years later, members of the Rank and File Movement including Reynolds, suffered severe repression and were purged from their jobs, but in the 1960s a new group of radicals emerged in social work. Many young people who had joined VISTA, the War on Poverty programs, and the developing community movements organized out of storefronts, welfare rights organizations or Black or Latino organizations, began to challenge government and professional policies as at best limited palliatives designed merely to "cool out" the unrest of the 1960s. After the unrest of the 1960s, new theorists emerged to define "radical social work" anew. Some of these theorists also saw a clear link between good social work practice and radical activity:

> Radical social work is little more than social work that has not compromised its own commitments to human welfare. It is social work that takes seriously the dilemma of a people-serving profession in a people-denying society and tries to resolve the dilemma by

finding ways for the profession to be of real service rather than accommodating itself to conventional arrangements...[19]

Two viewpoints co-exist in the debate about radicalism in social work. One which continues with strong force from the 1960s argues that that the ideology of specialization, elitism, and "businesslike career structures" is part of social work professionalism and this ideology serves the "ruling class" of society.[20] Yet an alternative perspective, such as those of Reynolds and Galper, sees social work values and ideals as very compatible with political radicalism, and even revolutionary zeal, since they place the concerns of people above profits, and seek to empower the poor, the downtrodden, and the discriminated against to fight for social change.

This study will explore this seeming contradiction, particularly in terms of the psychological and subjective struggles of radicals who entered the social work profession with highly idealistic values. We will view both perspectives as having validity. On the one hand, it is clearly possible for some activists and radicals to sustain a professional social work career and maintain their radical political ideology. They do not do so easily or without tremendous sacrifices, sometimes materially, and sometimes psychically. It is not an easy task to create a radical professionalism, and it is greatly dependent, as we shall explore, on the specific career experiences of radical professionals and how they interpret the successes and failures of their efforts.

On the other hand, the pessimism of critics of professionalism has powerful support as we move beyond the individual careers of radicals to evaluate the success of radical professionalism as a social movement. For here, as we study two decades of collective efforts to influence the social work field, its politics and its practice, we find far less success. Indeed, the viability of radical movements in the professions is clearly bounded by the pull of careerism, upward mobility, and the norms of professional conduct. As we shall explore, the more militant prescriptions of radical activists, not only in social work, but in other established helping

7

professions, are severely constrained by the
employment market and the pull of mainstream
ideologies and institutions which dominate the helping
professions.

Is there a Radical Career Path?

In choosing to explore the careers of radical
social service workers over time, we ask the question
of how different are self-labelled radicals from their
peers in the professions. Do they enter the profession
with a commitment to radicalism or come to this
viewpoint after experience in social work? Do they
remain in the profession over the long haul? How do
they react to professional training, often critiqued
by sociologists and radical social workers, as
training for conformity and acquiescence[21]? What type
of jobs do radicals take, what actions do they
participate in at their jobs, how do they perform
their work, and does it differ from others? As these
social workers are faced with opportunities for
promotion or upward mobility, do they abandon earlier
precepts and ideals or abandon more conflictual
strategies?

These questions have not been adequately tackled
for a variety of reasons. Studies of radicals have
always been plagued by methodological problems[22]. For
one thing, radicals have good reason to be suspicious
and non-cooperative with researchers due to the
reality that often in the past such research was put
to repressive uses[23]. Most radical groups do not keep
a large quantity of official records or membership
lists, because of these fears. For these reasons,
access to populations of radicals is of key importance
for research, and it is doubtful that anyone but an
"insider" who was well known and trusted by subjects
could secure cooperation.

Secondly, traditional survey methods have strong
limitations in describing the issues involved in the
"radical career." The lack of 'official' records of
radicals is problematic, as well as the issue of
defining radicalism or activism. Also survey data can
only describe attitudes or behavior at one point in
time. It does not easily allow us to capture the rich
texture and continuing changes in people's lives the
way qualitative studies do. I chose an ethnographic

approach to this study to examine the longitudinal dimension of radical ideology and professional careers, to examine the feelings of pain and success, the trials and tribulations, and perceived successes or failures of radical social workers over a two decade period.

Testing Radical Prescriptions:
Radical Professional Social Movements

The first half of this book will focus on the career paths of the radical social workers interviewed, highlighting the social psychological and ideological struggles of individuals. The study would be incomplete, however, without returning to radical social movements, which will be the focus of the second half. In this sense, the whole is larger than the sum of its parts. For while as individuals, radical professionals may be able to retain their ideologies and beliefs, as past or current members of political organizations, those studied also were public persona which advocated certain strategies to other radical professionals. Their actions as political actors also need to be evaluated and studied.

Virtually no literature exists which studies the past public pronouncements and prescriptions of radical activists and compares them with ensuing political events that followed. For example, did the political activities advocated by radical social workers make sense, even to those committed to such projects? In fact, I suggest that both incumbent political or professional leaderships and more radical segments have some interest in avoiding this assessment. For the dominant leadership of organizations, there is strong incentive to ignore the noisy calls to arms, for even in proving its falsity or failure, they would tend to legitimatize the radicals and run the risk of antagonizing previously militant professionals in their organizations. Many radicals who abandon militant prescriptions have a similar interest. Moreover, in times of political quiescence of radicalism, as the late 1980s appear to be, past advice and strategic prescriptions often prove embarrassing to the radical activists themselves. In reviewing the success and failures of radical social movements in one profession, social work, the important issues common to many radical social movements are raised. Historical and economic reasons for the militancy of social movements need to be probed, as well as the reasons why militancy often abates. This analysis is sympathetic to radical movements, but is also critical of the failure of both social science and the movements themselves to critically evaluate their past slogans and prescriptions. Movements which do not evaluate themselves over time fail to learn from their histories, and are unable to analyze their current perspectives critically.

Catalyst: A Voice of Radical Social Workers

This book will explore the careers of radical social workers who were associated with the collective which published *Catalyst: A Socialist Journal of Social Services*. Founded in 1976 in New York City, the collective's members clearly distinguished themselves as a radical left-wing center within the social services:

> ...we are all dissatisfied with the traditional liberal analysis of the problems facing us and the strategies put forth to meet them. We are convinced that the field (social services) needs a new forum to provide a socialist perspective...[24]

At the time that I gathered the information for this book, *Catalyst* was the longest consecutively published left journal in the social services in the United States, surpassing the publication of the leftist *Social Work Today* in the 1930s (published 1934-1942). In early 1989, "Catalyst" ended its existence as a collective and contracted with Haworth Press to publish a journal under the name of *The Journal of Progressive Human Services*.

Between 1976 and 1986, forty three individuals were members of the *Catalyst* Collective. As will be described further, most of these individuals were active in a variety of left-wing groups in the social services including the Radical Alliance of Social Service Workers (RASSW), the Bertha Capen Reynolds Society (BCRS), and the Union of Radical Human Service Workers (URHSW), as well as in *Catalyst*. Although the numbers of participants in *Catalyst* and its location in the Northeast mitigates against its members being representative of all radical social workers, the demographic profile of these "baby boomers" (age range of 30 to 48 in 1986) closely parallels the social class, racial, religious, and geographic characteristics of the radicals of the 1960s and 1970s as reflected in other studies[25]. Although *Catalyst qua* organization did not form until 1976, the majority of subjects were radicalized between 1966-1971 representing a sub-set of those radicalized by the social movements of the 1960s and early 1970s, particularly the New Left, the student movement, the civil rights movement, and the women's movement.

The degree of influence of *Catalyst* might be subject to some debate. As with any radical organization, there are difficulties in relying on official records. For example, data on the number of copies of journals sold may be misleading because political tracts or copies of journals are often informally circulated. Further, many readers such as those who are prominent leaders in the field or even average social workers may be reluctant to admit the influence of radical literature on them. However, given the limited number of active left organizations in the social work profession, *Catalyst* and its associated organization, the Institute for Social Service Alternatives, appears to be the group with the most national following which arose in the aftermath of the 1960s radicalization.

A further review of the organization, ideology, and history of the *Catalyst* group will be provided in Chapter 2. In Part II of this study (Chapters 7-9), we will return to analyzing aspects of the history of *Catalyst* in relation to the rise and fall of radical professional social movements.

Methodology

Because I was a key participant in the formation and early years of the *Catalyst* collective (1976-79) as well as a member of several related radical social work groups (Radical Alliance of Social Service Workers, Bertha Capen Reynolds Society), I was able to gain a unique access to these radical activists. In addition to the primary research tool of the in-depth interview, lasting between two and six hours, I was also able to gather a large amount of historical data about each subject. For example, articles and memos written by interview subjects, applications to social work school, and other documentation of previous views (some from two decades ago) were used to assist interviewees in remembering past events and also in confronting interviewees with ideas and viewpoints with which they now may have differed. I was also able to secure a complete body of resumes which allowed for the development of a data base on the careers of those interviewed. Because many interviewees were known to me and other documentary evidence was available, resume information which can be unreliable could be revised for veracity.

Since I wanted to secure a group of radical professionals who were highly committed to radicalism, rather than those who may have joined the radical collective merely out of passing interest, in-depth interviews were limited to those members or ex-members of *Catalyst* who had served for at least two years on the collective. A total of 24 people were contacted and interviewed between June 1986 and February 1987, at their homes, offices or other locations. No subject refused to participate in the study. A demographic description of the research group suggests a plurality of females, generally from the Northeast, from Jewish or Roman Catholic families of origins, with a slight plurality of people from professional or business families of origin[26].

An interview protocol was developed that allowed for open-ended questions and a give-and-take between interviewer and interviewee. Subjects were asked to describe in relatively chronological fashion what led them to choose social service work as a career, how they felt this work was or was not compatible with their political views, how they experienced their professional education, and how they experienced their jobs, whether they had held one or ten positions. Subjects were asked, with the help of available documents, to retrospectively comment on and evaluate how their work and professional activities complemented or contradicted their political views.

In the second part of the interviews, I asked a series of questions aimed at securing information about these radicals current views about professionalism, social service work, and politics. Subjects were asked to evaluate a variety of positive and critical statements about social work, and its compatibility with radical politics, as well as to provide their own current views on the possibility of being an active radical within the profession.

The complete minutes of the meetings of the collective were helpful to me in framing my questions and developing some of the history of *Catalyst*. Additionally, on June 15, 1987, a two and one half hour "oral history" interview was held with six key informants who had been active for long periods of time with *Catalyst*, in order to secure a fuller historical record and to allow these informants to give their views as to the development of the collective.

All names of subjects are fictitious, and their workplaces, educational institutions, and geographic locations are not identified, in order to protect the confidentiality of the subjects.

Organization

Chapter 2 orients the reader to the basic contours of radical social work as it came to be defined in the 1960s and after, as well as provides the reader with an introduction to the *Catalyst* collective.

Part I of the book will focus on the individual lives of these radical social workers. In chapters 3-5, I analyze the development of the radical career with particular focus on the social psychological struggles of radicals with demands of education and work. I will review how the subjects came to be radicals; how they initially chose human service work; how they experienced professional training; what career choices they came to make and why, and what experience they have had in the job market. In Chapter 6, I return to the subjective viewpoint of radicals about politics and work. How two decades after the intense criticisms of "professionalism" and "cooptation," do these subjects now interpret their worklives? To what degree can social service work

13

provide a radical career?

In Part II of the book, I will seek to draw conclusions about radical professionalism as a social movement. In Chapters 7 and 8, I evaluate the subjects' accounts of their efforts to organize at their workplaces, their attempts to organize the poor or others through community organizing strategies, and their efforts to introduce radical precepts into therapy, casework, administration, planning, teaching and other work roles. In Chapter 9, I will analyze the rise and fall of militant activity among this group of radical professionals and develop an historical framework which seeks sociological, political and economic reasons, beyond the mere allusion to the "conservative times" of the 1980s, to account for the rise and fall of radical professional movements.

Notes

1. See for example, Daniel Moynihan,<u>Maximum Feasible Misunderstanding</u>, New York: The Free Press, 1968; Daniel Bell,<u>The Coming of Post-Industrial Society</u>, New York: Basic Books, 1973; and Seymour Lipset,<u>Rebellion in the University</u>, Chicago: University of Chicago Press, 1976.

2. see for example, Matthew Dumont,"The Changing Face of Professionalism,"<u>Social Policy</u>, 1 (1), 1970, pp. 26-31.

3. Andre Gorz,<u>A Strategy for Labor: A Radical Proposal</u>, Boston: Beacon, 1964; Serge Mallet,<u>La Nouvelle Classe Ouvriere</u>, Paris: Editions Soliele, 1969; Alan Touraine,<u>The Post Industrial Society</u>, New York: Random House, 1971.

4. Wini Breines,<u>Community and Organization in the New Left, 1962-1968: The Great Refusal</u>, New York: Prager, 1982.

5. see Michael Maidenberg and Philip Meyer,"The Berkeley Rebels Five Years Later: Has Age Mellowed the Pioneer Radicals?,"<u>Detroit Free Press</u>, seven part series, February 1-7, 1970.

6. see Emile Durkheim,<u>Professional Ethics and Civic Morals</u>, New York: The Free Press, 1958; T.H.

Marshall,"The Recent History of Professionalism in Relation to Social Structure and Social Policy,"Canadian Journal of Economic and Political Science, 1939; Talcott Parsons,"The Professions and the Social Structure,"Essays in Sociological Theory, New York: The Free Press, 1954.

7. The best historical treatment of the origins of professionalism as part of a "collective mobility project" is Magali Seffreti Larson,The Rise of Professionalism, Berkeley: University of California Press, 1977.

8. Gilb, Corinne,Hidden Hierarchies: The Professions and Government, New York: Harper and Row, 1967.

9. see, for example, Marie Haug and Marvin Sussman,"Professional Autonomy and the Revolt of the Client,"Social Problems, 17 (3), 1969, pp. 153-160; Elliot Freidson,The Profession of Medicine,New York: Harper and Row, 1970; Elliot Freidson,Professional Dominance, Chicago; Atherton, 1972; Julius Roth,"Professionalism: The Sociologists' Decoy,"Work and Occupations, 1:1 (1974), pp. 6-23; Ivan Illich et. al.,Disabling Professions, Boston: Marion Boyars, 1977.

10. Jerome Agel,Rough Times, New York: Ballatine Books, 1973, p.80 (excerpts from the journal The Radical Therapist).

11. Barbara and Alan Haber,"Getting by With a Little Help from Our Friends,"in Priscilla Long (ed.),The New Left: A Collection of Essays, Boston: Extending Horizon Books, 1969, p. 302.

12. Ibid,pp. 302-304.

13. Irwin Epstein,Professionalization and Social Work Activism, Unpublished Ph. D. dissertation, Columbia University, 1969, p. 34.

14. see for example, William Schwartz,"Public Issues and Private Troubles: One Job for Social Work or Two?"in R.Klenk and R.Ryan (eds.),The Practice of Social Work, 2nd Edition, Belmont,CA: Wadsworth, 1974, pp. 82-99; Carol Meyer,Social Work Practice, Second Edition, New York: The Free Press, 1976; Carel Germain

and Alex Gitterman,<u>The Life Model of Social Work Practice</u>, New York: Columbia University Press, 1980.

15. National Association of Social Workers,<u>Code of Ethics</u>, Silver Spring, Md.: NASW, 1988.

16. For a variety of empirical and anecdotal descriptions of the radicalism of social workers, see Norman Polansky <u>et. al.</u>,"Social Workers in Society: Results of a Sampling Survey,"<u>Social Work Journal</u>, 34 (4), 1953, pp. 74-80; Alfred Kadushin,"Prestige of Social Work: Facts and Figures,"<u>Social Work</u>, 3 (4), 1958, pp. 37-43; Seymour Lipset and Mildred Schwartz,"The Politics of Professionals," in Howard Vollmer and Donald Mills,<u>Professionalization</u>, Englewood Cliffs, NJ: Prentice-Hall, 1966, pp. 299-310; Harry Specht,"The Deprofessionalization of Social Work,"<u>Social Work</u>, 17 (3), 1972, pp. 3-15; and Charles Grosser,<u>New Directions in Community Organization</u>,New York: Praeger, 1976. Polansky and Lipset and Schwartz include data about cross national trends to radicalism among social workers.

17. Cited in Ann Withorn, <u>Serving the People: Social Services and Social Change</u>, New York: Columbia University Press, 1984, p. xii.

18. Bertha Reynolds, <u>An Unchartered Journey</u>, New York: Citadel, 1963, p. 173.

19. Jeffrey Galper,<u>The Politics of Social Services</u>, Englewood Cliffs, NJ: Prentice-Hall, 1975, p. 189.

20. This argument was most forcefully made by the British radical social workers who organized the journal <u>Case Con</u> in 1970, see Roy Bailey and Mike Brake (eds.),<u>Radical Social Work</u>, New York: Pantheon Books, 1975, p. 145.

21. The argument that professional schools and other education socializes initiates to conservative professional norms runs through much sociological and radical literature. The most hard hitting and succinct example of the critique of social work education is Richard Cloward and Frances Fox Piven,"The Acquiescence of Social Work,"<u>Society</u>, 4, 1977, pp. 55-65.

22. see Kenneth Keniston, Radicals and Militants: An Annotated Bibliography of Empirical Research on Campus Unrest, Lexington,MA: Heath and Company, 1973, Introduction.

23. see particularly, Kirkpatrick Sale, S.D.S.,New York: Vintage Books, 1974, p. 548; and Lipset, Rebellion..., pp. 111-113.

24. "Why Catalyst?,"Catalyst, 1 (1), 1978, p. 2.

25. The demographics of the population appear similar to the composition of the New Left in the mid-1960s. For example, the high number of Jews is consistent with many studies of radicals: see Astin (1968), H. Astin (1969), Everson (1970), Flacks and Neugarten (1966), Gelineau (1964), Haan *et. al.* (1968), Mankoff (1970), Meyer (1971), Smith *et. al.* (1970), Solomon (1964), Somers (1965), Useem (1970) and Watts *et. al.* (1969). The over-representation of children of professional families is also consistent with the research, see H. Astin (1969), Braungart (1969), Doress (1968), Flacks (1967), Gelineau (1964), Geller (1972), Liebert (1971), Lyonns (1965), Mankoff (1970), Meyer (1971), Miller (1970), Smith *et. al.* (1970), Somers (1965), Watts *et. al.* (1969) and Westby (1970). The preponderance of subjects origins in large urban areas is also suggested in the previous surveys, though the location of *Catalyst* in New York City obviously affects this outcome.

There are few studies of radicals in the professions, but the small number again confirm a similar social class, racial, and religious picture. See Resnick's study of the Medical Committee for Human Rights (MCHR) in Joel Gerstl and Glenn Jacobs,Professions for the People: The Politics of Skill, New York: Schenkman, 1976, and preliminary data on the radical professors group of the late 1960s/early 1970s, the New University Conference (NUC) by Fred Pincus and Howard Ehrlich,"The New University Conference: An Empirical Analysis of Former Members of an Organization of Academic Radicals" (Paper presented at the American Sociological Association, August 1987, Chicago, IL.).

26. The demographic profile of the participants in the current study are as follows:

Gender:

Male   10
Female   14

Age at time of study:

30-35 yrs. old   7
36-40 yrs. old   9
41-50 yrs. old   8

Place of Birth:

New York City area   12
Other Northeast   3
Midwest   6
South   1
West   2

Religion of Family:

Jewish   14
Roman Catholic   7
Protestant   3

Social Class of Families of Origin:

Business/Managerial   2
Professional   11
Storekeepers/Farmers/
Sales   6
Working Class   5

R A D I C A L   S O C I A L   W O R K

Shortly after the formation of the radical collective that would come to be called the "Catalyst collective" in 1976, I remember sitting with Marcia Cohen at a Chinese restaurant on the Upper West Side of Manhattan and batting around a number of potential names for the new journal. We came up with dozens, some of which we were convinced were excellent while some were just plain humorous. One of our favorites besides "Catalyst," which had the dynamic implications of a group of radicals sparking a chemical change among social workers and their clients, was "Out In Left Field." Mostly it was a play on words; I always liked baseball and I liked the pun on politics and baseball. It now seems hard to imagine that when we proposed it at a meeting, we actually thought the group might take it seriously.

Yet the two names provide more than an anecdote. "Catalyst," the far better name, implies power and effect, that radical social workers and other professionals could successfully influence and impact on the broader world. Over the years, many members of the collective and other radicals in the professions, have sometimes felt more "out in left field" than in a vanguard of social change. Complaining that they were voices in the wilderness, marginal in their fields and in the society at large, some over the years might criticize groups like *Catalyst*, including its name, as being overly optimistic.

In addition to the constant question of how influential radicals in the professions can be, the name game raises the question of how radicals see their relationship to organized occupations. Radical social workers have fluctuated between seeing themselves as being oddities in an oppressive field, who in fact should feel guilty or hesitant about what they do for a living ("out in left field"), to feeling they were uniquely situated in a field which had great potential for radicalizing many colleagues and clients ("catalyst").

This chapter will orient the reader to the dynamics of radical social work over the last two decades as well as provide a brief history of the Catalyst group.

Social Workers as Oppressors and Agents of Social Control

During the tumultuous 1960s, social workers, along with a variety of groups in society, were often viewed as the "enemy." Poor people, minorities, the handicapped, children, prisoners, and other disenfranchised people often came into contact with social workers when they were being denied a welfare check, when their privacy was being invaded by social workers conducting "midnight raids" on their apartments looking for a "man-in-the-house," or when their children were being removed to foster care or an institution.

1960s' criticism of social work initially began with liberal social critics who held high status and power positions, rather than from client groups. For example, Sargent Shriver, in launching the War on Poverty programs, criticized social workers as having deserted the poor to focus on the more arcane and esoteric intrapsychic phenomena; lawyers working for the new storefronts associated with the War on Poverty led the way in suing departments of welfare to overturn repressive regulations and arbitrary treatment of clients by some social workers; and academic writers criticizing mental hospitals and psychiatric power, attacked the major professions of mental health apparatus as a key element of social control in society which labelled the poor and others as "deviant," creating non-persons who were severely stigmatized[1].

As the Civil Rights movement spawned the Black Power Movement and other new movements for empowerment, in 1966, a new organization, the National Welfare Rights Organization, was created to organize welfare recipients to fight for their rights. Although there were always some social workers who supported this movement, and organizations of social workers later developed explicitly to support welfare rights, welfare clients and their allies frequently attacked social workers as representing a repressive system which intentionally sought to control the behavior of poor people and deprive them of minimal subsistence [2].

The militant attacks on professional power and privilege at welfare offices, and later at hospitals, schools, prisons, and child welfare institutions by clients themselves (just as militant demonstrators challenged the power of doctors and teachers by the late 1960s), along with a growing student and anti-war movement which stressed the hypocrisy, deceit, and collusion of professionals with political and business leaders, led to a New Left critique of professional status which was extremely renunciatory.

Young radicals of the 1960s who were social workers or training to be social workers, tended to see themselves as 'privileged' and even as 'oppressors' of the poor, particularly the Black and other Third World groups, who were after all a profound source of their radicalization as a result of the civil rights movement, ghetto riots, and Black Power movement. Rather than see themselves as potential allies, much less leaders of social movements, many New Leftists saw the only good social work (or psychology or education or law) as that which put itself out of business entirely.

Newly radicalized professionals were uncomfortable with their new roles and status and often made to feel guilty about their career choices by their peers [3]. Those who did not give up their careers altogether, adopted two main strategies as radicals in social work. One was to desert the more 'repressive' institutional roles in welfare departments, mental hospitals, prisons, child welfare institutions, and the roles of caseworker, therapist, or groupworker, to become active community organizers allied to community action agencies, welfare rights organizations, or "alternative" organizations. Community Organizing as a specialty, previously a marginal area of study in schools of social work, grew dramatically in the 1960s and early 1970s, and social workers participated in some of the most militant organizing efforts of the period[4].

As late as 1971, a radical role in Social Work
was defined by a leftist professor of Social Work, as
one which involved primarily organizing of the poor or
providing service to alternative movement
organizations[5]. In his typology, social work students
or practitioners could serve the 'movement' by being
(1) "an alternative model-builder" i.e. serving as an
organizer for community groups (2) a "part-time
movement conspirator" i.e. serving with S.D.S. or
other left groups utilizing organizing and leadership
skills (3) a "radical media messenger," i.e.
publishing radical press releases or programs (4) a
"life-style actionist" i.e. setting an example of
different values by rejecting middle class life styles
(5) a "new movement organizer" i.e. creating
alternative organizations and (6) a "human
liberationist" i.e. experimenting with communes and
other alternative life-styles. Of interest, is the
complete absence of any role for social workers
working with individuals and small groups (the work
role of the vast majority of social workers); of any
role for social workers working for bureaucratic
agencies since they were seen as part of the "system";
and of any role for radical social workers in
organizing their own colleagues.

The second characteristic stance of radical
social workers, along with radical lawyers, doctors,
professors, and other middle class radicals of the
1960s was a call for de-professionalization.
Consistent with slogans like "power to the people" and
"participatory democracy," radical professionals
argued that the clients should control their own
destiny, and that the "people," particularly the poor
and working class, needed, at a minimum,
representation in the professions, but, optimally,
control over the professions. Barbara and John
Ehrenreich suggest that what was unique about the late
1960s and early 1970s was the development of a
"negative class consciousness" among middle class
activists in which radical professionals would
voluntarily surrender power and encourage the
oppressed to take over the roles:

> 'Demystification' was the catchword. Radical
> doctors wanted not only to free their

professions from the grip of the 'medical industrial complex' but to demystify medicine. Radical lawyers would open the law books and make elementary legal skills available to the people. Radical psychiatrists would lead the assault on psychiatric mythology and show that any sensitive community person could easily replace them...Credentialling barriers would tumble. The rule of experts would be abolished--by the young experts...[6]

In social work, the "negative class consciousness" of radicals took the form of support for the new paraprofessional movement and for indigenous community residents without professional training assuming the many roles in social service; support for ending all psychiatric labelling and social control over people by the repressive mental health system; and support for militant demonstrations which sometimes targeted the profession of social work itself as the enemy[7].

While a few groups of radical social workers emerged in the late 1960s, such as Social Workers Action for Welfare Rights, it is not surprising that organizations aimed at radicalizing and influencing other social workers were not characteristic in this period. If social workers were the enemy, the oppressor of the poor, why organize them as a group?

Social Workers as Allies of Clients and Victims of the System

Among some social workers, a gradual change in ideology occurred between 1970 and 1975. By the time the *Catalyst* collective was formed in 1976, a growing body of radical social work literature promoted a very different view of activism than that which prevailed in the mid or late 1960s. The key differences can be summarized as follows:

(1) Rather than social workers being only "agents of social control," they could serve to help people as well as potentially harm them. Social workers could play a role in helping people develop a leftist consciousness through direct practice (casework, groupwork, even psychotherapy) as well as through

advocacy, planning, and, of course, community organizing.

(2) Rather than feel guilt at the 'privilege' of 'middle class' life, social workers were part of a 'new working class' or even the old proletariat. Rather than only focus on activities which served the poor or clients, social workers had a key role as *employees* of public and private agencies to organize in their own interests in unions, radical caucuses, and other worker organizations.

(3) While many radicals were, and are, attracted to employment in alternative organizations, there was also a key role for radicals in 'traditional Establishment' organizations where most social workers worked. Potentially, the key institutions of the Welfare State--the welfare system, hospitals, schools, jails, nursing homes, mental hospitals--were the very key areas of oppression which radical social workers could only change by struggling within them.

These ideological changes can be attributed to three phenomena: (a) the widespread employment of young "baby boomers" in the social services by the late 1960s and early 1970s (b) the entrance of Marxism into the social sciences in a significant way in the late 1960s and early 1970s; and (c) the downturn in employment resulting from the Recession of 1973 along with the widely publicized "fiscal crisis of the state" in the mid-1970s.

As the "baby boom" generation grew up and had to engage in full-time employment, the tremendous growth in the welfare state in the 1960s opened up a large number of employment opportunities in the social services. Welfare departments at this time, as well as many community action agencies, required a B.A. or less to secure a position. Often these jobs combined a minimal career commitment and the opportunity to work with the poor, Black and other Third World people or others designated as 'oppressed' (the mentally ill and retarded; drug addicts; street people and hippies) appealing to young idealistic radicals of the 1960s. Many young caseworkers and organizers initially saw their positions as only temporary. However, as the new occupants aged, they had *both* considerable incentives to remain in the field (particularly the vast increase

24

in agency funded tuition for graduate Social Work
education as well as accrued seniority and benefits
for those who remained on leave from employment while
training), *and* certain barriers to leaving the field
("baby boomers" faced more competition for entry to
the higher status professions such as law and medicine
than social work, and would have to accumulate
considerable more capital to pursue a Ph. D., M.D., or
J.L.D. than to obtain a Masters degree in Social Work,
for example). Of course,these demographic trends are
merely suggestive of the growth of a large core of
idealistic entrants to social services, not in itself
dictating major ideological changes.

The second change which allowed social workers to
view themselves as progressive social actors in their
own right, was the entrance of Marxism into the social
sciences, the academy, and the professions. By 1969-
1970, a variety of new journals, strongly influenced
by Marxism, had emerged. Some like *Radical America* and
Socialist Revolution were aimed at a general left
public, while an array of radical professional
publications emerged including *The Health/PAC
Bulletin*, *The Insurgent Sociologist*, and *The Radical
Therapist*. The newly emerging groups of radicals in
academia (the New University Conference, the Union of
Radical Political Economists), in law (the National
Lawyers Guild), in health and medicine (Health/PAC,
Medical Committee for Human Rights), and in science
(Science for the People) came to view themselves less
as 'privileged' elements of the 'ruling class' or
'middle class' than as part of a 'new working class'
oppressed by capitalist institutions along with their
clients/patients. They viewed themselves as capable
either of transforming their professions, or at least
struggling within the established professions to
polarize the professional associations around the
issues and recruit newly trained professionals to
left-wing activism.

Leftist theory filtered into social work
initially through other disciplines: particularly
sociology, economics, and education, as well as
through the health care and women's movements[8].
Perhaps the most important influence in shaping a
radical political analysis for social workers was the
publication of Frances Fox Piven and Richard Cloward's
Regulating the Poor in 1971[9]. Though Piven and

25

Cloward did not focus on the particular strategies necessary for radical social work, by its seminal historic analysis of the welfare system, the book helped radicals locate the social control function of welfare in the economic workings of capitalism. While a number of other articles providing a Marxist or critical perspective on social work were written in the early 1970s[10], the key works that developed a socialist approach to social work practice were not published until 1975: Jeff Galper's *The Politics of Social Services* and Bailey and Brake's *Radical Social Work*[11].

A key influence of Marxist thought was the growing belief by radical social workers that they had a valid self-interest which was not counterposed to the interests of their clients. Further, the possibility that conditions for social workers would deteriorate through 'proletarianization'--a word that began to emerge in the mid-1970s to describe worsening conditions for professional and white collar workers-- strengthened support of unionization and employee militancy as a radical goal.

However, I would suggest that neither the growth in numbers of New Left influenced social workers nor even the influence of Marxism by itself would have had as profound an impact upon social workers without the severe downturn in the economy beginning in 1973. With the Recession of 1973, young professionals for the first time began feeling the effects of unemployment, wage freezes, benefit cutbacks, and shortened hours. As the recession continued, budget cuts stretched from the federal government to state and local governments and fell on social welfare client services provided by the State. In most dramatic terms, the near bankruptcy of New York City in 1975, and the political use to which it was put (layoffs of 100,000 workers, imposition of tuition at city universities, cutbacks in social services, hospitals, firehouses, etc., forced use of municipal unions' pensions to bail out the City) exemplified the more theoretical descriptions of public spending crowding out private capital from the markets and therefore requiring a "tightening of the belt" from unions, public employees, and welfare state clients[12].

For social workers, the national contraction of

jobs and the deterioration of working conditions as a result of federal, state, and municipal cutbacks, reinforced the view that social workers were vulnerable workers, and that their self-interest was the same as their clients. Virtually all radical social work literature from 1974 on refers to the ravaging of the welfare state by the government, harming services to the poor, the unemployed, and working class *and* social workers themselves. Further, the failure by the mid-1970s of the Democratic Party to vigorously oppose the cuts at either the national or local level led to increased bitterness even on the part of mainstream social work groups. The years of cutbacks and perceived bi-partisan support for them, were brought forth in the very first paragraphs of the journal *Catalyst*:

> ...Few people who pick up this journal will have escaped the effects of the current crisis in the social services. If you are a social service worker, you have probably observed your agency or program being whittled away, along with your job security. If you are a client of any of the social services, you may wonder how the government and big business think you can survive with what little you get. From health care to housing, and from employment to income maintenance, there has been a massive attack on all the social services...There have been cutbacks and crises before in the social services, but never have the leading liberal politicians who helped build the welfare state led the attack. They have made a political choice, opting for austerity in social service programs, using slogans like 'less is more,' 'life is unfair,' and proclaiming the need for more efficiency...[13]

And so in the mid 1970s, a new ideology of radical social work emerged as massive cuts in social services were occurring, which particularly struck a generation which had come of age at a time of expansion in social services. It was a troubled time for social workers and other state employees after four consecutive decades of expansion in the number of state employees. And *Catalyst* emerged in a period of time in which a Marxist critique of the social services had begun to inform many young leftists who had entered the profession, some with reluctance and others with idealism.

The Formation of the Catalyst Collective

The origins of Catalyst, as a Collective publishing a socialist journal, and, as an attempt to develop a broader social movement of radical social workers took place in what appeared to be a particularly optimistic period for leftists in Social Work.

In New York City, a fairly large radical organization called the Radical Alliance of Social Service Workers (RASSW) was formed in 1974[14]. RASSW published a bi-monthly newsletter entitled *The Alternative View*, held several well attended forums and conferences, and developed a broad committee structure. The group's ideology and activities reflected the key components of a Left program in Social Work in the mid-1970s: antagonism towards the leadership of the profession and the liberal political leadership, encouragement of unionization and an employee identification for social workers, organizing for a massive 'fightback' against budget cuts by united groups of workers and clients, as well as developing critiques of the Welfare State, specific social policies regarded as repressive (such as workfare), opposing racism and sexism, and attempting to develop a 'radical practice' within Social Work[15].

Groups like RASSW and *Catalyst* hoped to develop a national organization of leftist social service workers (as broadly defined as possible) which would change the direction of the profession, ally it with labor, and with militant community and political groups. A radical journal in the social services, had been noted as a critical strategic need at least a year or two before *Catalyst*[16]. Importantly, such a journal was never framed to be an academic or literary exercise, but was viewed as a tool for organizing a movement of leftist social service workers and clients.

In the Spring of 1976, I discussed the idea of a radical social service journal with noted author,

Richard Cloward, who strongly endorsed the idea. With the aid of several others, letters were written to a number of prominent left-wing figures in the field to gauge their interest and possible support. The response was enthusiastic. Additionally, early on, we met with individuals involved in publishing *Social Policy* and *The Insurgent Sociologist* to gather facts about publishing, financing, and otherwise negotiating the business of a journal.

At the same time, a number of RASSW members and ex-members were forming a study group in New York to read the new radical social service literature as well as Marxist theory. At the first study group meeting, I raised the idea of of a radical journal. By the Fall of 1976, a group of about ten people began to meet to develop the political and practical objectives of a left journal and by 1977, a core of about seventeen people interested in undertaking a radical journal had been organized. Politically, the group was heterogenous, ranging from committed Marxists to those who described themselves as political neophytes. The key cleavage, politically, was greatly one of experience and definition; those who had been active for many years on the Left were generally more directive in their prescriptions for the journal and more formed in their views. This group constituted about half the group. The other half had less political experience, and sometimes felt that their ideas were not sufficiently well formulated for them to engage in political argumentation.

In addition to choosing the name "catalyst" because of the group's belief that a radical journal could help unite divergent left elements in the field, radicalize the profession, and lead to new activism, the group also formed the Institute for Social Service Alternatives (I.S.S.A.) in 1977. While the establishment of ISSA as the official publisher of *Catalyst* was necessitated by tax and non-profit laws it was always felt that ISSA might become a future center for organizing, radical research, and sponsorship of forums and conferences. As participants recalled in the oral history meeting, "*Catalyst* was only the first task of ISSA..."

Radical Egalitarianism

From the earliest Catalyst meetings, there was clear consensus that the publication of a journal was to be a collective endeavor. Basing itself broadly on collectively published journals such as *Radical America* and *Socialist Review*, the group never considered employing a formal hierarchical organization. Rather, all members were to be full participants in all of the journal's activities. The tasks of the journal, from publicity, to securing subscriptions, to reading manuscripts, to copy editing, to galley proofreading were originally done entirely by the voluntary labor of the collective. To this end, the Collective developed a system of rotating membership on committees which perform tasks necessary for the journal's publication.

In order to centralize and coordinate the myriad tasks involved in publishing a journal, bi-monthly business meetings were held. The meetings occurred at the homes of Collective members and usually lasted from two to three hours. They were chaired on a rotating basis. Because, by early 1977, broader political issues were already losing the floor to the concrete technical issues of publishing a journal, the Collective began to hold monthly "political retreats." Like the business meetings, they were held at members' homes, though usually in more festive fashion with food and drink. Over the years, political retreats ranged from the highly theoretical (the nature of Marxism and socialism, the role of the Democratic Party) to concrete issues in the journal (what audience should *Catalyst* strive to reach?) to the interpersonal (tension in the Collective, sexism by male members) to areas of people's worklives (how could the precepts of radicalism be applied to the individual's own workplace?).

Between business meetings, political retreats, and committee and sub-committee meetings, Collective members put in a tremendous amount of time. At a minimum, most members had responsibilities calling for one meeting a week, but, often these responsibilities could entail several nights a week and weekend work.

The radical egalitarianism of the Collective, which continued well into the mid 1980s, created several organizational dilemmas over the years. One dilemma was the balance between informal recruitment of new members in order to increase the number of people to do the work of the Collective and to meet the desire of the group to expand versus the group's need to retain a political identity and also the high interpersonal expectations of Collective members. At first, friends of members were simply invited to join. Beginning in the Spring of 1977, the group, concerned about both the political unity of the Collective and its size, developed a procedure for joining Catalyst which entailed the potential new member being interviewed by two Collective members. If the person was acceptable, she/he would join and serve a "trial period" in the group which would last three months. At that point, the group would vote on inclusion. Initially, the procedure was not seriously adhered to. But, later, major battles occurred over some potential new members.

The Collective gravitated between almost exclusionary procedures, because of the concern to secure members who were sufficiently "politically developed" and who were interpersonally non-sexist, cooperative, and hard workers, and almost a complete 'open door' policy, particularly later (after 1980) when recruitment to the Collective was a matter of survival. In a sense, the issue of setting boundaries for Collective membership pleased no one. When past and current Collective members were interviewed for this study, many felt the group had been too intolerant of newcomers over the years, while others felt that the group became less radical over the years because of the more 'open door' policy[17].

A long time Catalyst member suggests group size and personal feelings had as much to do with the fluctuation between exclusionism and openness to new members as their political ideologies:

> I think it has to do, first, with the size of the group. In the heyday years, (we) didn't need new people. (It) was harder to bring new people in. I had strong feelings about new people myself. But this was partly psychological too. We all felt very close and

in a small group, new people can be destabilizing...(You say) "keep it the way it is"...now later, we had a lot of turnover (in the early 1980s). Of necessity we didn't do that (exclude people) anymore. Plus the group had changed enough that there wasn't much pressure to be careful in recruiting new members...

The second dilemma of radical egalitarianism had to do with the all consuming schedule of activities of the Collective, and the need of many members to reduce activities due to child care obligations, increased work responsibilities, and geographic re-location. Indeed, at least on the surface, the reasons for almost every departure from *Catalyst* was increased work pressure, family responsibilities, moving or similar issues[18]. As early as 1977, the Collective began to experiment with an "associate member" category which would allow someone who could not undertake full committee responsibilities to at least participate in some tasks and in political retreats. With one or two exceptions, this experiment did not succeed. There was wide agreement that Catalyst was not able to deal well with differential levels of commitment. For the most part, Collective members uncertain of their commitment felt pressure to fully participate or completely depart from the Collective.

The committee structure and number of details to be attended to in publishing a journal were reduced somewhat over the years. Some work such as maintaining mailing lists and checking distribution problems were contracted out. The increased use of computers since 1980 has also saved considerable labor. Nevertheless, the organizational structure of Catalyst continued to be a major source of controversy.

Almost everyone interviewed expressed at least frustration, if not anger, at the amount of 'detail work' involved in the journal, and the excessive amount of time spent struggling with these issues. One ex-member bitterly complained that *Catalyst* was "an ongoing psychodrama in which people acted out their desires to be radical on an interpersonal level." In an article by former Collective member Nancy Aries[19], a more developed argument critical of the collective structure was made. Aries argues that the Collective

32

remained wedded to a 1960s form of organization at a time when people's lives had changed. With increased family, work, and other responsibilities, it was no longer possible for most people to devote themselves completely to all the tasks of a radical collective journal. Further, the collective organization began to turn inward on itself; it presented barriers to new members, particularly those who could not commit themselves rather fully to membership. Political work in the 1980s, suggests Aries, requires new forms of organization which allows people to become differentially involved in activities, and groups which tolerate people's different levels of interest and activity.

While not all Catalyst members and ex-members agreed with Aries, all ex-members of *Catalyst* interviewed felt that their needs, personal and political, were eventually thwarted by the structure. Many members initially joined Catalyst in order to be active in radical politics; yet the details of publication often took over the time for other political activities.

A second frustration came from those who sought more political theoretical training. One member points out the problem humorously:

> of course I was excited to join Catalyst...to be accepted, me who knew so little, into this group. And I wanted to learn theory, to learn Marxism. Of course, I don't know if we ever get to do this (laughs)...

Like political activism, political education had to take a back seat to the tasks of publishing. Most of the education function was assigned to the political retreats. But by 1979-1980, even retreats became more focused on organizational and interpersonal problems, and subsequently, retreats were abandoned entirely.

A third need strongly identified by Collective members, was that of securing support and assistance with their own "work struggles." Several members felt overwhelmed by the increasingly thorny problems of being a radical social worker, particularly as some members moved into supervisory and administrative positions. While some retreats focused on combining work and politics, and, at one point, the Collective had dinner together before meetings specifically for mutual aid around work problems, the interviews suggested that several people were frustrated that Catalyst was not able to help them more.

Given the tremendous personal demands of being a Collective member, both in terms of detail work, and political and personal commitment to constant discussion of interpersonal issues, it is not surprising that many organizations, Catalyst among them, have finally moved away from an egalitarian structure. In 1989, the journal contracted with a publishing house to publish as an academic/business venture.

There is the possibility that it was not only the prevalence of the 'detail work' that frustrated the many members and ex-members of Catalyst, but the very different agendas that people had. For example, some ex-members attacked the group as overly academic and theoretical; while others expressed the opposite view. It may be that the relatively small group structure which was composed of politically heterogenous members just could not meet all members' needs. It is possible that if the group decided to accent only political activity, it might have lost those more interested in theory or in discussing their personal problems, and *vice verse*. Nevertheless, it is important to keep in mind the ambitious agenda of the small group which created tension and ambivalence between instrumental tasks (putting out a journal); affective tasks (such as discussing work problems); and intellectual tasks (developing political theory and strategy for radical change).

Funding for the journal was always a knotty problem. Collective members early on agreed to assess themselves a fee based on their monthly earnings to support the journal. One Collective member who happened to be quite wealthy agreed to donate a substantial sum of money. This was believed to be only a temporary measure, necessary only until the journal was published and sufficient subscribers obtained. However, the journal never became self-sustaining. The wealthy member continued to subsidize the journal for more than six years. This money plus money from subscriptions and sales, and parties and fundraisers, barely kept the journal afloat. By 1981, fiscal problems combined with flagging energy and logistical problems prevented any semblance of a regular schedule of publication. Over the years, a variety of strategies were discussed to finance the journal, including securing foundation grants and publishing a collection of reprints from *Catalyst*.

The difficulty of economic survival was shared by almost all radical magazines which emerged from the 1960s and 1970s. Journals or periodicals which survived generally did so only by becoming academic periodicals supported by universities or in a very few cases (such as *Mother Jones*) by successfully becoming more slick magazines and becoming business ventures [20].

An Optimistic Period

The first few years of *Catalyst's* existence was marked by optimism among radical social workers due to the emergence of a number of local groups throughout the nation and the degree to which Catalyst Collective members were able to both promote the journal as well as voice the ideas of radical social workers to others on the Left.

Early in its history, the Collective could see itself as part of a growing movement. In its earliest years, *Catalyst's* founding coincided with the spontaneous formation of radical social service groups in Wisconsin, in Boston (the Union of Radical Human Service Workers), in New Haven, in Chicago (the Chicago Alliance of Social Service Workers), and in Philadelphia (the Philadelphia Radical Human Service Workers), among others [21]. While the Collective never had the resources to keep in close contact with these groups nor apparently felt it was politically feasible to act in a coordinating role, the news of each group's emergence was stimulating and exciting to Collective members. There was a strong sense that *Catalyst* was part of a burgeoning radicalization which would continue to grow.

The early Collective was considerably more active in speaking to left audiences, and potentially 'radicalizable groups' in its first years, when compared with later years. In the three years of 1977 to 1979, Catalyst Collective members addressed: students at several major Schools of Social Work and alumni groups at a number of schools, radical social workers in RASSW, social workers at professional conferences as varied as National Association of Social Workers, the American Orthopsychiatric Convention, the Council on Social Work Education convention, the Association of Child Care Workers, the Family Service Association of America, the National Conference on Social Welfare, and the Policy Training Center in Boston (which was developing classes and research material for radical human service workers), and groups of leftists through a radio presentation on N.Y.C's WBAI, through a forum at the Free Association in N.Y.C. which gave classes and presentations, at NAM (New American Movement) functions, at meetings of the Benjamin Rush Society (a radical psychology group), at meetings of the Red Apple Coalition (a group of radical publications) and through co-sponsoring a conference on "Marxism and Science" with groups such as the NY School for Marxist Education, Health/PAC, and MCHR.

Perhaps because the group was new, the Collective was approached for endorsement by a wide variety of left-wing groups, was able to gain some press coverage (ranging from *The Daily World* and *In These Times* to the reprinting of 'Why Catalyst?' in the National Federation of Student Social Workers newspaper), and was able to develop contacts with a diverse number of groups (unions such as the Pennsylvania Social Service Employees Union and organizations like the National Association of Black Social Workers). Indications of Catalyst perceiving itself as an independent activist left organization, included its endorsement of demonstrations (such as an anti-nuclear rally at Indian Point) and requests to co-sponsor the board game "Class Struggle."

The first issue of *Catalyst* appeared in February 1978 and reflected what would be the general format of *Catalyst*: a book-sized (the first issue was 112 pages) quarterly journal with rather long articles interspersed with a few graphics, poetry, and advertisements for other left journals. Issue 1 began several features: a "News Bureau" coordinated by two *Catalyst* members, which would continue in some form throughout the journal's history; a Book Review of a major work; and a "Notes on the Literature" feature (which continued, sporadically, over the course of the journal's history). Between the first issue and the delayed publication of the first completed volume of *Catalyst* (Volume 1 was completed at the end of 1979), subscriptions rose from less than 350 in early 1978 to more than 1,100 with an apparently strong amount of single issue sales[22]. At this point, growth appeared adequate, with the collective primarily expressing frustration only with the slow pace of publishing and difficulty in obtaining quality manuscripts.

Over the course of the first volume, the journal began to appear more attractive and professional due to better communication with printers/typesetters and additional photographs and graphics. A small number of letters began to appear including a debate on the nature of 'radical therapy'[23] and letters of welcome as well as advice from social workers who had at one time been activists of *Social Work Today*, the 1930s radical journal[24]. Significant articles in issues 2-4 included reportage on the fiscal crisis, an early published article on gays and mental health, a review of Social Work's treatment of the women's movement, an article by a Collective member on the experience of Social Work School, a photoessay about one's client's life on welfare, a bibliography on Professionals-as-Workers, and a report on the organization of a settlement house by a Collective member and a co-worker.

Calendar year 1980 represented the first year that *Catalyst* was able to maintain its goal of publishing quarterly. The improved publication schedule made for shorter, more compact magazines (about 90 pages) with livelier graphics and photos. Notable articles in the author's view include the publication of material on *Social Work Today* and the Rank and File Movement, two articles critical of radical social work practice and arguing for social workers' impact as employees[25] as well as a strong defense of the radical therapy position[26], articles on collective bargaining and union issues, an article by a Collective member on teaching social work, and an article on developing workplace 'stress groups.'

Back 'Out in Left Field'?

By the early 1980s, a crisis which had already been somewhat apparent in rising interpersonal frustration, declining energies, and logistical problems, became more evident. During the early 1980s, ten of the remaining twelve original Collective members would leave; the total number of collective members listed on the masthead would decline from nineteen in late 1980 to nine by 1983 and 1984; subscriptions would drop by half; and activism within the social service Left appeared to fall.

Generally, most Catalyst members and ex-members tend to ascribe the crisis to personal and organizational issues: interpersonal strife, exhaustion, members' increased work and family responsibilities, financial problems in the journal, and decisions that perhaps other forms of radical activity would be more useful than work on the journal. A Catalyst member suggested the convergence of age (now closer to a mid-30s median) and internal problems:

> (It was) a combination of getting tired because (the) journal was dragging. They (members) were changing, people were getting to be 35 or 40. If you look at any political movement, you worry about people at that age. Family demands...people hitting their professional strides...Yes, and these were people influenced by the 1960s, who weren't going to make those mistakes, if you will, of drop-out ism...but it wasn't just age or mobility either. When there is no end product, it is very demoralizing. If it was an exciting period, people might have managed to pull their personal changes and that (*Catalyst*) together. But the journal wasn't giving us anything but aggravation...

The decline in *Catalyst*'s success also paralleled, of course, the Reagan election:

> After Reagan's election, all of us on the Left felt so defeated that...may have contributed along with everything else to the

sense of nothing happening, and it was harder
to mobilize...(Catalyst member).

While this book will later probe these and other
more theoretical reasons for the decline in social
movements in the professions (see Part II), there is
strong evidence that the Reagan period did correspond
with the decline of organized radical social service
movements. Not only was *Catalyst* hard pressed to
secure manuscripts and maintain subscriptions, but
many local groups such as RASSW and URHSW folded in
the early 1980s. The large number of early speaking
engagements, presentations at conferences, and press
releases of Catalyst fell to an almost non-existent
level. Efforts to resurrect a new movement of social
service radicals, such as the development of a Human
Service Activists Network (HSAN) did not manage more
than a few meetings[27]. Significantly, as we will
develop in this book, the content of 1980s radicalism
was far more defensive, far less hostile to the
organized profession, and less overtly socialist or
militant than that of the 1970s movements[28].

Only *Catalyst*'s prior commitment to publish two
special issues with guest editors actually enabled
four issues to be published in calendar year 1981.
With Special Issue 9/10 on "The State of the Black
Community in Capitalist America" guest edited by June
and Richard Thomas and Special Issue 12 on "Lesbian
and Gay Issues in the Social Services" guest edited by
Scott Wirth, Rani Eversley, and Nancy Rubin, as well
as issue 11, *Catalyst* for the second time fulfilled
its quarterly commitment. In 1982, however, only two
issues were printed; in 1983, only one; in 1984, only
one; in 1985, three; in 1986, only one; and in 1987,
only two. Paid subscriptions declined to between 522
to 720 (dependent on whether one counts issues given
free to libraries, authors, sponsors, etc.)[29].

Catalyst actively sought new members to replace
the stalwarts who had left by 1982. Between 1981 and
1985, ten new members were recruited. However, many
individuals stayed for only a brief time period. Some
in fact came to a meeting or two and were
disillusioned or disinterested. Of ten new recruits,
only four would stay for a significant amount of time.

When I interviewed former members of Catalyst in

1986 and 1987 most of them were rather despondent about the results of their efforts. Although two people actively involved in Catalyst were more optimistic, citing an improved financial picture through fundraising, a little more stability in the new smaller collective, and the emergence in 1985 of a new national group of radical social workers, the Bertha Capen Reynolds Society, the demise of the journal as a radical collective endeavor in 1989 tends to support the pessimism of the others interviewed.

Indeed, from a purely instrumental perspective, the vast amount of work and finances to successfully produce a quarterly journal overwhelmed the group, and neither the number of issues published, subscriptions sold nor the public impact was as great as the journal's originators hoped. Moreover, the absorption with the demands of producing a journal paradoxically reduced some Collective members other political activities. Until recent years (with the joint 1987 conference with the Bertha Capen Reynolds Society), the ISSA organization had failed to develop as an activist organization in its own right, but had served primarily as a vehicle for publishing the journal, a reversal of the activist ideas of the original Collective.

While some could conclude the decline of *Catalyst* (formalized by it contract to become a new academic journal entitled *The Journal of Progressive Human Services* in 1990 under the aegis of the Haworth Press) was inevitable as the left is now so marginal to the professions, there is the danger of circularity in this conclusion.

For by the late 1980s, there was a widespread feeling generally in America that the Left had declined or vanished. The question then reduces itself to a kind of chicken-or-egg phenomenon: to what degree did actions taken by leftists themselves, such as those in Catalyst, reduce the strength or appeal or militancy of the Left, or, on the other hand, to what degree was any radical movement doomed to failure by outside factors in the society which were leading to the advance of conservatism throughout the United States beginning in the late 1970s? What is the relationship between events at society's macro level and the smaller scale efforts of individuals and groups of radicals trying to affect social change? To what extent has the Left faded, or has it, as reflected by the development of Catalyst into a more academic journal, been absorbed as a legitimate part of the social institutions of America? The Left might be marginal, or it could have so "bored from within" such institutions as academia and social services, as to have successfully reduced the need for radical change and militant actions[30].

This book will try to tackle these questions, at least in regard to the case study of radical social workers. First, by reviewing the retrospective accounts of radical social workers as to their own professional and political development between the 1960s and 1980s, we will examine the possibility of the 'Big Chill' occurring among radical professionals. Further, by examining the changing political behavior of radical social workers over the years, we will try to separate the actual political behavior of radical professionals from their ideological views.

Notes:

1. I have argued elsewhere (David Wagner,"Collective Mobility and Fragmentation: A Model of Social Work History,"Journal of Sociology and Social Welfare, 13 (3), 1986, pp. 657-700) that the crisis in social work in the 1960s, as in the 1930s was a combination of elite attacks on social work and pressure among potential client groups (the poor, the working class, etc.). For Shriver's attacks on social work, see Neal Gilbert and Harry Specht,The Emergence of Social Welfare and Social Work,Itasca, IL: F.E. Peacock, 1976, p. 321; for the best description of lawyers often in an antagonistic position to social workers in the 1960s, see Ira Glasser,"The Prisoners of Benevolence,"in Willard Gaylin et. al.,Doing Good: The Limits of Benevolence, New York: Pantheon, 1981, pp. 97-170. The revolt against the mental health system and the professionals that staffed them were greatly influenced by the works in psychiatry of Thomas Szasz (see particularly The Manufacture of Madness, New York: Delta, 1970), and in sociology of Erving Goffman (particularly Asylums, New York: Anchor, 1961). By the late 1960s, many radical academic critics and students had greatly absorbed the critique of psychiatry as an agent of social control.

2. In many of the more recent professional discussions of the welfare rights movement it is frequently forgotten that many social workers felt challenged, and opposed the movement for welfare rights. For a good history of the welfare rights movement, see Chapter 6 of Frances Fox Piven and Richard Cloward's Poor People's Movements, New York: Prager, 1978.

3. For a contemporary view of the discomfort and guilt felt by early New Left activists who entered "straight" jobs in the "Establishment," see Haber and Haber,"Getting By..."

4. The specialty of Community Organization in social work goes back to the late 1930s, but no more than a tiny number of students trained in this area of social work until the mid-1960s. Moreover, the early Community Organization students were primarily interested in managing and coordinating social welfare organizations such as united ways and community chests. For a discussion of the growth of C.O. in the 1960s, see Grosser, New Directions.... Examples of the militant activities of social workers in the 1960s include the confrontational organizing against landlords and school principals in the Lower East Side of NYC under the leadership of Mobilization for Youth (MFY) which led to severe red baiting (see Moynihan, Maximum...). Social work academics, notably Frances Fox Piven and Richard Cloward, helped spark the welfare rights movement through their calls to "flood the welfare system to topple it," see Piven and Cloward,"A Strategy to End Poverty,"The Nation, May 2, 1966, pp. 510-17. In 1969, welfare rights organizers were joined by some radical social workers and students in disrupting the annual conference of the National Conference on Social Welfare by blocking all the doors at the convention until attendees agreed to make significant financial contributions to NWRO (cited in John Ehrenreich,The Altruistic Imagination, Ithaca: Cornell University Press, 1985, p. 199).

5. John Erlich,"The 'Turned on' Generation: New Anti-Establishment Action Roles,"Social Work, 16:5, 1971, pp. 22-27.

6. Barbara and John Ehrenreich,"The Professional Managerial Class,"in Pat Walker,Between Labor and

Capital, Montreal: Black Rose, 1979, p. 39.

7. The militant demonstrations against the profession itself, such as noted above (footnote 4) tended to paint social workers, rather than political leaders and business elites, as enemies and often aroused hostility among rank-and-file social workers. By the 1970s, radicals in social work sought allies among their colleagues by targeting outside enemies or by at least separating the responsibilities of most social workers from those responsible for major policy decisions.

8. The most influential books from outside the social work field in this period (based on a citation review) include Alvin Gouldner,*The Coming Crisis of Western Sociology*, New York: Avon Books, 1970; from health care, Barbara and John Ehrenreich (eds.) ,*The American Health Empire*, New York: Vintage, 1971; from the women's movement, Robin Morgan's (ed.) *Sisterhood is Powerful*, New York: Vintage, 1970, which included an article specifically addressed "to our sisters in social work"; from economics, Richard Edwards, M. Reich and T. Weisskopf (eds.),*The Capitalist System*, Englewood Cliffs, NJ: Prentice-Hall, 1972; and from education, the translation of the works of Brazilian educator Paulo Freire particularly *Pedagogy of the Oppressed*, New York: Continuum, 1984, originally published in America in 1972.

9. Frances Fox Piven and Richard Cloward,*Regulating the Poor*, New York: Vintage, 1971. My view of this book as key is confirmed by a study of citations in the first twenty issues of *Catalyst* itself.*Regulating the Poor* is cited in 16 different articles. Other major works cited were James O'Connor, *The Fiscal Crisis of the State*, New York: St. Martin's Press, 1973 with thirteen cites, Harry Braverman's *Labor and Monopoly Capital*, New York: Monthly Review Press, 1974, and Jeffrey Galper's *The Politics..* with twelve cites each.

10. see particularly, Martin Rein,"Social Work in Search of a Radical Profession,"*Social Work*, 15:2, 1970, pp. 13-28; and Robert Knickmeyer,"A Marxist Approach to Social Work,"*Social Work*, 17:3, 1972, pp. 58-65.

11. Galper,The Politics...; Bailey, Roy and Brake, Mike,Radical....

12. The business community by the mid 1970s was calling for widespread cuts in the public sector, particularly in social service spending citing a "capital crisis," see Business Week, Special Issue,"Capital Crisis: The 4.5 Trillion America Needs to Grow,"September 22, 1975.

13. "Why Catalyst?,"Catalyst, 1:1 (1978), p. 1.

14. As with the study of all radical groups, membership information is a tricky issue. RASSW, like SDS, operated greatly on the principle of participatory democracy with fairly permeable boundaries for membership. My own notes from the annual conference of RASSW on June 14, 1975 indicate a speaker cited 125 members and a mailing list of 600. A note in the minutes of Catalyst in 1979 show RASSW had a mailing list of 1,200 at that point.

In 1974-76, which informants agree was RASSW's most successful period, a number of meetings held were extremely well attended. Perhaps the biggest was RASSW's May 22, 1976 Conference on Radical Social Work which drew about 300 people. At the oral history, informants agreed that RASSW was the largest group of radical social workers prior to the Bertha Reynolds Society which they had known of. But again any exact measure of membership would require another study.

15. see The Alternative View, Volumes 1-3, 1974-1976.

16. A need for a radical journal was voted as one of RASSW's objectives at the annual meeting on June 14, 1975. See Alternative View, 2:1, Sept. 1975, p. 2.

17. There was a widespread consensus at the oral history that the wholesale recruitment of "newer members" in the 1980s led to less politically radical collective members. Several informants cited this fact as one of the reasons the Collective began to shy away from its identification as "socialist" (at a 1983 meeting, for example,the subtitle of Catalyst was only narrowly saved from deletion). On the other hand, other informants felt embarrassed about some early exclusions of people, and said they regretted their

actions.

18. Of course, people often cited these concrete reasons when other more political or personal issues also contributed to their decision to leave the Collective. One of the purposes of the study, see particularly Chapters 7-9, will be to determine to what extent other more structural factors accounts for the difficulties in being a radical professional.

19. Nancy Aries,"Small Changes, Big Changes: Restructuring Political Organizations for the Eighties,"Catalyst, 4:4, 1984, pp. 59-68.

20. Russell Jacoby's powerful critique of the absorption of radicals into the academic and journalistic establishment very much parallels my view. For his comments on the press and journalism, see Chapter 7 of The Last Intellectuals, New York: Noonday Press, 1987.

21. A series of meetings were held in 1979 between representatives of *Catalyst*, RASSW, UHRSW (Boston), CASSW (Chicago), PRHSW (Philadelphia), and radical New Haven social workers (no group name). The exact purposes and objectives of these meetings are not clear, although documents examined by the author discuss a "socialist human service workers group." The minutes of *Catalyst* (October 16, 1979) note, however, that one organizer of the meeting hoped to have the left groups "bore from within in NASW." The opposition of *Catalyst* and other groups to this proposed strategy is evident from the minutes; and apparently this was one reason for the failure of the groups to coalesce.

It should be noted that many radical social service groups were small regional collectives, and the ones named are only those I am aware of through their communications with *Catalyst* or personal experience.

22. Information on subscriptions had to be 'pieced together' by the author from several sources. The best information is available from 1981 and after when the journal computerized the list, and broke down subscriptions between paid and free copies to certain libraries as well as to sponsors and authors (both of whom received two free issues). The early subscription data (1978) are available through the minutes.

Unfortunately, the highpoint of subscriptions occurred during a point, 1979-1980, when the journal's mailing list was handled by a contracted out service. I interviewed several members of the Collective and Mimi Braun, formerly of Transactions, (phone interview, June 4, 1987) to obtain the estimate of *Catalyst*'s subscriptions.

A problematic feature (see footnote 29) is the citation of numbers which sometimes include free issues with paid subscriptions, and sometimes do not. The minutes of *Catalyst* reflect a decision made in early 1980 to continue for a time sending journals to those who had not renewed after the first volume. This practice was then discontinued except for some libraries and other left journals. A further problem is that there is no good source of single copy sales, which was at times quite high.

23. See <u>Catalyst</u>, 1:2, 1978, pp. 90-92, and 1:4, 1979, pp. 145-148.

24. See <u>Catalyst</u>, 1:3, 1979, pp. 119-120 and 1:4, 1979, pp. 148-149.

25. Marlene Webber, "Abandoning Illusions: The State and Social Change, <u>Catalyst</u>, 2:2 (1980), pp. 41-66; Paul Adams and Gary Freeman, "On the Political Character of Social Service Work," <u>Catalyst</u>, 2:3 (1980), pp. 71-82.

26. William Caspery, "Psychotherapy and Radical Politics," <u>Catalyst</u>, 2:3 (1980), pp. 27-36.

27. Information on the Human Service Activists Network (HSAN) is primarily from the informants at the June 15, 1987 oral history. There was disagreement as to whether the group met once or twice or slightly more and over the exact numbers who attended meetings. However, there was widespread agreement that it was short-lived and generally unsuccessful in unifying the declining small groups of radical social workers in the early 1980s.

28. Evidence of this trend include the continued disputation of the 'socialist' label by collective members, until the term "progressive" has finally

replaced any more explicit identification both in the journal and in other leftist organizations in social work in the 1980s. Increased representation of faculty, high administrators, deans and directors has been noted in the late 1980s in groups such as Bertha Capen Reynolds Society. The focus of much radical social work activism of late has been the historical preservation of the works of Bertha Reynolds and cooperation with the professional associations in social work around anti-intervention, peace, and aid to the homeless and other liberal to left causes. Little, if any, criticism of top leaders in the social work profession or its organizations, has been voiced for many years from left-wing social workers.

29. In this period, better subscription information is available. Actually listed as "active subscriptions" for each issue were:

Issue 11	620
Issue 12	694
Issue 13	586
Issue 14	608
Issue 15	575
Issue 16	522

However, for each issue, two additional columns followed. One was marked "sponsors/free subs" and the third was marked "other." The third column remains somewhat ambiguous even after an interview with the collective member who maintained the list. The third column for Issue 12 (Gay and Lesbian Issue) is marked as "special purchases," while the third column in issue 14 is marked "authors." Since measurement of the journal's impact can arguably be made to include all those who received each journal by mail, we can also arrive at higher figures by adding the three columns as follows:

Issue 11	687
Issue 12	841
Issue 13	671
Issue 14	717
Issue 15	773
Issue 16	720

30. We will return to this analysis later in the book. The term "bore from within" was used by V.I. Lenin to

describe the communist strategy of infiltrating social democratic or labor parties and trade unions to attempt to move the rank and files of these groups to the left. Indeed, throughout the 1970s and 1980s, some groups of radicals, particularly the Communist Party USA, has advocated such strategies, and many radicals believed that by becoming active members in the National Association of Social Workers and other professional groups, the left would gain legitimacy and new adherents. There is evidence that a large number of leaders in social work, in the professional organizations as well as academia are radicals, some openly and some more covertly.

Of course, the question becomes do these organizations move to the left, or as the 1960s New Leftists warned, do those who bore from within become co-opted by the institutions they attempt to bore into? We will argue that in general the left-wing critique and movement is weakened by absorption into the mainstream of social services (as Jacoby, 1987 argues that radical intellectuals have been absorbed in the academy), though in social work there is also evidence that the left wing critique of the profession has been weakened by paradigmatic and structural changes in the profession itself which make it a less salient target for protest (see Wagner, 1986).

PART I:

*The Moral Careers of Radical
Social Service Workers*

3

BECOMING RADICAL

What exactly does it mean to "be radical?" How do people come to define themselves as radicals and what events and factors do they feel were most influential in this process? This chapter suggests some of the important aspects of radicalization discussed by our subjects.

Family Backgrounds

As in previous studies of radical activists done in the 1960s and 1970s, most subjects came from families who were liberal or moderate Democrats who were at least somewhat in favor of civil rights, labor, and government social programs[1]. Of the subjects interviewed, most described their parents as "liberal," a few classified their families as "moderates" or "apolitical". Only one person described herself as a "red diaper baby," a daughter of Communist Party members (at one time in their lives), and only a small number described their families as "conservative."

Although the subjects spent a great deal of time speculating on the influence of their families-of-origin on their later political identification, none of the individuals came to political radicalism as a simple reflection of their family's views. Typically, for those from liberal families, there were key moments and incidents of discovering family hypocrisy and failings. Naomi, for example, from a Jewish professional, liberal family, described a close relationship with her mother who did considerable volunteer work and strongly believed in the welfare state. However, when Naomi was an adolescent, she:

really couldn't understand her (mother). In my school, all these mothers were helping with the marches in Selma and elsewhere..I

50

couldn't understand why she had no interest
in this...the others did...

Similarly, Barbara, from a white, Catholic,
working class family of strong Democrats, found that
interracial dating in high school revealed her parents
strong latent opposition to integration:

> Boy, was that an uproar...if I wanted to find
> out how my parents really felt about Blacks
> that was the way..and it triggered something
> in my mind,that something was wrong, wrong
> with them, wrong with my town, the way people
> treated the poor, the way people were
> persecuted for the color of their skin...

Even among the people who were able to trace some
past experience with the Left far back into their
parents' lives, this was a hidden strand, which was
not talked about in their childhood or was even
repudiated. Richard, from a Jewish professional
family, recalls:

> Well, now, years later, I can see my family
> was part of a Jewish Left subculture...my
> grandfather was a socialist...but this was
> never talked about in my family...its taken
> me years and years to unearth the hidden
> strains...

While the specific political orientations of
these radicals are not shaped by their families of
origin, the families were obviously influential in
providing some of the early value clusters to their
children, and, like the families of the radicals
studied by Keniston and others, they did often impart
idealistic and egalitarian principles. The only major
difference between those originating from liberal
families and from more conservative ones, is the
relative clarity the latter have as to the exact time
of their radicalization and the degree to which
radical politics has meant a more significant rupture
in their lives. For example, Agnes, whose family is
conservative, sees her radicalization as dramatic:

> It wasn't just becoming political..it changed
> my whole life, my whole world view, how I
> relate to people, to my job, my family...and

51

its kind of scary...not only my family, but most of my friends are apolitical or conservative or liberal...I think because of this I stay away from labels, like socialist or Marxist, it's kind of threatening...

The Time and Setting of Radicalization

As our study includes people ranging in age from 30 to 48, it is not surprising to find a wide variation in the ages at which individuals 'became radical,' in the years in which they became radical, and in the influences upon subjects which they define as "radicalizing" them.

At one extreme is Alan, who at age 13, watched a TV ad for a small socialist party (which had "equal time" airing) and promptly subscribed to their newspaper, becoming a self identified Marxist as a teenager. At the other end of the spectrum is Agnes, who was 33 and a graduate student in a social work, when she heard a prominent radical address a class and was profoundly influenced by the speech.

However, neither Alan nor Agnes were typical. The majority of subjects identified their radicalization as occurring during the 1966-1971 period when social movements such as civil rights, the anti-war movement, the New Left, and the student movement were at their height. For these subjects, the "cutting edge" issues were clear: the War, the draft, Black Power, Community Control, Welfare Rights, etc. One major difference between the "60s radicals" and those who were radicalized later was a *general tendency* among the former to have adopted a more clearly articulated ideological worldview than those who came to their radicalism later. Howard, upon arriving at a college known for its protests in the late 1960s, recalls:

I began going to SDS meetings...out of curiosity, at first, it was real exciting. But soon it became important to know exactly where you stood...I mean the Weathermen people were yelling about 'white skin privilege,' the Progressive Labor (Party) people about the worker-student alliance, and so forth...I knew I had to read Marx and Lenin and everyone, so I could identify what

52

the heck was going on...where I stood...

By contrast, other subjects identify joining the *Catalyst* Collective as their first affirmation of a specifically leftist politics. Rita, who joined *Catalyst* in 1977, remarked early in her interview that she "was always political...always humanistic." However, when I asked her to review her life prior to 1977, Rita notes she did not identify herself as a leftist during this earlier period. Rather when she started graduate school, a fellow student who was in already in *Catalyst*, told Rita "your thinking is like a Marxist." Rita then became a reluctant joiner:

> My experience always started with myself and moved out...I hadn't hung out with political people...certainly never called myself a socialist or socialist-feminist...not until I was in *Catalyst* anyway...though I instinctively was one...there was this hitch with joining (*Catalyst*)....I associated groups like this with collectivism...I had never been in a group like this and it felt like it might be oppressive, I was really resistant at first...

Rosa, who is currently in her early 30s and went to college in the mid-1970s, had a similar experience. While in college, she had a boyfriend in a radical group, but she felt that"they sat around and it was alot of rhetoric. I was struggling with what does this have to do with everyday living?" Several years later, upon moving to New York and becoming a social worker in a ghetto community, Rosa felt interested when she heard about *Catalyst*: "For me, it was hard to live in NYC and not be radical...and be a social worker...the contradictions were so obvious." Yet joining *Catalyst* was a difficult decision, and her identification was more clearly non-ideological than ideological:

> People would get involved in ideological arguments (in *Catalyst*)...to me, since I wasn't exactly sure what my views were anyway, I didn't know if I wanted to have discussions where we went around and talked politics...I felt "what am I going to say?," I'm getting out of here...

53

Of course, any discussion of "radicalization" raises many definitional questions. An interesting example of the variability of people's interpretations of similar political events and their political attitudes is expressed by Mitch and Richard, both of whom are the same age and attended college at the same time. Both Mitch and Richard describe themselves as "followers" at college, trailing along during the many campus demonstrations, but trying to avoid arrest or any potential trouble to their careers. Neither were interested in the organized Left. Yet Mitch declares that he identified with the New Left and considered himself a "radical." Richard, in describing the same series of events, is more critical:" I wasn't a joiner nor an activist nor radical. I was too individualistic at this time." Richard considers himself to have not been a radical at that time, at least in part, it seems, because of a more rigorous definition of radical ideology linked to Marxism, a perspective he would later adhere to. Retrospectively, he views his past political orientation as mainstream:"Yeh, I think I still supported McGovern in 1972!" Richard declares; separating his later viewpoint about the two capitalist parties from his earlier views.

The differential definitions of radical political ideology and different paths to self-definition will be examined below in terms of the distinction between activist and theoretical orientations, and between Marxist, Feminist, and New Left ideologies.

Activist versus Intellectual Orientations

When asked to describe how they "first became radical,"subjects differed considerably in stressing a single event, a series of readings, a milieu of activism or a combination of events. The manner of radicalization, which I have divided into intellectual, simultaneous intellectual/activist, and activist, have important ramifications for political ideology and for how subjects came to identify as professionals.

Very few radicals identified a purely intellectual conversion to radicalism. For these few subjects, a particular article, book, speech or class provided the "intellectual framework" for a developing belief system which had previously been present in only an inchoate form. James replied immediately to the question of how he became radical as follows:

> Yes, I remember exactly. It was in 1970 and I read an article in *Monthly Review*...it was on debt and the economy, I think...it made things click in my head, the way no liberal analysis had..after this I started reading everything I could get my hands on...on economics, political economy, the Left...

Far more typical of the study were those interviewed who described a completely activist orientation toward politics. What is most striking about these subjects is their pride in not being terribly concerned with reading or political theory. This theme appears in the quotations from subjects who were radicalized at very different times:

> (Joseph, radicalized in the early 60s): I remember I was in one of the first major demonstrations against the bomb...I was proud to be part of it...I wasn't sophisticated, but I knew it was immoral...I've never been (an) intellectual...in fact I've always had problems with this...my politics always came not from having read, whatever, but really out of what I believe is morally correct...

> (Renee, radicalized in mid to late 60s):...I always felt I wasn't an intellectual...radical politics didn't mean reading to me or engaging in some sort of intellectual pursuit, being political was *doing* things, not thinking about ideology...

> (Josie, radicalized in late 70s): I don't know...how I came to it (politics)...it wasn't intellectual, but from my gut...the way I judge anything is whether its against my principles and whether I feel comfortable with what's going on...

In fact, an intellectual conversion to leftist political ideology appears to be almost stigmatized, as James explains,"part of me has always (been) ashamed that it was an intellectual conversion." While the importance of activism and de-emphasis on theory certainly characterized at least parts of the New Left, an almost equal number of *Catalyst* members came to radicalism through a combination of strong engagement with a social movement and reading (either in study groups, in the classroom or through independent reading stimulated by their political interests). Those radicalized in the 1960s or early 1970s more consistently combined intellectual study with activism than other subjects. The subjects suggest a strong interaction between social movements and theoretical reading:

> (Jacqueline, radicalized as a VISTA worker after college, circa 1970): Yeh we were organizing Latinos around community issues, the grape boycott, everything...participated in trying to organize a union for VISTA workers...I met this guy, he was in or around the CP (Communist Party) and I started going to a study group...used to read everything that came into alternate press...I really got a political education...

> (Sam, radicalized while working at City job, circa 1970): There was so much happening at the time, we went to all the demonstrations, active with the union, and there were a lot of city employees who were on the Left...they started reaching out to me, and they got me to join a few study groups. Yeh I read everything in those years, but I was ready for it, I was really disillusioned with liberalism by this time...

While the distinctions above should not be overdrawn (since most of the "activists" did eventually come to do theoretical reading at a later point in their lives) their differential accounts of radicalization point to interesting differences. Those who cite intellectual conversions or a combination of involvement with social movements with study are more likely to be male, radicalized in the 1966-1971 period, and be more strongly influenced by Marxism than the purely activist radicals. Moreover, the activist orientation towards politics is closely allied with the "missionary zeal" towards social service work which allowed some subjects to strongly identify with their chosen profession of social work. In a similar vein, future occupational interests can be related to this split; the activists are more likely to be administrators today, and those who combined activist/intellectual orientations are more likely to be in "movement" or "movement like" services (e.g. labor unions) or in academia or planning a career in academia.

Ideological Orientations of the Subjects

Identifying the dominant ideological orientations of the radicals interviewed turned out to be a far more difficult task than I envisioned. After all, all of those interviewed had been members of a group which had a label of *socialist* for at least two years. Yet nearly all those interviewed questioned the relevancy of "labels." Typical of the many comments were Bea's:

I don't know what I am. I've never been comfortable with any of these labels....I suppose my thinking is more socialist-feminist at this point...although I still don't completely know.I've never been sure what it means to be a socialist...I get involved in politics...but not heavily into political distinctions...I judge political events by actions rather than (the) theoretical...

At times, it was difficult to determine whether these comments reflected genuine unclarity, discomfort with left "sectarianism," a discomfort which certainly characterized the group, uncertainty about the interviewer's judgements or a discomfort reflective of collective's past battles over political labels. For some people, ideological stances came out by a process of elimination in which the individual ruminated until arriving at something comfortable:

(Jacqueline): My politics have gotten more certain. Though I don't like the label of socialist (pause) I'm not a social democrat (pause) we need a revolution (pause)..but I'm not comfortable with Communist or Marxist, because (I'm) not sure what alternative structure (I) would like to see, what would work in the US ...

The considerable hesitancy and ambivalence of subjects in attempting to label themselves suggests the problematic nature of labelling as well as the absence, at this time, of a strong left culture and community in the United States. Any classification is subject to interpretation and re-interpretation by the interviewer and interviewee, and is time and place bound. In fact, one of the key points of the study was to view "radicalism" and "radicals" not as a fixed category, but as a dynamic, ever changing orientation, with a heavy dependence on attachment to particular social movements present at the time. For this reason, I tend to share the subjects' own reluctance to classify themselves.

Nevertheless, for the reader to more fully understand the lives of these radicals, some attempt at labelling is necessary. A close analysis of the interviews does enable us to suggest the major ideological influences on our subjects.

Organizationally, the subjects were not strong "joiners" of classically defined political parties. Only two subjects were ever members of Marxist-Leninist parties. Two other subjects were associated for a considerable amount of time with the New American Movement (NAM), with one moving to the merged Democratic Socialists of America (DSA) in the early 1980s. Two other subjects were part of a brief effort at "pre-party formation" in the mid-1970s, the National Interim Committee for a Mass Party of the People (NIC/PAC). All of the above were male, five of the six were Jewish, and five of the six are now in their forties (six years older than the median age of the entire group).

As for the two-party system, only one person displayed any involvement in the major parties (local activism in the Democratic Party), although some people mentioned support for individual candidates in campaigns. It might be noted, however, that this was prior to the Jackson campaign of 1988 which may have involved a number of subjects. Perhaps because the median age of our study participants was only 36, there is less involvement than expected in 1960s groups like Students for Democratic Society (SDS), with only some people mentioning this. A number of subjects note that SDS was not present at their campus or had already split apart when they became politically active. A few people were well aware of SDS, but felt it was "elitist" or "condescending" and never joined the organization.

There was a scattering of affiliation with movement groups of the 1970s and 1980s which are less centralized and formalized in their membership and commitment demands: several subjects were (or are) involved in women's organizations (like CARASA, the Coalition for Abortion Rights and Against Sterilization Abuse), Central American and other solidarity groups (like CISPES, Citizens in Solidarity with the People of El Salvador), anti-nuclear organizations, study groups of various sorts, gay and lesbian organizations, and religious Left projects.

Nevertheless, there appears to be a relatively low level of affiliation with groups which were not occupationally connected as opposed to groups that were linked to professional activism. In addition to *Catalyst*, a third of the population was involved in the Radical Alliance of Social Service Workers (RASSW), several in the 1960's Social Workers Action for Welfare Rights (SWAWR), in the newly formed radical Bertha C. Reynolds Society (BCRS), in radical planning groups (the Urban Underground, the Planners Network), in other left social service groups (such as URHSW, the Union of Radical Human Service Workers, and CBHN, the Coalition for Basic Human Needs), and in radical psychologist groups. The strong involvement of this group with radical professional movements, and relatively low level of involvement with extra-professional radical groups, might suggest that the radical professional groups can be considered a social movement in its own right, perhaps attracting different individuals than other radical movements.

In an effort to present the ideological orientations of subjects, interviewees' self definitions and reported past memberships were analyzed as well as inferences made from other statements made by subjects. Despite the reluctance to self-label and the imprecision of such labels, both Marxism and Feminism were overwhelmingly identified as influential ideologies for the majority of those interviewed. Among those influenced by Marxism, there

59

was considerable questioning and ruminating about various aspects of what the subjects saw as Marxist precepts: the working class as agency for change; the question of the vanguard party; the ultimate collapse of capitalism, etc. However, interestingly there was no contemporary movement away from a general identification with Marxism, despite specific questioning of various versions of Marxism. One subject, Monica, who at 30 was the youngest person interviewed, expressed a movement from Feminism to Marxism:

> Interviewer: Would you say your politics have changed at all since you began to identify as a radical?
>
> Monica: No, they haven't...except I used to say I was a Feminist (pause) now I'm more of a Marxist (pause) I used to see issues more of patriarchal control, now (I) see economics and money as kinda the bottom line...and, of course, this incorporates sexual oppression as well...

Sam, in a series of ruminations also generally returns to a Marxist view:

> Interviewer: What do you think now of what you were studying (in Left study groups)?
>
> Sam: Definitely there was truth in it. I became an anti-capitalist certainly and I'm a socialist (pause) I'm not sure if I'm a Marxist or Leninist anymore (pause) I don't know whether capitalism will destroy itself without a revolutionary vanguard, but I'm not really involved with that (pause) I would like to think that change would occur peacefully (pause) but probably not...I still have the Leninist leanings, I guess, yeh...

Those heavily influenced by Marxism, even including those also influenced by Feminism, still tended to be more male, and they also tended to be over 35.

Feminism appeared to be the other major theoretical orientation of the population, including

some overlap with Marxist or socialist thought.
Feminism tended to provide a theoretical framework for
the younger members of the population (under 35) many
of whom joined *Catalyst* after its inception. For
example:

> (Josie, age 32): I guess I got political when
> I went to college..I got very involved in
> women's issues. I took some very militant
> women's rights courses...it was more of a
> personal thing...at 15 I wasn't very affected
> by reading Feminist stuff, but at 19 I
> was...I began to label my problems and what I
> saw as part of sexism...

> (Brenda, age 34): I always considered myself
> a Feminist (pause) it came early on (pause)
> I guess a reaction to the traditional
> structure...I read Feminist literature in
> college...took a lot of women's studies
> courses...

Like Marxism, there is little or no attrition
from this basic belief system, although specific
tenets of past political perspectives were sometimes
questioned, and, of course, like socialism, there are
many variants of feminist theory. Like many subjects,
Barbara, referring to her Marxism and Feminism, sees
politics as a life long commitment:

> (My politics) are not just something I think
> and feel. I live it. I don't know how to live
> another way. Its weird!...I can't understand
> how other people can become 'non-political.'
> Sure I get tired and want to take time or go
> away for a year. But I can't ever see saying
> 'that was a phase in my life' or 'those were
> my political days'...

A third major influence on the population was New
Left thought. In contrast to Marxism and Feminism, the
precepts of the New Left, at least when viewed in the
1980s, appear even more indeterminate than either
Marxism or Feminism (even with the many variants and
splits which have occurred among these theories).
Indeed no one identified themself as a "New Leftist."
However, some subjects in their belief in the poor and
minorities (and also students and other elements of

the population defined by Marcuse as part of the 'periphery') being a vanguard for change; in decentralized authority and local control; and in participatory democracy and skepticism about Leninist parties (to cite but a few ideas) reflect the New Left movements of the 1960s[2]. Those who were profoundly influenced by the New Left include nearly two-thirds of the people studied.

What makes "New Left" ideology difficult to analyze in the 1980s is its superordination on the one hand by Marxism and Feminism, and, on the other hand, a detachment from past radicalism by many former New Leftists. For example, when the people who were active in and influenced by the New Left were analyzed with regard to current ideology, only a few people remain who were not now (in the 1980s) more clearly identified with Marxism or Feminism. Since the 1960s, subjects who remained wedded to radical ideologies generally gravitated to strong Marxist or Feminist perspectives. Interestingly, the few remaining people who did not strongly embrace these perspectives are now the least likely to identify with the left at all. These subjects are George, who was the only person interviewed to clearly repudiate his past politics and no longer identified as a radical; Mitch, who describes himself as primarily a "left liberal"; and Joseph and Ann, whose current orientations are more complex, but who generally suggest they are a little more "conservative" now than in the 1960s and 1970s.

There was some sympathy and comments which could be interpreted as sympathetic to other ideologies, particularly anarchism or radical ecological perspectives. However, none of those interviewed posed this a major identification, but mentioned aspects of this thinking in addition to ideologies such as socialism or feminism.

While a detailed review of Marxist, Feminist or New Left ideology is beyond the purpose of this work I do suggest that *specific* ideological orientation is certainly *one factor* in how radicals understand their work lives. As will be explored further in Chapters 5 and 6, those subjects who have had a strong socialization to Marxism will have a relatively more difficult time identifying with social work and with maintaining strong professional loyalties. Those with more of a Feminist political orientation will experience somewhat less tension between radicalism and professionalism. Further, the Marxist orientation toward the working class as the vanguard for social change has provided more support to the "professional-as-worker" strategy for radical professionals, that is for unionization and employee caucuses, and for an educational role vis a vis clients and students. The Feminist and New Left perspectives, while not counterposed to Marxism, find their stronger influence in the development of a "radical practice" in the human service professions: i.e. the use of therapy or teaching to raise consciousness on the part of clients or the use of community organizing techniques to organize clients for community and personal empowerment. Further, to the extent the ideologies can be separated, emphasis on different client populations (the working class, the poor, women, etc.) for professional services and political organizing would be suggested by these ideologies.

Notes

1. The best studies of radical youth and their families are probably still the early ones. Kenneth Keniston's Young Radicals: Notes on Committed Youth, New York: Harcourt, Brace and World, 1968 has a wealth of information about family backgrounds, as does the series of studies of New Leftists by Richard Flacks (see R. Flacks,"The Liberated Generation: An Exploration of the Roots of Student Protest," Journal of Social Issues, 23:3, 1967, pp. 52-75; Flacks and Neurgarten,"The Liberated..."; and Flacks,Youth and Social Change, Chicago: Rand McNally, 1971).

2. For the best summaries of the ideology and contributions of the New Left, see Sale, S.D.S., particularly pp. 3-11; and James Miller, Democracy is in the Streets, New York: Simon and Schuster, 1987.

4

BECOMING SOCIAL WORKERS

What leads people to choose social service work, and what leads radicals to choose such work? This is a particularly interesting question because a great deal of research has suggested radicals tend to major in the social science and humanities areas[1], which may suggest a self-selection process is at work in career selection [2]. Yet, on the other hand, a large number of the people interviewed were not politically radical when they chose social service work. Could their conversion to radical ideologies then be a function of the professional training and socialization they received? This would be somewhat surprising in that many observers have argued that professionalization in general, and social work schools, in particular, have a conservatizing influence on neophytes[3].

This chapter will review what our subjects said about their choice of social service work as well as their experience of professional training.

"Missionary Zeal" and Social Service Work

It became evident in talking with subjects that most chose social service work out of strong feelings of "missionary zeal." While many had only vague ideas about the field prior to entering professional training, subjects generally saw counseling, community organizing or working with people in general, as a kind of "calling." Their comments bespoke a quasi religious feeling:

(Rosalind): One becomes a social worker to do good (pause) it's a way of serving, it's a way of understanding the human condition and acting on it and changing it and I needed to do that, you know...It goes back to what I described when I was nine years old (pause)

understanding that this (poverty) was wrong,
thought of it as being evil that people
should suffer this way...I was going to be a
good person when I grew up and I was going to
help people.

(Bea):...and I thought that if I wanted to
change the world, which, of course, I wanted
to do, that I would have to be a social
worker!

(Ann): I wanted to save the world...I thought
about the Peace Corps. That was the ideal
world. But (failing that) I could work with
children and help save the world...

To what extent was this "save the world"
orientation a "political" one? This is a complex
question because it raises interconnecting issues of
humanitarianism and political action: the historic tie
between women's caretaking role and human services
(the strongest "missionary" orientation was among the
women interviewed), the religious overtones to a
"mission" (notably almost all the Roman Catholics in
our study had strong missionary attitudes), the upward
mobility strivings of subjects from working class
families (these subjects displayed strong zeal; while
only half of those from professional/business families
did), and the role of family socialization (a number
of subjects who were from professional families had
parents who were psychiatrists, psychologists or
social workers, which may have influenced their career
choices).

To explore this complex dynamic, we can separate
subjects into those who displayed strong "missionary
zeal,"but were not self-consciously leftist at the
time of their career choice, those who combined strong
zeal for social service with radical politics, and
those who did not display any feelings of "missionary
zeal."

Nearly half of those who described their desire
for social service work as a "mission" were not
politically radical upon making a career choice. For
these subjects, human service work was a value choice,
a means of "doing good" and getting paid which
involved people rather than material concerns or

profit:

> (Rita): I always had a sense of honesty and
> fairness...and people would tell me their
> problems (laughs) sometimes I feel like I was
> a social worker from (the) time I was
> five...and then when I worked as an
> executive-in-training in a department store,
> it hit me, this wasn't productive work...if
> you have to spend all this time in a job, it
> should be meaningful to you...and I began to
> have strong feelings about things that
> operated for profit (pause) I didn't like the
> way the women were treated (at the department
> store)...

> (Brenda): I think my career and my beliefs
> stem from my Catholic background, some of the
> values that are implicit in there, although
> certainly (you) run into a lot of
> contradictions...but still the right to work,
> the equality of all people, civil rights,
> there all in there...

In addition to the humanistic and religious
values displayed by this group, there was a strong,
but latent, sense of feminism among these subjects
choosing social service work. In many cases, subjects
would come to a more developed ideological position
later in their careers. And, in many cases, the
problems inherent in social service work which may
interfere with "missionary zeal" also became apparent
to the subjects as their careers progressed.

A slightly larger group of people who displayed
strong "missionary zeal" also identified themselves as
leftists upon embarking on professional training in
social service. While these individuals echoed the
same idealism as the subjects above, they also raised
different themes. They differed primarily in being
attracted to social service, not to counsel people on
a one-on-one basis, but to become community
organizers. These subjects were all profoundly
influenced by the New Left and saw social service as a
way of being paid for "doing radical work."

Jacqueline, for example, had worked as a VISTA
volunteer and on an alternative paper prior to

deciding on a career in social work. She wanted to earn more money and have a "more meaningful job" than her secretarial position afforded. While she considered other professions, the possibility of organizing attracted her:

> (I) thought there would be some way of combining my political beliefs with a job...figured I could do community organizing that I'd get paid for, instead of earning $25 a week like I did working (as non-degreed organizer)...I had this image of social work trying to meet people's needs and educate people too (pause) like the Black Panther Party was doing...

For Joseph, the decision to go to Social Work School was overtly political, helping him overcome difficulties with school and career, which he attributes to psychological issues. Earlier in his life, Joseph had dropped out of college, spent much of the 1960s as a street worker with gangs and later as an owner of a small building rehab business. Becoming "political" around 1970 influenced him to enroll in a program which combined completing his undergraduate degree with a masters in Social Work:

> My decision was totally wrapped up with my politics...it helped me get the credential and become a professional...I knew exactly what I wanted to do: organize the white working class. No one else was doing it at that time. This goal kept me there (in school) and helped me overcome my inferiority complex...

For a number of people, the choice of concentrations in social work school was a critical barometer of their politics: they associated community organization with radicalism, and social casework, groupwork or psychological theory with conservatism:

> (Renee):I got to school still not knowing what I would do...and then at Orientation, there was this faculty member talking about Community Organization... It sounded exciting (and) they were talking this language... talked about the 'power structure,' 'the

power structure,' you have to research the power structure. It sounded activist and militant and the casework people were boring. I switched to community organizing (as a major)...

A few subjects did enter the helping professions without the kind of enthusiasm noted above. This group included some of those most socialized to Marxism through prior affiliation with leftist parties. Further, for three of these individuals who are now in their forties and had worked in various welfare departments, their own occupational experience made them question how "radical" the goals of social work could be:

(James):I saw my job (at a welfare department) as social control more than anything else, I guess...and community organization, this wasn't real at welfare...you discovered it meant being little more than a spy, telling (management) what clients were thinking so they could do something about it.

(Alan): I knew zip about social work. I figured it was the same stuff that we did in welfare (department) with big words...I had no conception that this was political,(but) I thought at a minimum, this was a way out of the welfare department which I hated...

Court questioned the basic precept of the "missionary" activists by suggesting strong limits to any political compatibility between work in a capitalist society and radical politics:

A lot of people get burned out because they expect too much!...I never felt that my jobs would be anything but screwed up in a political sense...It depends what you're hoping for. Naturally if your image of yourself is that you're going to get paid a fair salary for undermining (the) capitalist society, then you're doomed to disappointment. I always thought that people who imagined that were just misinformed.

Those who sought to combine leftist political views with careers in the social services (particularly community organization), while numerous in our study, clearly were associated with a particular historical period. The subjects entered professional school in the early 1970s, having been strongly influenced by the New Left and the anti-poverty wars, VISTA, and welfare rights organizing. In contrast, the remaining subjects entered the professions with a less explicit political orientation and were *then* socialized into radical politics; or, in a few cases, were radical upon entering the professions, but viewed social service work as being somewhat problematic from a radical perspective.

Upward Mobility as a Goal

Studies of social workers[4] and literature in the sociology of work and occupations[5] suggest that social work and other human service professions have historically provided a bounded upward mobility for women excluded from higher status professions and business, as well as upward mobility for males from working class and minority families (the latter being true since the 1960s).

Indeed, despite the quest for a radical job, the subjects interviewed often spoke of a social service career as their best opportunity for income and status. Overwhelmingly, the female subjects felt limited to what Etzioni classified as the "semi-professions." Jacqueline, upon saving some money to go to school, felt her choice to be Social Work or Library School; Rosalind began college, having come from a working class background, with nursing, teaching or social work as her perceived career possibilities; Monica felt her choice was between special education and social work; and Agnes initially went to college to be a nurse, but upon deciding that she didn't have the "mechanical hands-on" skills to do nursing decided to try human service work. For Rita, who worked in retail; Rosalind, as a hotel clerk; Agnes, as a unit clerk in a hospital; and Brenda, as a child care worker, there is a strong sense of achievement in having earned degrees in social work or related fields.

The opportunity for upward mobility is

significant as well for men from the lower social economic classes. Joseph, whose parents were garment workers, spoke with great esteem of the social workers who first hired him as a non-professional. When he was admitted back to college in a joint program with a M.S. in Social Work, he says,"I was in tears when they admitted me. (I) couldn't believe (that) someone believed in me, and would offer me this opportunity." Sam, from a farm family, was able to take advantage of what had been a generous tuition reimbursement program in the public sector in the 1960s to go to graduate school:

> I had no money saved up after three years in New York City. But the welfare scholarships were available to go to Social Work School. At full salary. I didn't think I would even get in (to Social Work School),(it) was almost a lark, but I was accepted...and I don't know, I was very vague about what social work even was...

At this point in their careers, subjects felt little contradiction between the "missionary zeal" of helping people and the practical virtues of mobility and career achievement. However, upward mobility as a sole motivation appears rare. Differing balances of idealism with career goals suggest three possible orientations: pure "missionaries," whose 'save the world' orientation is pre-political and often combined with strong career aspirations, political missionaries, who are self-consciously leftist upon choosing the human services, usually majoring in community organization (combining the goal of radical politics with paid work), and careerists,some of whom are also leftists, but whose primary attraction to the social services is career mobility, often arriving fortuitously in the professions through the availability of scholarships and employment benefits such as leaves of absence. The conflicts that appear for subjects once in paid employment (see Chapters 5-6) also suggests that the mediation between mobility goals and political and idealistic motivations are most possible at the early stages of a career.

Professional Education as Radicalizing

Typically, the definition of what constitutes a

"profession" has been linked to a socialization process in higher education where initiates are invested with certain professional norms and acculturated into a unique subculture distinguishing professionals from others[6]. These norms are hardly radical, but in Merton's terms "neutral, objective, disinterested...values inherent in the scientific process"[7]. Yet when professional training is addressed as an aspect of liberal arts education, theorists have suggested that certain social factors such as freedom from occupational commitment, the aggregation of large numbers of "roleless" youth, and the influence of a liberal to left faculty is conducive to the development of radical student movements[8]. While radicals have typically criticized the professional norms and culture of universities, some studies have indicated that the period of professional training can indeed be a period of significant radicalization[9].

Because of these conflicting views, I was particularly interested in how the study's subjects experienced professional training. Were these radicals socialized to professional norms and ideology in school and did they adopt the same norms and values of professionalism which have been characterized as politically conservative?

Significantly, professional education, at least at the graduate level, had an almost universally politicizing effect. While at school, those subjects who had not identified as leftists at earlier points began to identify themselves as such. For many subjects who had already defined themselves as politically leftist, school provided the possibility of increased political activism, theoretical education, and commitment. Secondly, while some subjects were critical of their education and certain values and norms imparted, professional socialization appears to have primarily resulted in greater commitment to both social service professionalism and radicalism. This suggests that the marriage of professionalism and radicalism is strong upon completion of professional training i.e. further heightening subjects' "missionary zeal."

Institutions such as schools of social work were not in themselves viewed as being hospitable to radical political ideology. Not surprisingly, they

71

provided an environment in which liberal values and political orientations were inculcated. Rather than being simple products of professional socialization and the inculcation of norms, subjects defined their political ideologies in *opposition* to the prevailing school culture. As studies of student activism would suggest, they were aided in this process by the availability of a limited number of radical role models (including professors), by having available time for intellectual activity, and by the presence on campus of large aggregates of students which provided opportunities for the existence of oppositional student subcultures.

Radical professors and fellow students were clearly the most important influences on those who came to define themselves as leftist in professional schools. George, for example, came to a School of Social Work in the mid-1960s, with an interest in groupwork he had gained from years of summer camp experience, but he had not defined himself politically. George remembers his school as not being very political, "it was before relevancy," he quips. However, a well known radical professor who taught a required course was influential. It was the very beginning of welfare rights organizing, and the professor urged the class to become involved in demonstrations of welfare recipients:

> It was very exciting. Before I knew it, I was getting arrested, blocking the doors of the welfare center...Somehow came to feel...that we were in the midst of this revolution...but it was greatly (professor) who was active in the school, not too many others...

Brenda, who entered graduate school in the late 1970s, with strong missionary idealism, but not identified with leftist politics, found her own education to be "extremely conservative":

> Oh, it was difficult! The politics were real conservative, (a) psychoanalytic orientation that I struggled with the whole time I was there. The majority of the teachers just looked at the intrapsychic...and I found it kind of blaming-the-victim stuff...maybe it

72

was my Feminism, but I found myself always arguing against the Freudian stuff...it seemed like all you were doing was sitting down and chatting with people on a weekly basis and if they didn't show up, then it was classified as resistance...

Brenda began to feel strongly that the curriculum and the atmosphere at the school was not what she went into social work for. She began to become active with some other students in school politics and met two professors who were known as radicals. Eventually they developed a seminar which focused on how "Social Work maintains the system."

Agnes, who came to Social Work School in the early 1980s, and was not particularly political or missionary, found that radical politics allowed her to overcome feelings of extreme alienation and frustration that she had felt in her first year of school:

I had figured I had to go to grad school to really learn it...to do social work. Wrong! (Laughs)...the first year was awful...I don't know why, maybe my expectations were too high...but the classes weren't good...I was confused (pause) I thought 'what is this?' 'What are these people doing?' They don't listen. This stuff is not what the real world is about. It lacked reality. And I didn't like the people...

Later that year, Agnes took a course with a radical professor, and heard the speech of another noted radical social worker. Not only did the course lead her to discover "there was something other than a liberal or conservative view" about the world, but it led her to develop a study group of radical caseworkers. Interestingly, the conversion to a radical ideology made the choice of social work as a profession feel less conflictual for her.

Of course, student status also allows the opportunity for students to interact with campuswide events and movements, not restricting them only to social service professors and students. For Rosalind, who entered a Ph.d. program in Social Work and

Psychology in the mid-1970s with "missionary zeal" and counter-cultural influences, but without a leftist political orientation, a campus strike of graduate assistants led her to contact with leftist students:

> There I was all of a sudden stopping trucks, writing the Teamsters Union, working out strategies for mass arrests...I was on the bargaining committee, a picket captain, a steward...I made friends throughout the University...and all the radicals were there. The Union became a magnet for the radicals...and I began to get a political education...

For those who came to professional school already identified as politically leftist, the time spent in school was characterized by an increase in radical activism, in a deepening commitment to study and integration of radical politics, and a beginning commitment to extend radical politics to the social service professions. For some subjects, the activities within the school; classes, field work internships, student government, union strikes; provided a maelstrom of activity in which to engage:

> (Bea): I was active politically from day one of school! All my friends were too. We were active organizing things on campus, involved in the union's strike, (we) wrote articles for the school paper...There were several study groups...my first year placement was great! A wonderful politicizing experience. The supervisors were (well known labor organizer, and a left activist)..I learned all about the labor movement..it was a hotbed of activity...

> (Barbara):It was a great experience! First of all, I was fortunate in my field placement. Here I was in this multi-ethnic community doing housing organizing..with a staff organized as a collective...with a Marxist as my supervisor...it was a wonderful exposure...I hated my classes, but this led me to get more active. Became head of student government and fought tooth and nail,it was a daily struggle...and that's why I liked

school. I got involved, of course, with
RASSW...I was going 20 hours a day...

(Joseph): School was great...I guess I became
one of the 'politically hip' people. We
organized a grievance committee, you know,
around people being counseled out of
school...it was a great thing, it was a real
thorn in (dean's) side...we were very
provocative, challenging the School on
everything...my field placement was great.
Trained by feminist organizer...we made the
community center a real community run
program...wrote the by-laws so that it would
be consumer controlled...

For others, the period of graduate training led
to increased political activity and commitment, but
not in the school environment itself. In fact, it was
quite often during professional school that subjects
joined radical professional groups such as RASSW,
URHSW, Health/PAC and *Catalyst*:

(Ann): Marxism really came alive to me at
this point. In Social Work School, for the
first time in my life, I felt I had to join a
political organization...I couldn't do social
work without doing political work at the same
time...You couldn't help people adjust to the
system, you had to do something to change the
system that made them the way they were...I
got heavily involved in RASSW. I felt
people's problems weren't individual...You
really have to do something about that.
There's no way in casework to do this, not
casework by itself...

While there are many factors related to the high
degree of radical activity subjects engaged in during
professional training, notably the relative youth of
subjects (most were in their twenties) along with
limited family and work obligations, the findings are
salient for two reasons. First, several of the
subjects who were young and already politically
identified with the Left, became *more* active during
graduate school than in the years immediately prior.
For example, Howard, Barbara, and Jacqueline, all
radicalized in the late 60s, had been less active and

organizationally involved in the years prior to school (the early 1970s), then while attending school. It appears that the aggregation of a community (students, faculty, etc.), the stimulus of intellectual learning, and, perhaps, the need to reconcile their professional training with their idealism led subjects to stronger political involvements.

Moreover, the relationship between professional school and radicalization holds steady whether subjects attended graduate schools in the 1960s, 1970s or 1980s. These findings of increased radicalization appears significant in that, as noted above, a considerable amount of literature on professionalization stresses its conservatizing nature, rather than its radicalizing potential.

Developing a Radical Professionalism

How did subjects reconcile their increased radicalism with the professional norms, paradigms, and ideology they were being socialized to? It is conceivable that radical professionals could reject professional norms altogether[10] or could experience tremendous tension, a "role strain" in Mertonian terms, between the two sets of norms (professional and ideological). Conversely, radical professionals could accept professional roles either by re-interpreting them or by selecting certain aspects of professional culture and rejecting others in order to find an occupational orientation and ideological view that incorporated both sets of norms.

The study shows that radical social workers can interpret their professional training to be consistent with radicalism. There is little evidence that subjects rejected professional norms, paradigms, and roles at this time, and, in fact, the identification of the subjects with a radical tradition in the social services reached its high point at the time of graduation from professional school. With the exception of several individuals, "missionary zeal" reached its zenith with professional training, and most of the population expressed optimism about being "radical social workers," "radical therapists,"or "radical organizers," at this time.

Virtually all of the subjects praised the

training they received in most areas of their education. This positive view of professional knowledge and skills was particularly apparent among the subjects who were trained in direct social work practice:

> (Mitch, describing his internship): Yes, it was a very traditional setting, a psychiatric clinic in a hospital.But I loved it. I had a stupendous supervisor. And all these other students were complaining about their placements...Its very ironic, I guess, here I was attacking the school for supporting certain traditions and I was working in a fairly traditional environment and enjoying it...

> (Monica, describing her internship): I wanted to do clinical work, but with a poor population where I could also do systems work, be an advocate. When I asked for this, my advisor looked at me, and said "Why do you want to do that?"But they gave it to me...and I was thrilled!...worked with children and adolescents, learned a lot about individual and family therapy, but also did a lot of concrete services...

Interestingly, even some of those who had viewed a social work career as problematic came to adopt the skill claims and basic paradigms of the profession:

> (Court): Yeh, I had had a lot skepticism about social work as a profession...had absorbed some of the critique of social work as an agency of social control... But, I learned a great deal about psychodynamics!...I developed a sense of skill, I learned I was good at what I did and there was a lot to know about child welfare...complex and demanding work which requires professional skill...sure I resisted and still do the elitist connotations of professionalism, but I began to accept it in so far as professionalism is a skill, a craft, a responsibility...

Alan, developed a similar respect for

psychodynamic skill and for the possibility of using therapy for radical ends:

> Once I got to School...I discovered that psychotherapy was part of social work and I liked this...I began to read Wilhelm Reich and follow the *Radical Therapist*. I was intrigued by it and generally persuaded by it...discovered I could do therapy. This gave me a context, because prior to this I had no idea what I was doing there (in school)...I finally felt that this was a way to combine my political beliefs with my career...

Subjects commented on the irony of their socialization to the profession. Mitch's comments are typical:"I fought professional socialization all the way...and, of course, it was happening anyway!" However, I would reject the view that such socialization was unconscious. Rather these new professionals developed a clear self-consciousness while undergoing training.

The radical counselors were hostile to what they saw as the dominant view of counseling among their peers in school: a private practice model of clinical work which focused on middle and upper class people so that young social workers or psychologists could increase their income and achieve status through the psychotherapy market. These people were characterized as "therapoid narcissicists" by Court:

> I have no patience with these people. They're just into status and they claim to be so big and skilled and yet they have a lot less skill than a good social worker in an agency...they operate in a really narrow realm of neurotic problems...

Rather, the radical counselors were committed to agency based social work practice, particularly for the poor, working class, and oppressed populations (rather than "middle class" or "upper class" people). Additionally, the radical counselors shared another set of norms. They opposed the narrow definitions of clinical work as being a 45 minute interview, and believed good counseling involved case advocacy for clients, provision of concrete services, development of groups (both therapeutic and self-help), and community organizing. The narrow specialization of clinical work bothered these subjects who adopted a "generalist" approach to social work[11]. The commitment to use all possible means to help clients, but particularly social action, was critical to the self-definition of these subjects:

> (Rita): I had trouble in school...with students and faculty who talked about clients in a de-personalized, clinical way...you know, the attraction for me was the many different ways you could help a client by intervening as a social worker. Being a generalist means knowing casework, groupwork, administration, and how to organize with clients...and then you can work in whatever situation the clients find themselves in and what they need, not what *you* need. Politically to me, that also felt right...

The complementarity of radical and professional norms was a more complex issue for those subjects who majored in community organization and in other non direct practice areas. The majority of community organizing students felt that organizing itself *was being radical,* particularly when organizing was combined with a commitment to the poor, the working class, minorities or other oppressed populations (women, gays and lesbians, the aged, the handicapped):

> (Bea):I had no idea at first that there was such a thing as organizing jobs and that I could continue my interest in this. And in school, there were all these clinical types, but here I could extend my political interests and be paid for it by being an organizer...as that became clear I was very happy to have been thrust, somewhat by chance, into Community Organization and have nothing to do with the rest of the school...I felt very unconnected with most of the school...

> (Josie): I had a negative, stereotypical impression of social work in school, and I still do... But...community organizing...we had a real thing...we were the political

people, we were the most militant, most
vocal...it was C.O., its political
orientation that interested and intrigued me,
not that feely, sort of touchy, feely
stuff...

A majority of the community organizers, like the
caseworkers, defined their professional norms in
opposition to what they saw a dominant clinical
paradigm involving work with middle class individuals
behind the closed doors of a therapy office.

A minority of subjects who were either community
organization, research or other non clinical majors,
found professionalization and radical values to be
problematic for two reasons. One, was the tendency of
more intellectually, academically oriented subjects to
look at training more critically and to therefore have
less connection with the radical tradition in the
social services. Secondly, and closely related, was
the fact that these subjects were cut off from any one
professional paradigm and feared, even prior to
graduating, that there was no place for them in the
social service employment market:

(Jacqueline, C.O. student in Social Work
School):I was very disappointed with C.O...I
mean they seemed to be fabricating a theory
out of nothing...and then my placements
really had nothing to do with community
organizing...we ended up doing casework and
groupwork with these schizophrenic clients.
When I said this doesn't seem like C.O., the
school said that's all we have now...I just
clung to a fantasy that there still was real
C.O. going on, somewhere, someplace, but, of
course, the school was out of touch with
it...

(Naomi, student in Ph.D. program in Social
Policy): It was a conflict (school). I didn't
fit into any of the functional areas of the
school, you know, retardation, aging,
alcoholism, whatever...I didn't fit in. I had
no professional identification. And I knew
I'd be in trouble later. I mean
professionally...in the sense of being an
academic. And I was right. It was highly

problematic. I wasn't considered a social worker, not a hard core academic, neither fish nor fowl.

The critical perspective of the subjects above including the problematic nature of "fitting into" an occupational area in the social service professions, the difficulty accepting uncritically certain professional paradigms, and ultimately the problem of identifying with the profession at all, would come to characterize many subjects later in their careers. But at the time of professional training, most subjects felt that radical politics and the norms and values of the social work profession were complementary. Indeed, the radical caseworkers and community organizers were following an historic tradition.

While many subjects *felt* they were defining their ideology and principles of professional practice in opposition to dominant norms of their particular school or to the majority of students in school at the time, the values and norms of agency based practice committed to poor people with an emphasis on advocacy, activism, and community organization reflect an historic tradition in the social work profession dating back to the Settlement House movement of Jane Addams and Lillian Wald. While the professionalization project in social work has led to an increased status quest with a particular desire to expand services to new markets (including the middle class and upper class in some cases) and to promote specialized and more highly psychiatric types of services, most textbooks, faculty, and schools in social work support, at least, in the abstract, the key principles enunciated: service to the poor, social action, and agency-based practice.

As Bertha Reynolds said, what might be different about such radicalism is that it treated seriously these high abstract principles of social work[12]. Subjects at the time of professional socialization had absorbed the values and norms of social service as taught in its most idealistic form. They did not challenge the basic precepts or techniques of social casework nor of groupwork or community organization. Nor did they reject the elements of a professional relationship which some in the 1960s challenged as "professional dominance." However, the subjects rejected as narrow and elitist, aspects of professional rhetoric and training which were not consistent with an "original mission" of social work as conceived of by radicals.

Rosalind describes this as "reclaiming social work for us as radicals, going back to its progressive roots." Rita stated "I identify with the social work of the 1930s, not today. I identify strongly with the values I perceive social work to have or at least once (have) stood for."

By the time of graduation from school, the vague "missionary zeal" of "saving the world" had become a more sophisticated quest for a radical profession which traced its roots to the historic traditions of social work.

Notes

1. The large number of studies done in the 1960s on radical students overwhelmingly found them likely to be social science or humanities majors (for a summary of the many studies, see Keniston,<u>Radicals...</u>).

2. Lipset,<u>Rebellion...</u>, p. 82.

3. See, for example, Geoffrey Pearson,"Making Social Workers," in Bailey and Brake (eds.), <u>Radical...</u>,pp. 13-45; Cloward and Piven,"Acquiescence...,"; and Mark Monchek,"Drawing the Lines: My Political Education in Social Work School,"<u>Catalyst</u>, 1:4 (1979), pp. 19-34.

4. See, for example, Alfred Stamm,"NASW Membership: Characteristics, Deployment, and Salaries,"<u>Personnel Information</u>, Silver Spring, Md.: National Association of Social Workers, 1969.

5. See, for example, Amatai Etzioni,<u>The Semi-Professions and Their Organization</u>, New York: The Free Press, 1969, and Nina Toren,<u>Social Work: The Case of a Semi-Profession</u>, Beverly Hills: Sage, 1971.

6. Classical treatments and definitions of the professions include Talcott Parsons,<u>The Social System</u>, Glencoe, Ill: The Free Press, 1951; Robert Merton <u>et. al.</u>,<u>The Student Physician</u>, Cambridge: Harvard University Press, 1957; and William Goode,"Community

within a Community: the Professions,"<u>American Sociological Review</u>, 22 (1957), pp. 194-200.

7. Robert Merton,<u>Social Theory and Social Structure</u>, Glencoe,Ill: The Free Press, 1949.

8. Lipset,<u>Rebellion....</u>

9. Two suggestive studies are on physicians, J. S. Maxmen,"Medical Student Radicals: Conflict and Resolution,"<u>American Journal of Psychiatry</u>, 127:9 (1971), pp. 131-134; and on social workers, Rubin Todres,"The Radicalization of Social Work Students,"unpublished paper, 1978.

10. This was the prescription of the radicals-in-the-professions movement suggested by Haber and Haber,"Getting By..." and the conclusion of John and Barbara Ehrenreich,"The Professional..."

11. "Generalist" social work practice is now a term used to describe the curricula thrust of major Schools of Social Work. Beginning in the early 1970s, a minority of graduate schools went from the traditional method divisions of Casework, Groupwork, and Community Organization to teaching "generalist" practice. Depending on one's definition of "generalist practice," it has arguably been central to social work since the 1890s settlement house worker or is relatively new. In either case, the assumption of generalist practice is that methodology or technique of social work is subordinated to client problem, so that dependent on client problem, the social worker might use individual casework, groupwork, organizing, or different interventions within the methods such as advocacy, providing concrete services, planning, etc. Hence, social workers in this view need to capable of providing a multiplicity of services rather than be defined as a pure clinician, groupworker, planner, etc.

12. Reynolds, <u>Unchartered...</u>, p. 173; The idea of the professions being based on such broad abstractions that a variety of "segments" can cite similar literature for very different purposes while presenting a "fictional unity" to the public may be central to this process. See Rue Bucher and Anselm Strauss,"The Professions in Process,"<u>American Journal</u>

of Sociology, 66 (1961), pp. 325-334.

5

Images of Success, Worlds of Pain

A large amount of information was collected in this study on the early to middle careers of radicals. All told, we talked to subjects about 150 different jobs they had held. Subjects discussed dozens of case examples of individual clients they had counseled or community groups they had organized or assisted. The data is rich and varied, and belies the ability of job resumes or purely objective measures to actually capture the complex experience of worklife.

Images of Success

Subjects were interviewed at a point which found most of the individuals approximately ten to fifteen years into a "career." A description of the group's occupational positions, professional credentials, and accomplishments provides a portrait of success and diversity. While the societal image of "social workers" might conjure up welfare workers or other low paid and low status positions, studies of the social work profession (particularly those with a Masters degree) indicate a substantial movement into positions of administration, supervision, private practice psychotherapy, as well as mobility into other fields such as business, health care, and education[1]. While the group in this study fared at least as well, gaining considerable mobility and occupying fairly high positions within the health, education, and welfare apparatus in the U.S., we were interested in whether these subjects, as radicals, *perceived* themselves to be successful or satisfied. Do radicals have different career patterns and objectives than other social service workers, or do they share similar objectives?

By virtue of their job positions and accomplishments, the group presents an impressive picture. The group includes: several high level administrators in state and city governments who control considerable funds and supervise large staffs, an official of a major labor union, several faculty members with significant accomplishments for their age, a business executive, and several social service administrators and organizers who have gained local prominence. Educationally, our subjects include six Ph.D.s, five doctoral candidates, and two winners of exclusive fellowships.

From a more activist perspective, the group has also achieved some success. A number of subjects have led major union organizing campaigns or been involved as officials in major union elections. Several subjects, as directors of local neighborhood coalitions or settlement houses, were involved in community organizing and local political struggles which received notice in the left press and/or in the mainstream media. One subject is a fundraiser for Left causes. Several others have played important roles in pioneering efforts in the battered women's movement, the homeless movement, and the housing movement. Many subjects, including some who are not currently academics, have made significant contributions to literature and theory in professional publications or in activist organs.

A review of resumes or a list of accomplishments, however, tends to *freeze* a conception of success based on a series of achievements. Self-consciously, professionals develop written documents or public accountings which seek to convince employers, educational institutions, professional associations and colleagues, of a linear progression into their current status. It is not only that job tensions, periods of unemployment, and the loss of jobs through quitting and firing are naturally minimized, but that the very sequence of jobs is presented as to appear rational and intentional. The entire concept of a career is perhaps a social construct of social scientists and the professional culture. As Barbara reflected in response to a question about her career:

> I don't know. It's not like I feel I have this *career* (her emphasis)...you know, like a career that's moving along...I just ended up doing different things...

Significantly, what may appear to the public or to sociologists as "success," fails to capture the underlying tensions and problems of work life and in professional 'careers.'

Worlds of Pain

Underlying the records of accomplishment of these subjects, which one might glean from their resumes, is a sense of pain, guilt, ambivalence, and tension which becomes evident once an in-depth discussion occurs. While there were some jobs which were discussed with pleasure, nostalgia or pride, there were many more jobs and specific incidents which evoked pain. Moreover, for *some* people, the entire experience of "straight" jobs in the "Establishment" as the radicals of the 1960s feared, was marked by a struggle for survival, sometimes successful, and sometimes just unbearable, in which one swallowed deep, held one's nose, and then went to work. A comment by Rosalind captures the dilemma:

> Let's face it, the job structure is not conducive to being a radical....these institutions are frustrating and discouraging, so that at best, maybe you have to decide to do something different and keep moving around...

One of my key interests was, to what degree do radical professionals feel this kind of tension alluded to above? What are the sources of such tensions? And what different patterns of coping exist for those who find the occupational structure to be hostile to their values or political ideology or even to their psychological well being?

In order to explore these broad social psychological/political questions without losing the subjective experience of worklife, we will examine several case studies indicating the divergent experience of careers: (1) Court, who perceives social service work as psychologically and politically non-conflictual, and states that he felt no major tensions in his jobs, (2) Ann, who found a great deal of job related tension upon entering social work; she framed this tension in psychological terms and resolved it by departing the profession, (3) Barbara, who experienced a great deal of tension in her social service jobs, primarily attributed it to the political structure of work; Barbara resolved this tension by departing the field, but in a very different direction than Ann and, (4) Renee, who experienced a great deal of tension in particular job positions which she attributes to the social structure, and through job change and mobility within the social services has escaped much of the prior tension.

Court: The Lack of Tension with Social Service Work

Court, a 42 yr. old subject, who is one of the few people interviewed still engaged in direct social work practice (counseling), is one of the small number of subjects who stated they "liked all their jobs" and who felt little tension between paid social service and either political values or psychological needs. Court's jobs were hardly prestigious. After graduating from college, he took a job in a welfare department, which he left for a while in the late 1960s to become a writer. He subsequently returned to the welfare department where he worked for five more years. After leaving to go to graduate school, he returned to work at a different division of the same agency. In recent years, Court has enrolled in a doctoral program in social work, but has continued to work in direct practice, as a medical social worker in a hospital emergency room.

I was particularly struck by Court's comments about fulfillment in his work. These work settings, a welfare department and a hospital emergency room, are considered to be among the most difficult in the profession, and many radicals interviewed had expressed a great deal of tension and stress about their worklives. In response to questions, Court noted his enjoyment of work with children, the contact with co-workers at the welfare department, his active participation in the welfare workers union, and most of all his enjoyment of struggling in bureaucracies. Recently, at the hospital where Court works, a private home care agency failed to follow up on their agreement to speedily assist a medically ill patient:

I enjoy being able to yell at them! I can give these people a really hard time for

failing to live up to this...I know this is
petty enjoyment, but you know...they deserve
this treatment. I like the bureaucratic
battles, and, if you lose, Ok, you're no
worse off, but sometimes you win...

Part of Court's comfort with his work seems to
stem from a political position developed early on
which separates him from the strong influence of New
Left politics and from those who felt that the freedom
from bureaucratic rules and institutions should be a
goal of the Left. Court never felt the "missionary
zeal" towards social service, but as noted earlier,
felt it was not possible to be paid to do "radical
work." He recalls:

Even before I was political in a very clear
sense...I always felt that society is not set
up to fulfill our expectations. It was anti-
human and I expected work to be screwed up.
So I have never felt that I should be
personally responsible and wear myself out
being guilty about the failures of society
(pause) I guess I believe in a very direct
day-to-day cynicism about dealing with
bureaucracies...

Court appears to feel less guilt than other
subjects about the types of authority that social
workers wield, such as removing children from their
natural parents and reporting child abuse cases. He
also rejects as utopian and ill thought out the notion
that decentralized, de-bureaucratized small agencies
are more conducive to good work and radical politics,
as many other subjects and some authors in social work
have suggested[2]:

Oh no, I'm a great believer in bureaucracy! I
think that you can appeal to the Weberian
sense of an ethical spirit in a bureaucracy.
You can say 'no, the reason you are supposed
to do such and such for a client, is you're
supposed to, and you're supposed to by these
criteria, if you don't do it, it's because
you're a bad bureaucrat and you're not living
by what you claim to be living by! And it's
amazing what you can accomplish with
this...Now these small agencies...that's all

personalistic, petty politics...little
fiefdoms...yes, social workers think they are
getting out of the bureaucracy, but it's
worse, there's no union, no formal rules, no
criteria. You're at the mercy of whosoever is
in charge...

In speaking to Court, the other feature which
distinguished him (and some of the others who
experienced less job tension) was his self-labelled
class and status security. He notes of his parents,
who were both professors from old Yankee/Dutch/Irish
lineage:

They didn't have this sense of struggle for
upward mobility behind them. Many, many
people...knowing implicitly or explicitly
that their relatives fairly recently came
over, were outcasts, had to learn English,
worked as industrial workers, rose in status
in whatever way they did...status...we never
had any question that we had a right to be
here (pause) in some small way our ancestors
had founded the place...

Unlike many others interviewed, Court appeared
less concerned about upward mobility. He stayed in a
welfare department as a 'line' level social worker for
many years. In his early thirties, as a result of the
urging of his wife and the availability of free
tuition, he did go on to gain his Masters degree, and
even then returned to the public welfare department.
Further, while Court subsequently enrolled in a
doctoral program, this was some time ago, and he
appears to feel unpressured about completing his
degree. In response to a question, he states he may
want to teach or do research one day, but he's not
sure. He enjoys direct practice social work. When
asked whether he has ambitions to be an administrator
or faculty member, Court is ambivalent, suggesting
interest, but not the clear ambitions that
characterized others.

As with the few other subjects who experienced
little tension in their careers as social service
workers, Court was not a "missionary," and was not
linked to the New Left, nor was he a Community
Organization major. He felt from the start that there

were strong limitations to the possibility of "paid radical work." Moreover, he is from a professional and Protestant family, both characteristics which showed low associations with high job tension. He also had less desire for upward career mobility than other subjects, which may account for his feeling less stress.

Job Tension and Its Interpretations

Ann, Barbara, and Renee's experiences in social service positions, described in the vignettes below, are more typical of radical social workers' experience with work: high job tension and struggles around remaining in the profession. However, significant differences in interpretation of work tension are revealed in the vignettes, as well as in the actions taken by each individual to resolve these tensions.

Ann: Job Tension as 'Burnout'

Ann, a 34 year old Jewish female from a working class family, entered social work with a strong "missionary zeal," highly influenced by New Left ideology and movements. Ann was only 23 upon entering a Masters program, having spent a year as a day care teacher. Ann "loved graduate school," feeling her field placements were terrific, and classes excellent. Almost immediately upon graduation, Ann found that her work problems had begun.

Finding the job market "was terrible for social workers," she accepted a job at a municipal hospital as a medical social worker in a pediatric unit. Ann found the work intensely depressing, overwhelming, and unrelenting:

> What could be more depressing than a big city hospital pediatrics in-patient unit? (I) went from a wonderful environment of stimulation to doing entirely child abuse and neglect...you only could work with the worst cases, abandoned, burned, dying kids. I can't imagine a more depressing place. The cases were unmitigated and...My first case was a 3 yr. old girl, she eventually died from a fire her brother set, the burn cases were the worst. The doctors often throw up going into

91

the rooms of burn cases. I was also making
life and death decisions on whether kids
would go home or not...finally I found myself
starting to get hardened and that's why I
left, that disturbed me, when I started to
feel like I would get cynical and detached...

After more than a year at the job, Ann left this
position for another job at a community mental health
clinic. She was pleased because mental health was the
area she had wanted to work in. Even before she
started, however, she heard it "was a terrible
agency." Ann took the job anyway, as she was desperate
to get out of the hospital, but found the "agency
politics" at her new job to be "awful." The
administrator who hired her was fired only a week
after Ann was hired. Ann had trouble even being
assigned cases, apparently because her role had not
been made clear to the new administrators. Ann further
noted that other clinicians weren't doing their jobs,
sometimes failing to show up for appointments with
clients. However, when she protested this, she was
firmly rebuffed. After three months she was fired.

Once again in the job market, Ann describes
herself as "really burnt out." She poured over
newspaper ads, but would eliminate most jobs as "too
depressing." Eventually a job in an art school came
up, and Ann, who had been pursuing art as an
avocation, described it as "an answer to my
dreams."Ann describes leaving social service jobs at
this point as not being a self-conscious choice:

I guess I was also desperate to get out of
social work (pause) although I never made a
conscious decision. I wanted to be in
something that was healing...to be an artist
at that time seemed great (pause) to work
with beauty and people who worked with beauty
as counterposed to seeing every type of human
suffering, sadness, pain, every terrible
thing you see in social work...

However, to some degree, the problems Ann had
experienced in social work followed her into the art
school position where she had a great deal of
difficulty with her supervisor, a college
administrator. Ann eventually was laid off from this

job, and after another period of unemployment began doing free-lance publishing work. A year later she took a job with a publishing house where she is currently an associate director of marketing. Ann feels she has done extremely well in the new career.

Ann's interpretation of the job problems she experienced are primarily situational and individualistic. Several times in the interview, she noted that if she could have gotten a social work job like her field placement, "she would still be in social work now." The other factors Ann highlighted, besides the 'depressing' nature of the hospital and mental health clinic, are psychological: her inability to conform with organizational rules and her own conflicts about mobility.

Ann feels she was very naive and idealistic in her earlier positions and feels she has greatly succeeded in her publishing career by being able to get along with her superiors and co-workers:

> I worked very hard at this when I got the job (pause) I mean after having so many negative experiences (I) felt this was my last ditch chance to see if I could survive in an organizational structure, because maybe I couldn't...Maybe I was just too ethical (pause) values and beliefs, I didn't want to compromise, didn't want to kowtow and kiss ass. But I realized (I) would not survive. (And) realized (my) friends knew how to 'play the game' and (I) had to learn that skill. Now it doesn't bother me much...

The other psychological theme raised by Ann was her discomfort, as a 'red diaper baby' from a working class family, with success. She muses:

> I have this confusion about mobility. A role confusion. Because of the values that I have, but these values about achieving success in the world and how you mix these two together is hard...Now there is a lot of resentment (from my parents) about my being successful. I feel a lot of conflict about it. In some ways (it's) more comfortable for me to be not successful....

Interestingly, Ann seems to have resolved some of the tension (at least momentarily) by viewing her prior problems in adjustment to organizations as her own psychological problems, and praising business establishments as superior to social service and non-profit organizations. In a sense, she has rejected her working class roots for her upward mobility into the business world.

While Ann's experience of social service positions as as leading to "burnout," as well as her discomfort with changing social class and status positions, is in many ways typical of those studied, in some ways, she is as atypical as Court. While it is extremely difficult to determine retrospectively which came first: Ann's primarily psychological interpretation of her career in social service, her growing comfort with a career in publishing or her detachment from radical politics (see Chapter 6), they seem intimately bound. Because she feels she has grown and matured and has been able to adjust to corporate life, a social-political analysis of the problems of work such as the journal *Catalyst* might offer, no longer appears relevant to Ann. She accepts as normal the demands of work in American society, and prides herself in her successful efforts to cope with them.

Barbara: "Burnout" as Interpreted Politically

While Barbara, a 36 year old Roman Catholic subject from a working class background, shares similarities with Ann in relation to social class and status and in suffering job tensions in social service work and eventually leaving what would be traditionally defined as the social service field (she currently is a fundraiser and administrator for a leftist foundation), there are considerable contrasts between her and Ann.

Barbara also came to social work with a strong "missionary zeal" and New Left influence. As a community organization and planning student, she was well positioned to move into higher level positions. However, she continually found herself "in the middle" of troubling assignments and agency politics. At her first job as a program planner for a settlement house interested in doing a 'customer evaluation' of its services, Barbara found the way the job was organized belied the agency's actual intent:

> You know, you bring in this kid right out of school and tell her to evaluate your program, boy is this a set-up! The program managers felt threatened, of course...as soon as there were problems, forget it. I had no power. My supervisor stopped supervising me. There really was no backing from the top. So ultimately, I took the program evaluation seriously, but the agency didn't...

As the agency began to cut benefits and staff began challenging the administration, Barbara felt "neither fish nor fowl" as she was neither labor nor management. This problem continued in her next position as a researcher with a non-profit organization. Again, problems arose at the agency, and as personnel became angry about conditions, Barbara was limited in what she could do both because of her staff position and her politics which were known to the Director:

> A small group of staff began to meet, hoping to form a pre-union core...it never panned out. And here it was again, those of us who weren't management and yet weren't line staff...the same position as (previous agency). Of course we met secretly anyway, but it was rough, not viewed as 'labor' by secretaries or as management by the directors...And then because the Director knew my politics she began to just dismiss me (pause) I would always raise the ethical questions or the more progressive beliefs, and I think she began to just say, 'Oh, Barbara, she's a socialist and that's why she's saying that'...there was no respect due me just as a simple employee...

A key distinction between Barbara, and Court and Ann, which will be key to our discussion of radical professionalism, is Barbara's frustration about the lack of political meaning intrinsic to her work. She sought relevance in her work as a researcher of the criminal justice system, but felt frustrated:

Yeh, I produced some good pieces of work (at research agency)...*but it had no impact*...oh some small things were done...So I felt like I was doing work which had no impact and except for two people I was close to, what I was doing wasn't appreciated, not by the organization, not by society. These reports could end up in the files somewhere. *One of the major issues, was, I'm doing this work, but I'm not making a difference in the world*...(author's emphasis)

Barbara's move out of social service work came as a result of being able to develop job positions for herself which were *politically relevant* and combined her skills in organizing and administration, but which were outside traditional 'Establishment' funding. After five years in the two social service agencies described, she quit to develop a women's resource center which a number of radical women in her study group had been exploring. Barbara reacted ecstatically to her new position as a project director for the center:

When I got this (women's project), it was the first time in my life (pause) I was so excited. I couldn't believe it. A new lease on life and I thought what did I do to deserve this?...

The women's resource center failed to materialize. Eight months later, Barbara got another position with a left foundation. The solution to work tension and to the dilemma of finding a 'radical career' for Barbara was to leave the more traditional confines of professional work for an alternative organization. While noting her job is not without problems, Barbara concludes:

Yes, (it's) definitely my best job...it's the one job where I'm best able to be a whole person, minute to minute, (pause) and still do political work outside my job (pause) it's a job where I can be a Marxist, a Feminist, a lesbian...it's there and it's not hidden, it's respected...

Barbara experienced her job tensions and conflict

in a political manner, blaming the structure of her
worklife, rather than herself. Her solution, for the
time being, was to leave the mainstream of
professional work. While Barbara's perceptions of
'Establishment' work is shared by many subjects, few
as of yet have been able to find as satisfactory a
solution. Two further points about 'movement work'
need to be noted: subjects like Barbara who have taken
these types of jobs have increased their political
activism at a time when most subjects have decreased
their levels of activism. Second, this type of work
exerts a certain cost. As Barbara notes, she makes
a relatively low salary, and feels that she may have
"locked herself into" limited job prospects in the
future. In this sense, Barbara has taken the opposite
route from Ann, opting for lower career mobility and
increasing political involvement rather than the
upward career mobility which Ann has achieved.

Renee: Resolving Job Tension by Moving within the Social Services: Finding a Radical Job Shelter

Renee, a 36 year old subject from a Jewish
professional family of origin, also experienced a
great deal of job tension. However, her 'career'
suggests a resolution to the dilemma of being a
radical professional through having successfully (for
the time being, for such a quest is always contingent)
achieved job positions within the social services in
which she feels she is able to be a radical, to
practice professionally, and meet her mobility and
status needs. Following Elliot Freidson's[3] description
of job positions as "occupational labor market
shelters," we might describe this goal, which Renee
shares with most of the radicals we studied, as a
quest for a "radical labor market shelter" in which
the normative occupational needs for income, security,
and status are met in addition to the achievement of
social space for "radical practice." As Renee puts it:

> Some of us want it all, professional mobility
> and radicalism (pause) a job should be
> politically relevant, fun, interesting,
> challenging, pay money and have a really
> fancy title...these are my contradictions. I
> want to be a good Marxist and put that into
> practice and have a lot of status and a big
> salary. Maybe it's contradictory, but...

97

For Renee, coming even close to such a goal took considerable time. Renee went straight to social work school after college, embracing the "missionary zeal" of social work. Upon graduation, she took a job as a social worker in a foster care agency which she describes as "awful." It was a conservative Catholic agency in which agency rules prohibited providing birth control information to teenage girls:

> I hated it, it was awful. I didn't fit in. I wrestled the whole time I was there with quitting and finally I did, though I was warned never to quit my first job before a year. I don't know, I probably would have gotten fired...

Renee obtained a position as a medical social worker where she stayed for over three years. At first, this was a very positive experience. She had a protective supervisor, enjoyed the work with patients, and found the large cosmopolitan hospital to be far more liberal than her previous work setting. Over the years, however, as her supervisor was changed, more pressure was put on workers through an increase in caseload size, and a union drive with which Renee was involved failed, the work felt more alienating. When Renee learned of a doctoral program which seemed interesting to her, she decided to leave the hospital:

> I felt badly burnt out at (hospital). I was depressed. The stress was high. And there were a lot of ways in which the changes in the department made it (the work) much harder...(I) wasn't really happy with what I was doing...My idea was to get a doctorate to be a social work teacher. I thought I could be more radical as a teacher than a practitioner....I guess I felt frustrated...

After Renee completed her course work, she sought out work while she wrote her dissertation. Two "awful" job experiences ensued. In the first job, as a social worker at a home health care agency, she felt good about her work with clients and her co-workers, and proceeded to do union organizing. Her social work practice was shortly thereafter called into question and she was fired. Renee believes she was fired for

labor organizing, and an unfair labor practice charge
was filed with the National Labor Relations Board
(which was ultimately dismissed). After some time out
of work, Renee secured a similar job with a public
health agency in a rural community. Here she felt
isolated as the only social worker on staff in an
agency which was extremely conservative. When on one
occasion, she defended clients on welfare, she had a
dispute with most of the staff. Renee was fired during
her probationary period for "not fitting in." This
reason was never explained, but Renee attributes it to
her 'hippie' style of dress, her 'New York' style, her
ethnicity, and political views.

After leaving the rural area, Renee found a
social work job with an agency serving battered women.
Suddenly, Renee felt like she was doing the type of
work she loved. It was good social work *and* good
politics:

> I leaped at the opportunity to work with
> battered women. I would have earned a hell of
> a lot more anyplace else with eight years of
> social work experience already, but I didn't
> care. I was motivated by politics, by the
> fact that work with battered women is
> movement like, it has a political flavor...Of
> course, there isn't this blaming-the-victim
> stuff because the principle of the work is
> that the women are victims...My values, some
> of which come from social work and most of
> which come from radical politics, I could use
> all of this at (this job)...

After a year and a half, funding for Renee's
position was cut, and she was extremely upset about
losing her job. She obtained a position, largely by
chance, working with the homeless. The position, which
Renee was still employed in at the time of the
interview (about three and a half years later)
involves counseling mentally ill homeless women,
developing and running a program for them, supervising
student interns and staff, and teaching at a
university affiliated with the project. Renee has
found the job tremendously rewarding:

> I was very lucky. This again put me on the
> cutting edge of something new--work with the

99

homeless--and also the cutting edge of where
the radicals were. It was an innovative
program and it was practice with the surplus
population, the poorest of the poor, the most
irrelevant to the needs of capitalism.
Moreover, I also was going to have power to
design a new program. It meant this job had
some real potential to implement my radical
thinking....

Renee describes radicalism as being brought in
subtly, through the "backdoor," since the program
aspires to be innovative, different from traditional
mental health services, and intended to "empower"
clients. Renee and the staff have used groups such as
a "current events" group to politicize the women
around housing issues, and have helped the tenants in
a hotel for formerly homeless women to take over the
running of the tenants council from management. Much
of this work is not formally sanctioned by her
administrators:

When I talk of it as a radical job, I don't
mean the bosses are radical. But what I do is
acceptable to them as long as I use their
terms. I may have to change the words around
a   little   bit...phrase   things
differently...(but) there is a sanction for
empowering or at least for innovation...

Renee feels that her career in social work has
become more radical "paradoxically at a time when the
country, and even the field has become more
conservative." Renee attributes this to her being able
to work with populations which are 'oppressed'
(battered women, homeless people), fields which
attract radicals and innovative social workers, and to
the fact that as her experience, skills and
credentials have increased, she has had an expanded
job choice. I asked if there was a conscious decision
in recent years to seek radical work:

No, but I guess there is self-selection. You
know if you're fired from enough conservative
agencies, you figure out, you don't want to
work in them (anymore). For the first time in
1983, I started refusing jobs that were
offered me. I guess I never had that luxury

before...I was looking for a job that was freer and where I (could) do more interesting stuff. I don't know if I articulated it in my head as 'I want to do radical work.' I don't remember. But even if it is articulated as wanting freedom, creativity, interesting and innovative...that's pretty conscious, I think, because it speaks of radical instincts behind these words...

Renee's career shows a different resolution at this point than Barbara or Ann's. She feels she has been able to find radical work in the social service field which is complementary to her values and yet not suffer in terms of day-to-day misery or even low pay and low status.

The Prevalence of Job Tension

How typical was Court's experience of work as compared with Ann's, Barbara's, and Renee's? A close analysis of the interviews[4] suggests Court's experience represented only a small minority of those studied. Only four others expressed complete satisfaction with their jobs or, in the many hours of interviewing, did not share a great deal of conflictual material.

Like Court, those few not experiencing high job tension tended to be from professional or business families of origin as opposed to subjects from working class or lower middle class families, they were more likely to be Protestant than Jewish or Roman Catholic, and they were likely to be older than those suffering extreme tension (in their forties at the time of the study). Perhaps most interesting, like Ann, Barbara, and Renee, those who suffered from job tensions were overwhelmingly likely to have entered the profession with the "change the world" missionary zeal discussed earlier[5]. Clearly this idealism, whether in the pursuit of a "radical job" or a general sense of doing good ethical work, ran up against a bureaucratic, institutional structure which was felt to be hostile to these goals. On the other hand, those like Court, who had more minimal expectations of being paid to do radical work, and, came to the social services, more by chance, experienced less tension. Finally, not surprisingly, there is a strong relationship between the experience of tension and changing careers and job turnover.

"Negative Career Events"

There is, of course, a considerable distinction between Barbara's decision to leave her positions at the settlement house and the research agency, and Ann's forced departure from the mental health center and from the art school or Renee's forced departures from the two home health care jobs. I was interested in developing some way of coding subjects who had been *involuntarily* separated from employment. The term "negative career events" is broader than firings or layoffs, since frequently professional employees are "eased out" or forced to quit, though this is not formally recorded. For example, Rita, was forced to quit a supervisory position at a child welfare agency when she refused to carry out practices which she considered discriminatory and illegal. Upon her refusal, her choice was basically to quit or be fired. Subjects were coded as having suffered a "negative career event" when they left a position held for a significant period of time under extremely adverse circumstances.

Twelve subjects experienced "negative career events" with many experiencing more than one. Those who experienced "negative career events" are overwhelmingly Jewish and Roman Catholic as opposed to Protestant. There is a strong relationship between social class of subjects' families of origins: those from working class or lower middle class families are more than twice as likely to suffer "negative career events" than their peers from professional or business families[6], and there is again a strong link between those who entered the profession with a "missionary zeal" and those suffering "negative career events"[7]. Not surprisingly, those who experienced "negative career events" were likely to be strong career and job changers[8].

While this study is not focused on "job burnout," the findings above, which are somewhat serendipitious, are worthy of some exploration. The association of tension and "negative career events" with those lower in social class and in ethnic/religious status as well as with a "change the world" ethic raises several possible theoretical explanations.

One logical explanation would cite societal discrimination against those from lower socio-economic classes and less than dominant religious/ethnic groupings. Indeed there is support for such an argument. Renee notes that anti-semitism characterized the rural agency from which she was fired; when Howard was running for union re-election, he was subjected to Jew baiting as well as red-baiting; and Joseph, after being forced out by his Board of Directors, was called "a dirty Jew" by the Board President. However, there were no expressed incidents of overt anti-Catholic sentiments nor can any precise account of class prejudice be made from this study. In any case, developing clear causal evidence of such motivations would be beyond the scope of this book.

A second cogent explanation would suggest that perhaps those suffering from "negative career events" were more politically active on the job or militant than others. There is again some anecdotal evidence to support this. Renee and Richard were fired from jobs after union organizing, Joseph and Bea ran into difficulties with their Boards of Directors when they moved into highly controversial, political community organizing, and Rita, was forced out after refusing ethically reprehensible orders. However, there is insufficient evidence to support this thesis. First, many of those who were active politically in their jobs did *not* suffer retaliation. Secondly, most of the subjects experiencing "negative events," did not interpret them politically; like Ann, they tend to cite lack of organizational sophistication as well as their high ethical, idealistic principles as causal factors. Brenda is perhaps representative of these subjects in her account of being firing by a child welfare agency:

> Interviewer: Do you think you were fired for political reasons?
>
> Brenda: Its hard to say. I wasn't playing the game right...as a radical or someone who is looking to try to change things you certainly have to become sophisticated in the way you try to do this...I took a very anti-authority stance and came up against a supervisor who

was very vindictive... But I think you can't consider it political, as my having been fired for taking a stand or anything. I think I was just not being very smart...No, I thought this supervisor was a stupid person, that's all,and I refused to go along with her ideas, it was not consciously political...

The above suggests to me a third possibility. While no doubt discrimination plays a role as well as political retaliation, the interviews support a complex interaction between "missionary zeal" and ethics and social class/ethnic origins. On the one hand, the subjects, particularly those with the ideal of "changing the world" or securing paid "radical work," were, like much of the New Left, unprepared for the institutional response of social service agencies which adhere to humanistic sounding values, but which function in the same bureaucratic and anti-worker fashion as the profit making sector of capitalism. Those subjects from non-professional families were further handicapped by a lack of familial socialization to the professional culture and bureaucratic norms of their new careers. Brenda, whose father was a road department worker, and Rita, whose father was a policeman, both stated in their interviews that they had trouble "closing (their) big mouths." Contrast this to the extensive pre-socialization that Court, whose parents were professors, evidently had even prior to starting work:

Oh, I remember the academic life when I was a kid. My parents were always helping the faculty with academic squabbles. They'd (other faculty) call all the time.'I'm being screwed,''I'm up for tenure, what do I do?" you know. And I knew from parents that academics always had to cover their asses...

The anticipatory socialization to middle class norms and conduct which is then applied to the professional worksite is more strongly embedded in those from higher social classes[9]. Closely related to this, is a bifurcation in occupational goals of those from different class backgrounds. For example, Naomi and Martin, never faced the major battles with social service bureaucracies, as they focused from the start on academic research (in fact, almost all subjects who are academics or preparing for academic careers have family origins in the professional class). While not minimizing the major political and organizational impediments to success in academia, we do suggest that perhaps the struggles in academia are different from social service work, such as being more time and ritual bound (tenure review, specific criteria for research and publishing, etc.) and that further, there is a self-selection process in which those from the professional class view themselves with more confidence in obtaining entrance into this "club" as compared to working class people[10].

The Allure of Mobility and Other Careers

As noted earlier, this is a highly successful group by societal standards. Despite the tensions noted above, few subjects experienced major periods of unemployment nor have most suffered what appear to be *long-term* career setbacks. In fact, the very mobility of these subjects somewhat contradict the predictions of *Catalyst* which postulated a "proletarianization" of professional work[11].

While one can argue that salary levels for many social workers remain low, in some cases still lower than blue-collar workers, and that working conditions are no better for these professionals than other workers once they are stripped of the professional mystique, the key predictions of the "proletarianization" argument have faltered. Rather than being forced to suffer long term job insecurity, a lack of advancement, and, therefore, resort to increased collective action, the social workers in our study have in fact successfully left "line staff positions" and moved into supervisory and management positions, into faculty positions, or, in some cases, achieved mobility in other fields.

Most of those interviewed were pulled toward mobility goals as much as pushed by negative circumstances. Court's work history indicates that he did stay at a welfare department (in a relatively low status position) for many years, but Court also received a Masters degree and is now in a doctoral program. While his goals are not completely clear, he will certainly have options to teach, do research, or engage in administration. Ann, one of the few subjects to actually experience some significant unemployment, did manage to leave social work for arts administration, and, afterwards for a publishing career. Renee describes herself as having been "burned out" at her hospital job, but could afford to resign and enter a doctoral program. She was also able to have sufficient resources (financial, family and friends, professional networks) to recover from two firings and eventually acquire a faculty/administration position. While negative events are not suggested to be a pre-condition for moving up, they hardly contradict mobility. In many cases, it is hard to tell if job tensions were not connected with feelings of blocked mobility aspirations or with some conscious or unconscious desire "to move on."

James puts this issue in perspective when he muses about the history of radicals-in-the-professions as a social movement, mentioning the issue of self-consciousness:

> Sometimes I think what this is all about has to do with opportunity theory, like Cloward and Ohlin's. A whole bunch of people whose mobility was blocked and who were educated, children of (the) professional class whose upward mobility was blocked because positions weren't open *or as a consequence of values, they didn't share*, so they were either driven to or gravitated to the public sector because they didn't share private sector market values...(author emphasis)

Indeed, most of the subjects expressed ambivalence about their past view of themselves as "proletarians" as well as some guilt associated with mobility. I asked Renee about her previous writings about social workers being part of the working class, asking her about her current viewpoint:

> I don't know if I ever totally believed it! I wanted to identify with the working class and liked to think of myself as working class, but I *felt* awfully middle class. There was this ambiguity about whether my identification as a social worker was professional or occupational...It had an interactionist effect. I can't say which came

first...but for a number of reasons, a lot of
it having to do with my own insecurity, I
stayed a line staff level social worker for
many, many years longer than the typical MSW.
I knew I was competent at what I was doing,
but if I moved up I might not be. I felt I
might be a lousy supervisor or administrator.
But also psychologically and ideologically it
was more comfortable to say 'I'm a worker,'
and 'yeh, the director of the agency might be
an oppressor, but I'm not'...(but) as I
became more confident about (my) self, about
my skills, about myself as a social worker
and a professional, my ideology didn't keep
me from doing supervisory work or from being
an administrator...

Indeed, the occupational character of the group
interviewed has changed considerably over time due to
upward mobility. The cohesiveness that shaped the
group as students or as young caseworkers and
organizers has been disrupted by rapid occupational
change. The key cleavages along these lines are
whether this mobility took the form of moving
vertically, or through moving laterally to different
or alternative careers.

Job and Career Changing: Coping with Tension and Finding a Radical Labor Market Shelter

There has been a considerable amount of job
changing, and, to a lesser degree, career shifting in
subjects' biographical accounts. I collected a job
history from each subject, with dates recorded as well
as relevant positions and names of employing
organizations, and developed a measure of job
changing[12]. The median number of positions held by
subjects in the last decade was five, with a mean of
4.7.

Women changed jobs far more often than men, Jews
and Catholics more often than Protestants, and
subjects from working class families of origin had the
most job changes. Younger subjects had higher job
turnover compared to the over 40 group. While, at
first, the last finding seemed obvious, since those in
their thirties are at a different cycle in their
careers than those now in their forties, the pattern

continued to hold even when the author reviewed the biographies of those now over 40 to analyze their job changes while they were in their twenties and thirties. One explanation might be the high concentration in our study of those now over 40 who were in public sector, civil service positions. It may be that these positions because of their relative security or some intrinsic or extrinsic nature (e.g. relatively high union and radical activity in these areas in the 1960s and 1970s) plays a role in these subjects' relative stability. Or it may be that, as the statistics suggest, there is a generational difference: with those who graduated college from 1968 or so on having a higher job turnover rate than those slightly their seniors[13].

There are high associations between job turnover and the high job tension and "negative career events" discussed above, not surprisingly. Again, we find those who entered the professions with a "missionary zeal" to have a job turnover twice as high as those who did not[14].

While changing job positions to escape tension is clearly suggested (as was the case for Ann, Barbara, and Renee), it is important to stress the simultaneous motivations of mobility and finding a "radical job shelter." Barbara left her job at the research institute because of the allure of working in an alternative radical organization as much as from the fact that she suffered job tension at the agency. Renee was as much attracted to going into a Ph. D. program as she was desirous of relieving her job tensions in the hospital position.

The group's considerable mobility is suggested by data generated by the author which suggests a rather mass move by subjects out of direct practice human service work. The human service professions generally classify as direct service all direct client contact positions such as caseworker, groupworker, therapist, community organizer, etc. Teaching, research, administration, planning or fundraising would be examples of non-direct service work. Of interest to us here, is the tendency of non-direct practice work to be of higher pay and status than direct service, and to remove the occupant from the initial choice of human service work which was most often related to counseling or organizing clients. Members of the *Catalyst* collective who were interviewed went from nearly four-fifths direct practitioners in 1977 to only one-fifth in 1987[15].

This movement has important ramifications. Career patterns indicate a high degree of mobility into administrative and faculty positions as well as an alternative route to "movement" or "movement like" jobs (e.g. labor unions). In addition to the fact that such mobility contradicted the jointly held belief in proletarianization, such occupational fragmentation also is subversive of the political strategies and goals that this population of *Catalyst* members held (see Part II of this book).

I was also interested in distinguishing between those subjects who stayed in the social services, but moved into administration or supervision (such as Renee), and those subjects (such as Barbara and Ann) who appear to have left the profession entirely. This was not an easy task to accomplish since there are many definitions of social work or human service work and many borderline cases[16]. Those leaving the social service professions to pursue a variety of jobs, from carpentry to labor organizing, increased dramatically around 1982 with eight of the fourteen subjects who had been in the original collective moving out of the social services. Interestingly, there is a slight trend in the years since 1982 for a return of subjects to the social services. At the risk of freezing the subjects in their current employment choices, those who have returned to the social service professions were labelled as "temporary" departers, and, those such as Ann and Barbara, who have spent at least five years outside the social service professions were labelled as "permanent."

Those who leave the field (at least temporarily) are more generally male, now in their late 30s, Jewish, from non-professional or business families of origin, have a Masters degree (only), and were more likely to have been community organization majors in Social Work School. There is some relationship between high job tension and "negative career events" and leaving (at least temporarily), but not a striking one. And there is no association between the "missionary zeal" discussed above and leaving the field. The data would seem to suggest that a combination of factors such as tension and opportunity (note the gender relationship) are operative.

Those who have more permanently left the social services, however, include more women than men, and more of those from lower social class families of origin (Ann and Barbara as opposed to Court and Renee, for example). Those who majored in community organization are nearly three times as likely to depart the field (Barbara, for example) than those who major in casework or groupwork. The high departure (both "temporaries" and "permanents") of community organizers would seem to reflect our analysis about "blocked mobility," since community organization as an area of employment has been in increasing decline since the mid 1970s[17].

This review suggests that the mobility of the population has different roots: high tension and difficulty at jobs leads to job turnover, but for many subjects, there is little consideration given to leaving the field (particularly for the female caseworkers such as Renee). On the other hand, the allure of "movement" jobs is strong, particularly for organizers, and the allure of high level administration is strong, particularly for men. Some subjects, of course, are driven by unanticipated events which may occur, such as Sam's run for union office, which he did not think would be successful. He is now in his seventh year at this position.

Current Positions and Occupational Goals
of Subjects

The subjects' employment at the time of this study reflects a picture of relative success with a significant trend away from direct practice to widely dispersed areas within and without the social service fields. Seven of the twenty-four subjects are not doing social service work. Of the remaining seventeen, only six remain in direct practice. The most common current position held was administrative. Only two subjects were in full-time faculty positions[18]. One subject is a Ph. D. student. Only four hold traditional mental health/social work counseling positions (and it should be noted that two of these four are relatively recent M.S.W.s).

110

While prediction of this population's future careers is beyond our capacity, subjects, in some cases, had made obvious plans to move on (such as enrolling in doctoral programs) or, in other cases, stated during the interviews, that they wished to move into a certain area. Even without the advantage of a crystal ball, we can at least account for obvious career plans now anticipated. The most prevalent trend currently is towards academia; the six now employed in this setting wish to remain, and are likely to be joined by three who are obtaining their degrees. Those in high administration or business indicated no plans or desires to move into different career paths nor did those who I have classified as being in "movement" work.

By combining the subjects' current employment statuses and the additional information gained in the interviews, a more complete profile of the population's careers is obtained. First, we note areas which are *not* trends for our population: unlike many graduates of professional schools in social work and psychology, there is no major movement towards private psychotherapy nor is there any major interest in the more prestigious professions such as medicine or law. Generally our study population clusters towards academia, counseling, supervising or low level administration in public or voluntary agencies, high level public administration, and full time "movement" work, in that order.

Most of those heading towards academic careers are from professional families, but professional families of origin are underrepresented in high level administration and movement work. Both of the latter areas attract subjects from more working class backgrounds. Interest in counseling positions is less affected by social class than by gender. Consistent with studies of the field[19] men are overrepresented in high level administration, while women are in counseling and low level supervisory positions. Religious background presents an interesting dichotomy, with Jews three and a half times more likely to be interested in academia than Catholics, while the percentages are reversed for counseling. Jews compose entirely all subjects in the high administration/business area, but Catholics

111

predominate in the small number of movement jobs. Surprisingly given the overlap in curricula in Schools of Social Work between Community Organization and Administration[20], most of those trained in C.O. did *not* move into traditional administration after the drying up of organizing jobs. Rather they have moved towards academia or alternative organizations.

Career direction, political ideology, the experience of job tensions, and "negative career events" interact in a complex fashion. The academics tend to have had a lower degree of job tension and "negative career events" probably because academic positions attract more individuals from professional backgrounds. Evidently, those subjects doing research or part-time teaching while securing higher degrees over the last decade experienced less tension. Some subjects who came to social services with a "missionary zeal" are now moving toward academia, but for the most part the current academics were not missionaries. The most salient associations between political ideology, job tension, and career direction occur at the extremes of the population: those like Ann who went into business or into high administration; and those like Barbara who went into "movement" work.

As will be further developed in Chapter 6, the high level administrators/business group are the only sub-group of the population to become generally detached from radical ideology. Those who are now in "movement" work, like Barbara, interpreted their previous job tensions more politically, and sought out employers who were more complementary to their ideologies ("labor market shelters").

Both academia and counseling positions provide 'job shelters' for the majority of the subjects who have retained their radical political ideology and idealism, yet have suffered job tensions. That these positions are prized for their autonomy (more than income or status) is evident from the interviews. Rita's account of her work as a therapist (below) and James' account of his teaching were typical:

(Rita): When you do therapy, you have autonomy. Its just the walls, and you and the client. Here I can be myself. And I can

112

integrate some of my political theory and practice...(I) can be satisfied because on a direct 'one to one,' you don't have to plan *through* people or maneuver around other people...

(James): The classroom is kind of given to you as your political terrain. I introduce myself in class as a democratic socialist, and I haven't had great problems...Teaching is satisfying personally and politically because it does give me (a) certain social space and says "this is yours"...

In this sense, the career goals of radical professionals are the same as that which sociologists have suggested to be the goal of classical professionals: job autonomy and control over work. Professional skills buttress the market power and ideological claims for professional labor to control their own work[21]. In forthcoming chapters, we shall explore to what degree the social space of "autonomous" professional work or a "radical labor market shelter" can *actually* be utilized for different ends by radicals than by the 'average' professional.

Notes:

1. See National Association of Social Workers, <u>NASW Data Bank</u>, Silver Spring, Md.: NASW, 1985, which indicates that only 57.1% of its membership are in direct service positions, while the remainder are in administration, supervision, consultation, research or policy development.

2. A good example of this perspective is Steven Weinman's, <u>The Politics of Human Services</u>, Boston: South End Press, 1984, calling for a small, local and de-centralized system of social services.

3. see Elliot Freidson,"Occupational Autonomy and Labor Market Shelters,"Unpublished manuscript, 1985. Freidson restores some dynamism to the concept of occupations by considering them as "opportunity points" for individuals and groups. Professional identification and adherence to a particular occupational group is not to be simply reduced to social class or status stratifications, but is a self-

conscious process whereby individuals use occupational identifications and job positions to bargain in the labor market, not only economically, but in relation to autonomy, skill claims, prestige, and job control. Drawing on these concepts, I extend this idea to radicals in the professions. Radicals use positions in the social services and elsewhere as bargaining points for their skill claims, and to accumulate credentials and professional identifications, since as radicals and professionals they gain opportunities to be autonomous of strong employer control, and to some degree free of repression, allowing more freedom to implement their political beliefs at work (along with their trades).

4. I did a content analysis of the interviews to assess the existence of job tension. Generally minor dissatisfactions were not included, but only longstanding conflictual situations experienced over a long period of time. Three interviews were too ambiguous to be coded.

5. Of the subjects able to be coded, twelve of the sixteen (75%) who suffered high job tension had entered social service work with strong "missionary zeal" , while only one in five (20%) who suffered no job tension entered the profession with a strong "missionary zeal." See pp. 242-243 and Table XII of David Wagner,"Political Ideology and Professional Careers: A Study of Radical Social Service Workers," Ph. D. dissertation, City University of New York, 1988.

6. Nine out of thirteen subjects from a business or professional family of origin suffered no "negative career events" while eight of eleven of subjects from working class or lower middle class families of origin suffered "negative career events." See Wagner,Ibid, Table XIII.

7. Ten out of twelve subjects suffering "negative career events" entered social service with a strong "missionary zeal," while only four of twelve who did not suffer "negative career events" entered with strong "missionary zeal."

8. Seven of the twelve people experiencing "negative career events" would leave the social services at

114

least temporarily and four others experienced more than average job turnover of 5.0 for the study. See pp. 246 of Ibid.

9. The issue of social class and academic life, and a similar point about the difficulty those from working class or poor families of origin have in adapting to academia is found in Jake Ryan and Charles Sackrey,Strangers in Paradise: Academics from the Working Class, Boston: South End Press, 1984.

10. Ibid.

11. In the first issue of *Catalyst*, for example, almost every article discussed this deterioration of conditions and long term trend towards 'de-skilling' and 'routinization' in the social services. See David Wagner and Marcia B. Cohen,"Social Workers, Class, and Professionalism,"Catalyst, 1:1 (1978), pp. 25-55, and Christopher Dykema,"Toward a New Age of Social Services: Lessons to be Learned from our History,"Catalyst, 1(1), 1978, pp. 57-75, for example.

12. To develop a measure of job changes, I coded each full time position as one entry and developed a count for each subject for ten years. I chose the period (1976-1986) for two reasons. As of the period of study, it corresponded to the ten years that *Catalyst* had been around. Moreover since the average subject was only 36 at the time of the study, the previous ten year period would have been quite difficult to code for many subjects since the years would include high school and college years.

13. see Table XIV in Ibid. Subjects in their forties at the time of the study averaged only 3 jobs in the decade studied, while those between 35 and 40 averaged 5 jobs, and those between 30 and 35 averaged 6 jobs.

14. See Ibid. Those who entered the social services with strong "missionary zeal" averaged six positions in the decade studied as opposed to only three positions for those who did not have such zeal.

15. See Ibid, Table 7. Of the 14 subjects who formed the initial *Catalyst* collective, if students and the unemployed are discounted, 11 were in direct practice in 1977 and only 3 in 1987. If subjects are added in

as they joined *Catalyst* the proportions remain about the same, the group going from 79% direct practitioners in 1977 to 25% in 1987.

16. Distinguishing which positions are in the social services can be quite difficult due to the many definitions of social services. Generally I adopted a combination of relying on the subject's own definitions ("Did you consider yourself a social worker at the time?") and their functional role, rather than place of work. For example, a person employed by a union as a counselor would clearly be in the social services, but not a full time elected union official. On the other hand, an administrator of a mental health program would clearly be in the social services, while an administrator in a leftist organization would not.

17. See, for example, Michael Reisch and Stanley Wencour, "The Future of Community Organization in Social Work: Social Activism and the Politics of Profession Building," in <u>Social Service Review</u>, 60 (1986), pp. 70-93, for a discussion of the decline of community organization. Community Organization as a field generally declined as the last vestiges of the "war on poverty" programs were cut, and, currently, most schools of social work have either eliminated community organization altogether or consolidated it with administration, management or planning.

18. The numbers in 'academia' are higher than those numbered as faculty because several subjects, at the time of this study, held primarily administrative positions within universities (sometimes combined with teaching), so are listed as working in that area, but not as faculty.

19. see, for example, National Association of Social Workers, <u>1983-84 Supplement to the Encyclopedia of Social Work</u>, 17th Edition, Silver Spring, Md.:NASW, 1983, p. 180.

20. Community Organization as a method area of Social Work arose greatly out of the community chest/federation movements of the 1920s, and despite its association with radicalism and "grass roots" organizing in the 1960s and 1970s, was often educationally linked to administration and planning.

After grass roots organizing positions declined again in the mid 1970s, most Social Work schools again re-oriented their curricula to the job market by stressing administration, planning or policy over grass roots organizing. For a classic formulation of community organization as a method area including administration and planning, see Fred Cox, <u>et. al.</u>, <u>Strategies of Community Organization</u>, Itsaca, Il.: F.E.Peacock, 1974.

21. See Charles Derber,<u>Professionals as Workers</u>, Boston: C.K. Hall and Co., 1982; Freidson,<u>Profession of Medicine</u>, <u>Professional Dominance</u>; Terence Johnson,<u>The Professions and Power</u>, London: Macmillan Press, 1972; and Larson,<u>The Rise of Professionalism</u>.

6

OCCUPATIONS AND IDEOLOGY

After a number of years in the social service professions, how do radical professionals now view themselves? Have subjects, in spite of the difficulties they experienced, come to identify themselves with professional social work, its norms, values, and symbols? Do subjects find their work complementary to their political values, and if so, what beliefs allow them to maintain the tie between radicalism and professionalism? Has professionalism and careerism absorbed the radicalism of these subjects through the "long march through the institutions" or is professional work radicalizing as professional socialization was found to be earlier in the study? In this chapter we will explore these questions by analyzing how subjects described themselves ideologically when interviewed in 1986-1987 and how they interpreted their careers at that point in time.

The Stability of Radical Ideology

In their 1968 article on the first conference of radicals-in-the-professions, Barbara and Alan Haber comment on the agony and guilt felt by many conference participants:

> But regardless of background, most of the participants expressed a common set of questions and mood of frustration: 'It's hard to be radical for long -- nothing happens. How shall we live? Where is the revolution? How do we measure and aid its coming?' They were people who had, by themselves or in groups, been seeking answers for a long time, but had not found any; people who felt to some degree that they were failing and who were anxious not to fail...And among the bona

fide professionals, at least, there was a great deal of guilt; for having 'opted in'; for wearing a suit; for having given up some of the badges of opposition; for making a living; for having had too little success as radicals-within-professions.[1]

Despite the profound changes that have occurred in the twenty years since Haber and Haber wrote, the interviews conducted for this study provoked a similar sense of guilt among many of the subjects:

(Naomi): I was concerned when you came to interview me, I was thinking now I don't do anything political since *Catalyst* (pause) I guess it gets into the question of what's political (pause)...do you have to be an activist?...

(Renee): When I talk about what I'm doing politically, or not doing, it's hard. Like a radical super-ego nagging at me...and the whole conversation is very upsetting...

The high level of guilt felt by many subjects seems to be a result of their extraordinarily high standards of idealism and activism dating back to the militancy of the New Left. Since the majority of our subjects were radicalized in the 1966-1971 period, they tend to associate radicalism with sustained ongoing militant political activity. Further, the influence of "social myths" and language must be noted. The media's recent construction of a "yuppie" class of ostensibly well healed middle class professionals who are obsessed with consumption and indifferent to political issues, also has an impact. Most of the subjects expressed disdain for the so called "yuppies," distinguishing both their political beliefs and daily lives from them. However, the subjects' very concern with the issue indicates the power of the myth: subjects wish *not* to be seen as "yuppies," and fear ascription to this category, much as the 1960s radicals did not want to be seen as "opting out" or "becoming part of the system." Not surprisingly, subjects who have achieved less economic success or social status seemed to suffer far less psychological tension about this issue.

Occupations and Ideology

However, it is important to theoretically separate political ideology from political activism. Political ideology is related to an internal belief system and serves as an evaluative framework to view events and interactions, whether these be international issues or one's own daily life. Political activism, on the other hand, relates to the degree of success in implementing these beliefs within a public arena of social action. Numerous studies of radical students in the 1960s[2] found that radical political ideology and actual participation in protest were two separate variables. Radical ideology, as with any other ideology, translates into social action only when a complex set of events occur including opportunities for expression and responsive audiences.

In spite of the subjects' tendency to conflate the two variables (ideology and activism), it is not surprising theoretically to find a high degree of ideological consistency from the 1960s to 1980s, at the same time as one finds some degree of diminution in their political activism.

Despite the guilt expressed by some subjects and considerable debate about what was "radical" in practice, I found subjects displayed a strong persistence of radical ideology. With few exceptions (see below), subjects retained a strong commitment to radicalism, including beliefs in the need for revolutionary change. Barbara's comments in Chapter 3 about "(not) see(ing) living any other way" were echoed by many other subjects:

> (Monica): I don't think it (my politics) will ever change, its hard to imagine...nothing upsets me more than hypocrisy and (I) can't imagine becoming, ever becoming conservative...(it's) very clear to me how (the) political economy works, that's fact and (one) can't pretend it doesn't exist...

> (Richard): I still feel very militant, (I) haven't felt my militancy diminishing. It's still worth struggling...and, of course, I see all sorts of people become less committed to radical politics as they advance, you know, get a co-op and a management job or whatever...

The problem subjects had in labelling themselves noted in Chapter 3 appears to indicate discomfort only within a relatively narrow region of the political spectrum. That is, subjects were reluctant to choose between the labels of socialist, Marxist, socialist-feminist, Marxist-Feminist, feminist, democratic socialist or anarchist. Yet, except for the few subjects who will be discussed below, there was little question that the population displayed a consistent leftist ideology. While the difficulty in constructing a common language of description is not insignificant, and, is indicative of the fundamental lack of a popular Left culture in the U.S. in the 1980s, it cannot be interpreted as a diminution in adherence to radical values or beliefs.

The finding is of interest for two reasons. First, given the current emphasis by the media on "yuppies" and the decline of radicalism, the stability of ideology in our population is striking. The average subject was radicalized seventeen years before this study, and despite the demise of the New Left and other social movements, still embraces the principles of radicalism. Secondly, the consistency of political ideology appears in striking contrast to the lack of stability of professional ideology and identification. As we shall see below, an analysis of the group's attachment to the social service professions indicates that these ties and bonds are far weaker, and have eroded for many subjects over the same time period.

The Vicissitudes of Political Activism

There is little question that, compared to the stability of political ideology, political activism ebbs and flows. Nonetheless, there was a noticeable decline in activity for most of the subjects, particularly in the half dozen years prior to the study.

For those who displayed a decline in radical political activism, a variety of reasons were noted. Increased work and family responsibilities were chief among them:

(James): I guess my activity has dwindled in the last four years...My job takes alot of

121

time, then my teaching, and then, of course, writing my dissertation...it's hard to sort out political activism, maybe alot of Left politics has to do with people being single and in their twenties and thirties...

(Sam): Maybe if I didn't have the union movement to keep my time active I would more actively search out more Left activity to be involved in (pause) because I certainly am very concerned about politics...

The second major issue cited by those interviewed was the "change in the times" in the 1980s. For some subjects the times appeared so quiescent that it was difficult to see what to be involved in. Court suggests a parallel with Karl Marx in the 1850s:

It's family responsibilities and the hours of work and school, but it's also *there is less to be active in*. Maybe the times are what is most significant. You know, after the revolutions of 1848, Marx returned to his writings in the 1850s. You can't always be active, particularly in the absence of movements...

Others recognized the presence of some social movements, but felt they were removed from these political struggles. Bea, who was a community organizer and an activist for many years, feels that the accent on self-help in minority and other ethnic communities and the exclusion of whites from some of these movements has made participation by white middle class radicals difficult:

I was forced to confront the fact that I was Jewish, white, female, and middle class. You know I kind of denied some of this for a long time...But I can't just go into Bedford-Stuyvesant and talk passionately and be a leader in that community...Remember the analysis of the Weathermen...That the only role for white political people on the Left is to educate, to work with people of your own kind, not others...I find this totally untenable and yet I find alot of people I believe in, politically, espousing these kinds of beliefs. At least in (New York City) there is an increasing separatism, a tribalism...

Others who were active in the anti-war and civil rights movements or in the New Left, feel less compatibility with newer movements:

(Renee): I guess you have to look at what has been going on. I mean the major political activism (beginning in the late 1970s) was stuff like the anti-nuke movement. Those of us older folks from the 1960s didn't get as into that. I mean, of course, I'm sympathetic, but it was different, much younger (people) and less politically radical. I felt that way with alot of the Feminist stuff by the late 1970s. By then you were also branded as being on the 'male Left' if you were a Marxist...

In analyzing the comments, two variables seem to be most salient about activism. First, there is a generational issue. Those who were currently most active tended to be younger (age 30-37) subjects who were radicalized in the post 1975 period. There may be a significant relationship between age and work involvement and family responsibilities, as well as political differences between individuals and movements of the late 1970s/1980s compared to the 1960s/1970s. Moreover, it may be that consistent political activism, at least for most people interviewed, has certain finite time limits. For example, most subjects who are still in the *Catalyst* collective are between the ages of 30 and 36 and were radicalized after 1975, whereas many of the older and longer term radicals are no longer involved. While activism is more fluid than can be captured by such generalizations, it appears that many of those who became radical in the late 1960s trailed off in their activities by the late 1970s, while some of the more recently radicalized began to trail off by the mid-1980s. Certainly the psychic energy and time commitment demanded by political activities cannot sustain themselves at the same level indefinitely.

Secondly, as we will analyze further in this

chapter, occupational position seems to relate to activism. This was clearest in the 'extremes' of the population I talked to: those who worked in "movement" jobs, and those working in high administrative positions. The former displayed the highest activism and the latter the least activism (as well as the least adherence to radical political ideology). Further, other occupational roles, particularly being a doctoral student or faculty member, also seemed to mitigate against militant activism. To some degree, this seemed a function of time, but also occupational ties provide a different locus for activities (e.g. lectures, speaking engagements or publishing articles for radical faculty comes to replace participation in demonstrations or picketing).

A Typology of Alternative Interpretations of Work Roles

How did the radical professionals we studied understand and interpret their careers in relation to politics? To what degree did our subjects find professional careers in social work compatible with or contradictory to radicalism? The Table below presents the four possible orientations people could have to radicalism and professionalism, including one orientation which did not emerge in this study:

TABLE I:

A TYPOLOGY OF ORIENTATIONS TO
RADICALISM AND PROFESSIONALISM:

Strong Adherence to Radical Ideology	Strong Adherence to Professionalism	Classification
+	+	"Mediated"
+	-	"Critics"
-	-	"Detached"
(-)	(+)	("Professional-ist")*

* Potential orientation not found in this study, see below.

The table above seeks to locate subjects along alternative ideologies. The first conceptual category is termed the "mediated" group: these radical social service professionals have remained attached to their political radicalism *and* identify strongly with a profession (social work in all cases), hence mediating radical and professional ideologies. The majority of our subjects, however, fall into two categories which represent a more "outsider" stance towards the social service professions. The majority are classified as "critics"; those who remain strong ideological adherents of radicalism, but do not strongly identify with the social service professions. I have included here both those who have broken their ties with the social services through career changes and those who engage in much the same work as the "mediated" group, but who interpret their work very differently.

The "detached" category is composed of only four subjects for whom radical political ideology *and* professional ideology have become weaker. For these four, career changing or changed functional roles within the social services (e.g. high administration) have simultaneously led to a detachment from both radical and professional identifications.

Logically, a fourth category could be expected to appear: social service professionals who have become detached from radical political ideology, but strongly loyal to and identified with the profession. None of the subjects fell into this category; whether this absence is merely chance or holds theoretical importance will be discussed below.

While the typology will suggest some strong associations between job locations and political ideology, the categories cannot be reduced to only a "position consciousness" of sorts. While administrators had a strong occupational consciousness which suggested a detachment from radicalism, counselors and academics were split between the categories of "mediated" and "critics." As Table II suggests, there is a relationship between ideology and work roles, and there are also relationships with demography, professional training, theoretical paradigms, and political ideology of the subjects.

TABLE II:

A Descriptive Typology of Professional Attachments

(Categories)

	"Mediated"	"Critics"	"Detached"
Gender:	Female	Mixed	> Male
Age	Youngest (med. age 34)	Median age 36	Oldest (med. age 40)
Religion:	Roman Catholic	Mixed	Jewish
Method Trained in:	Social Casework	Community Organization Social Casework Social Policy Psychology	Casework
Theoretical Paradigm:	Social Work theory: particularly systems theory	Social Science theories: particularly Marxism	N/A
Political Ideology:	Feminism> Marxism: consciousness-raising; "empowerment"	Marxism>New Left >Feminism Critical Theory Organizing methodology	New Left radicalization (only)

127

Occupations and Ideology

	"Mediated"	"Critics"	"Detached"
Time period of Radicalization:	post-1975 dominant	1960s-early '70s dominant	1960s
Current Occupational Positions:	Counselors/ Supervisors Academia	Academics(more social science) Movement work Organizing Counseling Policy/Research	Administrat- ion Business
Radical Labor Market Shelter as Objective:	yes	yes	no

The "Mediated" Category: Social Work as Subversive Activity

The subjects classified as "mediated," a significant minority of the subjects studied, saw social work professionalism as being consistent with radical political endeavors. Typically these subjects were females who were trained in clinical social work and had a strong adherence to Feminist theory (though often co-existing with Marxism and other ideologies). They "mediated" their occupational life with radicalism through an ideology of consciousness raising and 'empowerment.'These subjects were strongly identified with the profession, whether currently employed as counselors, supervisors or academics, (the first two roles were most common) and they had all developed a self-conscious strategy of bringing progressive values into social work. These individuals believe that while others in the profession may not subscribe to these values, they can wage a kind of subversive struggle through their daily praxis which reflects the best historical traditions of social work. The intimate knowledge and connection with social work's history, with its theories, and with certain client populations allowed these subjects to feel they did "radical social work."

A few subjects implied that the organized social work profession itself was radical. Court approaches this view in stating:

> There is a radical potential (in social work). That's why the far Right doesn't like us. They know, they know, they're much smarter than the Left. They know social work is inherently subversive activity...

While Court borders on being a professional loyalist, most subjects were careful to distinguish their views from those of the organized profession. While they thought social work could be a "radical profession," they were critical of aspects of the profession (professional associations, educational institutions, and certain tendencies in the field such as the increase in private practice psychotherapy and the 'clinicalizing' of the profession). They distinguished a positive "good sense of professionalism" based on skill, from the "elitist" connotations of professionalism. In contrast to the "critics" and the "detached," however, they *do* identify strongly with their roles and training as social workers and associate themselves with the terminology, theory, and symbols of the profession. They are also disposed to consider the profession a relatively hospitable place for radicals. When questioned about how they reconcile their radical political ideology with strong identifications with a profession they had criticized so intently (through *Catalyst* and other leftist groups), the "mediated" group suggested an interpretation of the values and norms of Social Work which self-consciously identifies with certain traditions in the profession, and a "stretching" of professional norms in which radical social work could be carried out in a guerilla fashion.

One way in which subjects were able to assert the complementary of social work to radical political ideology was through an association with past values and traditions:

> (Brenda): It's funny. I identify with social work, but that doesn't mean I'm not critical of it as an institution...you can be cynical about social work, and the schools are just like businesses....*but when you look at the basic values and how the profession started, which is what I identify with,* it's there. It's there! Implicitly, its radical...

> (Rita): I identify strongly with the values I perceive social work to stand for...people like Bertha Reynolds. I'm proud of certain people in social work history and want to be identified with them. If people want to think it is no good (social work) (pause) I have never found it repulsive to be thought of as a social worker who does good for poor people. That's no insult. That's fine! But I do have trouble identifying with some of the people in the field today. *But the roots of social work are progressive...*

In addition to a strong awareness of the historic
tradition in social work, particularly of the early
Settlement House movement, the Rank and File Movement
of the thirties, and the 1960s community organizers,
those who identify with social work "stretch" concepts
which are liberal in their origins to radical ones in
a self-conscious manner:

> (Renee): There are good norms and bad norms
> in the profession. The bad sense of
> professionalism is that identification as
> part of the ruling class or as a social
> control agent, the need for status and
> prestige, the unequal relationship between
> client and worker, the 'I'm better than you'
> feeling. But professionalism can also mean
> competency and skill...If you really believe
> in the "mutuality" that is taught in Social
> Work School, which I do, and I teach my
> students, then you sit down with clients and
> help figure out together what changes need to
> be made in their lives or what resources
> they need, you help them sort it out, you
> don't *do for* clients, you help empower them
> to gain control, to gain greater power and
> resources...and then there are the phrases
> like "self-determination,""advocacy,""empower
> -ment,""respect for individual
> differences,""change strategies," they
> (students) get this drummed into their heads.
> There are a lot worse things to teach a
> student. They are not exactly 'power to the
> people,' but they don't contradict radical
> notions either, and they can be used in a
> radical way, which is why I like them...

Rita makes a similar point in describing her five
years as a social work supervisor at a child care
agency. The agency was an old traditional sectarian
agency hostile to professionalism and reliant on
volunteers for labor. Rita's experience was that she
and the other social workers were the more progressive
force:

> They were extremely anti-professional, but I
> mean professional in the best sense of what
> skilled social work can be. I don't mean
> elitist crap. To them (the volunteers and the

agency) these (children) were little savages
who needed socializing...But I was able to
hire a staff and do the kind of work we
wanted. We could use words like 'advocacy' to
do tenant organizing, to constantly raise
issues of concern to the kids, to raise the
banner of self-determination to protect the
rights of the kids against the agency's
norms...I guess we were undercover radicals.
*It was radical thought under the guise of
(pause) or camouflaged as good social work
practice...*

Perhaps the most distinguishing feature of the
"mediated" group is their view that the 'personal is
political.' For the "mediated" group, feminist theory
and the consensual affinity group radicalism of the
1970s and 1980s allows them to see political gains as
being achieved through the accomplishment of personal
transformations. The ideas of Paulo Freire[3] were also
frequently cited by these subjects who saw counseling
and teaching as a process of "conscientization" or in
its more Americanized form, "empowerment," a word used
by almost all subjects in this group. What
differentiates this stance from some of the "critics"
who are also employed as counselors or teachers, is
that radical ideology often remains implicit for the
"mediated" group, embedded in the process, while many
of the "critics" find consciousness raising in the
absence of ultimate political radicalization and
changed power relations to be insufficient.

To highlight this important distinction, the
political understandings of Rita and Monica can be
contrasted with two "critics," James and Bea. Rita
suggests, in describing her work at a hospital, that
struggling for change and being a radical is part of a
process that is not based on outcomes; she also
suggests that doing humane work with a radical
consciousness is "radical:"

We struggled to get the hospital staff to
discuss all these issues...I don't think we
we're very successful. But I've never felt
success is measured by an outcome. That's
something I feel very strongly about, about
being a social worker. Just to get people to
think can be a success. That's why I like

132

Freire, I think I always felt that the effort
to make people conscious of their oppression
on a very personal level was what I was
doing...I think living your life with
conscious political choices is radical, its a
political statement. Sometimes the best you
can do is be as conscious as possible of both
the system you're working in and the larger
political ramifications, how you fit in...

Monica, when asked about what a "radical
practice" in social work might look like, at one point
gave a case example which reflected her belief about
the close ties between psychological oppression and
political empowerment, and how pointing out these
connections could be radical:

I've been working with this woman and
(welfare) is giving her a horrible time. She
has this very controlling, awful caseworker
there. (We) spent a lot of time talking about
her family and how her sister constantly
tries to control her. And as she is talking
about Mr. B, who is the welfare caseworker, I
thought this sounds so much like her sister
and how she couldn't deal with this guy, how
she was totally intimidated. I began to ask
her if she saw any similarities and she made
the connections too. If we can keep helping
her say 'screw you' to this sister of hers
who dominates her, hopefully she can
eventually confront Mr. B and the welfare
bureaucrats. I don't know. This feels like an
example of how I see therapy being radical.
Maybe it isn't. And it (is) certainly not
radical in an overt way...

While the "mediated" group saw good counseling,
therapy, teaching and organizing as providing a
"conscientization" process in which oppressed people
could regain some control over their lives by learning
to confront authority figures and being better able to
make personal decisions unencumbered by personal
oppression, several "critics" explicitly rejected
"process" as political. James, in discussing his
teaching, suggests that his classes have a more
participatory and involving quality to them than many
traditional classes. But he draws a distinction

133

between process and content:

> But to say that stuff like this (the
> classroom process) is radical seems to me to
> be an extraordinary gutting of the term. Of
> course, I need to be sensitive to how people
> learn. But you do both, you teach well and
> you teach radical content. Then hopefully you
> have an effect. At least a few people each
> year say that my class re-politicized
> them...We used to think of 'radical' as
> meaning significant changes in society, but I
> don't even know how the term is being used
> now...

Bea, another "critic," when asked to describe
what politically radical organizing would be, as a
former organizer, drew a distinction between simply
working with the oppressed and the actual political
content involved:

> I know a lot of people feel it's radical to
> be working with the homeless or other
> populations like this. But that's not in
> itself radical. If your goal is to empower
> the powerless, fine, but then the work you do
> must move things forward in some measurable
> way. Even if you're an organizer working on
> low-income housing issues, *that's not
> political*, not unless you use the organizing
> to move into political education, to deal
> with the class structure in housing and the
> politics in the City which shape it. But just
> to be out there being paid as an organizer
> and even being a good one, that's not
> radical...

Another important distinction between the
"mediated" subjects and many non-radical social
service professionals, and some of the "critics," is
the desire of the former to be associated with certain
oppressed parts of the population which provide the
client base for their services. Renee, Rosa, and
Rosalind all have been active in working with battered
women, Monica in abortion counseling, Renee and
Rosalind, with the homeless, Brenda with trade
unionists. While many social service workers have held
similar positions, there is a strong movement among

professionals towards service directed at more middle class populations. In contrast, these subjects define their radicalism and professionalism in terms of their commitment to the poor, to women, minorities and "the oppressed" generally:

> (Rita): I've never worked with (the) middle class,(I) can't relate (to their problems). Social Work should be with the poor, with working people.(This is) another conscious choice. It's difficult for me, and its my own class bias and politics, but the kind of empathy I feel with working class and poor people, I don't feel with people who have money...

In sum, the "mediated" group sustains its commitment to a radical social work professionalism by mediating the norms, symbols, and trappings of the profession through association to a 'progressive' historical tradition in Social Work, through a process oriented practice which utilizes the terms of the profession to "conscientize" clients or students in a guerilla fashion, and through selection of a client base for social services which includes women, the poor, the working class, minorities, and "other oppressed people."

The "Critics": Social Work is not a Vanguard of Change

As noted in Table 2, those labelled "critics" include more males, almost all subjects who trained in Community Organization, in research and policy and Psychology (as well as several subjects trained in clinical social work), and subjects who tend to draw on social science theories or organizing methodology to mediate their occupational choices with their political ideology. Occupationally, the group is far from homogeneous. Those studied who were currently counselors or academics were divided between the "critics" and "mediated," with the former believing they are challenging the core theories or normative values of the professions rather than upholding historic traditions.

In addition to counselors and teachers, the group includes those doing movement work and organizing. Some subjects were categorized as having left the social services, while other subjects remain in the social services. What the group shares is a continued attachment to radical political ideology, but a diminution of professional identification with social work (or any other profession) as well as with the trappings, language, and paradigms of the professions. Further, rather than process being "empowering," "critics" suggest political ideology should be made explicit and success measured through actual politicization of clients or students.

This alternative of interpreting social service work includes both those who were alienated early on in their training from professionalism as well as others who came to this view during the course of their professional careers. Many "critics" also came to the profession with high "missionary zeal," and *at one point in time* were able to mediate radical and professional identifications successfully. Barbara suggests a common theme for the "critics" as she describes her "naivete" and "confusion" about social work as a radical endeavor:

> I used to think when I was 18 or 22 or even when I was in Social Work School, that, you know, social work was this vanguard, which now I think is total bull. It got me to Social Work School, I wanted to work and change society and this seemed the one profession to do it. But as I think back on it, that was stupid, because even when I was younger, working around the anti-war stuff and civil rights, that wasn't social work, those were social movements, but, of course, there aren't always huge movements to attach (oneself) to, so social work was a way to, on a daily basis, grind this out. I don't think the profession as a whole embraces that. As a political person, I was naive to believe that social work was going to provide leadership...in terms of real change, it's not the social work profession that does it. But you understand how my mind worked, *it got murky in my mind-here is this whole profession set up to help people-so I thought this was my calling. But its not a radical profession, it's a profession....*

The examples of Richard and Bea below suggest a synergistic pattern in which ideology and career events interact: political discomfort with professional education or employment can lead to disillusionment, while educational or professional disillusionment can lead to different ideological stances. While Richard suggests the first pattern, Bea's experiences suggests a two stage model of becoming a "critic."

Richard: The Professional as 'Homeless' and Marginalized

For Richard, political ideology interacted with career goals in such a way as to distance him from certain areas of occupational mobility and professional loyalty, almost upon completion of the professional degree. Richard entered the professions (Psychology) with a "missionary zeal" greatly influenced by his mother's career as a social worker/psychotherapist, by summer camp experiences, and by the idealism of the late 1960s. During college, Richard was attracted to a humanistic and civil libertarian approach to Psychology. When he went on to get his Masters degree, he found he had increasing problems "fitting in" with his surroundings:

I was a very non-traditional Psychology student. I was critical of mainstream Psychology. You know, critical of the medical model and psychopathology...and then critical of psychological research, of the studies, of the normative basis of it...in a way, this was the kiss of death for me because I was very isolated at school...

Richard's conversion to Marxism, which occurred while he was taking doctoral courses and trying to gain admission to a Clinical Psychology Ph. D. program, further distanced him from the mainstream:

In the middle of my graduate training, I became a Marxist...this reinforced my feelings about Psychology. But now I was two steps removed from traditional Psychology. I had an oddball theoretical perspective to begin with. Now I felt further marginalized.

137

(This) put me in a hole. Now sometimes I
think 'If only you had been a good boy!'
(pause) but the seeds were already sown. I
(would) never get into a mainstream
program...

The "hole" Richard refers to was partly a
reflection of his own ambivalence about mobility,
political ideology, and professionalism. On the one
hand, Richard applied several times to Clinical
Psychology Ph. D. programs; yet he refused to take
many of the quantitative and testing courses required
to gain admission. Finally, as a result of his own
political/professional interests and his failing to
get into a "mainstream" program, Richard gained
admission into a Counseling Education program where he
eventually earned his doctorate.

Since Richard completed his Ph. D., he has worked
in a variety of social service settings (with short
ventures into adjunct teaching and a brief full-time
job as a union organizer). Richard's criticisms of the
human service professions and lack of identification
is fueled by a combination of his strong Marxist-
Feminist-Critical Theory ideology, and by an
occupational structure which has limited his options.
With a Ph. D. in Counseling Education, he has found
the job market extremely difficult and has
contemplated returning to school in other areas,
including Social Work. Feeling, however, that he had
already spent enough years in school, he has attempted
to gain the years of psychological supervision
necessary to secure a license. In 1986, Richard
received notice that his application to take the
licensing exam was rejected due to the nature of his
training. These setbacks have, not surprisingly, led
to an uneasy professional identification:

(Interviewer): How would you identify
yourself currently if asked what profession
you are in...?

(Richard): (That's) a difficult question. A
short answer can be dismissed. Technically
I'm not to call myself a psychologist because
I'm not licensed. So I've stopped using the
word. I wrestle with this. I've left it and
come back to it (the profession). Sometimes I

say, 'I trained for this, I'm going to insist
on some way-some way of becoming a Marxist-
Feminist psychologist!' To carve out some way
(to) stay in the field. At other times, (I
say) 'no' they won't allow me to call myself
a psychologist, I can't stay in the
field...so then I consider myself an
educator, a mental health educator, a
psychotherapist, a Marxist with a background
in Psychology. I wrestle with it right up to
this minute...It's like I'm a homeless
person, I'm marginalized in the
professions...

While Richard's structural difficulties with the
employment market are somewhat unusual in this study,
and obviously affect his professional identification,
it would be overly deterministic to view his status as
a "critic" as purely situational. Richard came to a
clear intellectual position of criticism while in
graduate school, and has self-consciously weighed his
options to "join the mainstream" of his profession,
but has rejected these alternatives. Further, Richard
has a clearly delineated view of what mental health
services should be, and clearly rejects the primacy of
professional paradigms. When asked about his several
positions as a counselor/therapist and its
relationship to radicalism, he gives a very different
answer than those in the "mediated" group:

I can't be satisfied with this (social
service work). I find the basic day-to-day
activity of these kinds of jobs typically
limiting, reformist, individualistic (and)
ultimately unsatisfying. I demand more
political, critical thinking, and a more,
political, critical context linked up with
action. I can't give that up! I wish I could
and accept that this is the only role for
leftists...

Richard agrees that there is a need for radical
therapy (and is one of the subjects still engaged in
this activity), but feels strongly that therapy and
consciousness raising *by themselves* are insufficient.
Unless therapy is combined with political education,
organizing, and a broad preventative approach to
health and mental health it will fail to achieve the

radical goals. To Richard, "empowerment," in a therapeutic context, means something different than it does to the "mediated" subjects: it suggests a therapeutic process which is overtly politicizing into left-wing ideologies and class consciousness (as well as dealing with issues of personal oppression) *and* such services should ideally be in the hands of the working class. The latter vision propels Richard toward an ideal of services which is de-professionalized and non-specialized: services housed in unions, movement organizations, etc. which could combine political organizing with counseling. This vision, shared by some of the other "critics," is a very different understanding of what I have called a "radical labor market shelter." For the "mediated" group, non-profit services to an "oppressed" population (battered women, the homeless) represents a sufficient approximation of an ideal employer; while Richard is seeking a model which successfully links mental health to political mobilization and Marxist politics. He acknowledges that this vision may be unrealistic, and may isolate him:

> (What I want to do) may not be possible. I struggle with what I see myself as. I came up with a 'mental health educator.' You know, in the sense of public health, since there is a long Left tradition in that field. But obviously if you look through the *New York Times* you're not going to find the type of job advertised that's broad enough for what I would really want to do...

Bea: The Two-Stage Career of a Critic

Bea, a 34 year old subject, shares some similarities with Richard, but because of her training in Social Work and previous attachment with the Community Organizing "segment" in this field[4], her career pattern is more appropriately described as a two-stage development from organizing to social science criticism.

Bea entered social work with high "missionary zeal," associating social work with political activism. She felt that becoming a community organizer was doing "what came naturally" as she was "always organizing anyway," and her description of Social Work

140

School shows little separation between political and professional organizing. But Bea left her first job as a community organizer at a settlement house after two years, because it lacked political impact:

> The job required you to do all sorts of little bitty kinds of organizing. Crime problems of middle and upper class people. These weren't the clients or the issues I came into social work to work with. (I) wanted to work with low income people on social justice issues...not just a small piece of the problem, (the job was) not at the level that I wanted to be doing things...

Indeed, Bea was able to find a position with impact. Hired to be Executive Director of a small coalition in a neighborhood undergoing massive ethnic and racial population changes which subsequently experienced a tremendous drive toward gentrification, Bea developed a major agency. Her accomplishments in the six years as the coalition's executive were not only in building up a significant coalition, but in achieving some major victories in organizing in a low income neighborhood including successful struggles around housing and community schools.

Bea's description of the first eight years of her worklife marks a first stage in the formation of a critical consciousness. Bea's lack of identification with social work as a profession proceeded her departure from the field. She describes having to go to a series of meetings at a Social Work School in order to obtain students for her agency:

> No, I never identified as a social worker, not when I was an organizer or executive. No, my interest was always as a sort of reformer of the field. I never identified (pause) I'd go to these meetings of field instructors (at Social Work School) and I'd say "I'm not like these people, not at all"...

Moreover, the nature of organizing and community leadership is such that a social work identification was not the most pronounced identity Bea wanted to share:

141

> It was a strange position to be a social worker, which is probably why I didn't identify that way. You know you're perceived in the community as a social control agent and it is a negative to be seen as a social work community organizer. Rather than try to change everybody's understanding of social work, I tried to just get to these people on the basis of goals (pause) And I certainly didn't have my diplomas on the wall...

Bea's lack of identification with professional social work reflects Bucher and Strauss'[5] analysis of the professions as being divided into "segments" of competing forces which *do not* share common trappings and symbols, despite the fiction of a "professional culture." In social work specifically, Epstein[6] and others have found that a true professional community is fictitious in that occupants do not share the same identifications and professional ascriptions. It is not surprising then that Bea and the other subjects trained in community organization did not identify with social work. Clearly, as suggested by sociologists of the professions, the "core nuclear skill" of clinical social work (particularly social casework) has dominated over other segments of social work historically and provides the key discourse in the field[7]. I suggest then that the first stage in the development of an "outsider" orientation may be adhesion to a subordinate segment of a field.

After her years of directing the coalition, Bea began to experience both severe job conflicts and personal tension. The Board of Directors began to attack Bea and her staff's efforts to politicize a Latino population and to bring them into the mainstream of the agency's services. Reflecting a very similar experience to other organizers interviewed, Bea describes herself as "trapped between funding sources, the staff, the Board. Being out there all by myself trying to juggle it all." Finally Bea set a date to leave the agency, and just prior, was awarded a one year fellowship. The year of study changed her occupational goals considerably:

> It was great. I got to study about immigration, ethnicity, Latin American culture, and I learned all these things about

what I had become interested in,
Anthropology, History, Political Science.
(That's a) lot more the way I look at things
now. Everything is related to world politics.
But having seen that,it was very hard for me
to go back to that sort of limited practice.
That's why I decided to (not return)...

Bea, in fact, has not returned to social service
work, but has done research and consulting. While her
future plans are not totally clear, Bea suggests she
would not return to social work, but is likely to get
a Ph. D. in the social sciences or do research.
Relative to her social work training, Bea is now quite
critical:

Social Work training is basically technical
training! We're trained to do things, but not
why to do things and not who you were doing
things with!...That's why I feel Anthropology
is a much more important discipline in terms
of understanding what you're dealing with.
Social workers are not trained to understand
that.

Having become alienated from the social work
field as well as from organizing, Bea finds the
intellectual mediation of politics and work, and her
interest in social science somewhat uncomfortable. For
unlike Richard, she would not describe herself as an
intellectual, but as an activist. Bea feels uncertain
now about where to place her activist energies:

I guess you can say I'm an activist in search
of activity or an organization, like a
homeless radical. I'm not quite sure what to
do, where to fit in. I find it more difficult
than ever to be actively involved in a
struggle...

The "critics" have then become detached from
strong professional identifications, though not from
the ideological basis of their politics. The group
mediates occupational life primarily on the basis of
social science theory. Some subjects have fairly
consistently occupied a critical position, while
others such as Bea went through a two stage process in
which they were first enthusiastically linked to

143

marginal segments and then upon experiencing certain critical incidents (e.g. Bea's unsuccessful struggle with her Board) developed a further attachment to intellectual and social science criticism.

I accent the interpretive process which Bea and other subjects went through in evaluating such career experiences. Obviously, it is only *one* possible interpretation. For example, Joseph, who I place in the "detached" group, was also trained in community organization, and suffered considerable tension from adopting an activist, political approach to a major community struggle. Although parts of his biography are quite similar to Bea's, his attempts to resolve his occupational/political conflicts led him to a degree of detachment from radical political ideology.

"The Detached": "The Left doesn't Understand!"

The small number of subjects categorized as "detached" share two characteristics: they currently occupy more powerful occupational positions than the other subjects, identifying as "managers" in "the search of excellence," and each subject expresses to varying degrees a critical attitude towards the Left, which they feel does not understand their daily struggles and concerns or is unrealistic about the nature of worklife.

The distinction between "high administration" and positions occupied by some of the other subjects is significant. While some subjects had experience supervising staff or managing budgets, these positions were mostly of "straw boss" quality; they reflected little actual overall control of agencies (several subjects ran small coalitions or alternative organizations which were greatly operated on consensual or participatory models of organization). This contrasts with the responsibilities of George and Mitch who operate parts of major public agencies, or of Ann, who makes significant business decisions for a publishing house. Further, those subjects who have held administrative responsibilities for neighborhood coalitions or trade unions identified themselves as community organizers or union activists responsible to a constituency. In contrast, the "detached" group identifies more with the system in which they work rather than with outside social movements.

Detachment from radical ideology is relative. George, who began the interview by stating,"I don't know how radical I ever was...and it's fading fast" was the only subject in the study who went on to repudiate much of his past political activity as a "folly of youth." We might suggest that if any sympathy with the Left and occasional donations or participation in events is taken to reflect ideological commitment, than the others labelled "detached" are to some degree still 'radical.' However, an analysis of the interview data suggests a significant weakening in radical ideology and a general feeling of irrelevance of political radicalism in the lives of the 'detached.'

Like other subjects' occupational choices, the choice of management represents only a contingent choice which as of the time of this study appears to be the end result of a process of painful occupational experience. The "detached" group experienced uniformly high job tension in their past positions, and all but one suffered very traumatic "negative career events." As the vignette of Ann in Chapter 5 suggests, careers in business or high management were *not anticipated* by this group, but rather were obtained only after *significant disappointments or failures* in other career ventures. While the allure of mobility should, of course, not be discounted, we get the sense that initially these subjects were "reluctant managers." The career histories of the "detached" group suggest that these subjects did not enter their managerial positions having discarded their political attachments, but have gradually become distanced from both the culture of the Left and of social service professionalism *after* they began to occupy their managerial roles.

George: Radicalism as a Folly of Youth

George received his Masters in social work in the mid-1960s, motivated greatly by exposure to skilled groupworkers in a summer camp. He became radicalized in the late 1960s through involvement with welfare rights organizing and the community mental health movement. To avoid the draft, George entered a doctoral program in Sociology, while continuing to work at a community mental health center. Initially, George sought the degree only to stay in school and gain credentials to perform human service work, but gradually he became attracted to Sociology as a discipline and to college teaching. After receiving a Ph.D., George went on to teach Sociology at two liberal arts colleges for a half dozen years.

George links the political activities he was involved in (which were considerable) to his status as an academic:

> Being in the academy probably was why I was involved with all these political activities. I think I stopped being active because I left academia. Once I had left academia, this sort of participation had to stand on its own as an activity...you know, (like) being on (*Catalyst*), this was something an academic does...

George distinguishes his current position as a director of state hospital services for children with his political involvement earlier in his life:

> Here I'm doing so much, affecting the lives of hundreds of kids and families...I guess one thing that distinguishes it, particularly from the kind of thing I was into as an academic in which I was heavily into theory, is a lot of it is rhetoric. I was pretty good at rhetoric. I was pretty successful in convincing people on what the line should be. I began to realize that this is crazy...Now if I think something is true or I know something, I guess I try to do it, and if it works, I guess I'm right, I knew something. But its not just asserting the right Left principles and line that wins a vote at a small committee meeting...

Like Ann and Joseph, a negative career experience propelled him away from his earlier jobs. In his second teaching job, George tried to teach radically, which he describes as attempting to "empower" the primarily working class human service students to learn on their own and think critically. George found that his outspokenness caused him to be regarded as an "obnoxious colleague" by his fellow professors. George recalls his experience in a similar fashion to Ann's

146

description of her lack of organizational sophistication:

> Basically the lesson was if you try to empower students, the University will try to destroy you. But I wasn't savvy enough to (see) that. I was very naive, I think if I ever did it again I could be successful. I mean I also thought that universities took learning seriously. But they don't. There's no bottom line to the bull...

While the exact circumstance of George's departure from the college are not clear (whether firing, non-renewal of contract or pressured to quit), what is most significant is George's interpretation of the experience. While he believes his difficulties were greatly situational and psychological, the dashed idealism of an academic career is clear in George's tone of bitterness in his account of these years. He associates this particular occupational context (academia) with the corresponding period in his life which included radical politics:

> This was a 'ridiculous period' (1970s). A lot of us were intoxicated, maybe by the success of the anti-war movement and civil rights. We thought that if we got together, had some meetings, a few of us could do anything...and this corresponded to my academic career. You know how these left academics, they have all these pretensions, like they are proletarians. (Its) basically romantic bull...

George now describes his occupational and political commitment as being one of "good government" in which he can develop humane and efficient services to the public:

> The commitment is to the search for excellence, to improve services to people when you begin to treat it (mental health) as a business. That you treat patients as customers who could go elsewhere, even if they can't, you dramatically increase the quality of care. The worst thing about bad government programs is that they don't give a

damn about the customers...

While George's "search for excellence" appears commendable, he interprets this goal in a context which is hostile to not only the Left, but to the social work profession:

The first thing I'd do is screw AAUP and fire all the faculty. Tenure is bullshit! No one on a faculty in social work has spoken out on anything anyway...(you) have to look at social work as a business, and let some of social work go out of business...In the old days you could just say 'give us the money and resources and we social workers could save the world.' Well, nobody believes that anymore, and even with all the resources we wouldn't eliminate poverty. Maybe we should eliminate welfare, start out with the basic fact that 60 to 70% of (the) country agrees with Reagan, that welfare is a mess...maybe social work needs some Boone Pickens...

It appears that George's success in his career as a "manager" along with growing isolation from his former peers in the professions and in radical politics, has led him to a new identification with the efficiency of business. He appears to associate aspects of his past life (politics, social work, sociology, previous friendships) with a lack of realism, youth, and the disappointments he suffered in his career.

Other "detached" subjects showed similar discomfort with aspects of Left politics and with the social services which they associate with past "negative career events" and personal uneasiness. Like George, Ann stresses an ideology of efficiency:

It (publishing career) has made me broader...I don't feel comfortable with radical groups anymore. Its hard to explain why. I feel alienated. They just talk to themselves. And its kind of condescending...And I want to be a participating member of society, not in a subculture. And the Left is one. I want to be able to relate to my in-laws who are Irish

Catholic working class, to be comfortable in
the South with my clients. It's a different
world...And (publishing company) is a very
efficiently run organization, most non-
profits aren't. (I) really like that. You
know we used to believe in collective
decision-making, but this seems dubious now.
I think hierarchy is necessary, and I'd
prefer an efficient one like (company) to the
social agencies I worked in...

Joseph also displays how high administrative jobs
can create a 'class consciousness' of position which
puts people at odds with unions and with the Left:

I'd never go back to that job (public
administration)! The staff were totally
incompetent and sat around doing nothing,
protected by the union...and the Left has
difficulty understanding what you need to do
to administer a program like this. I mean you
have to run a housing program with money from
somewhere. You either raise rents...or forget
it...Yet the community groups are always
attacking you, even when you're doing the
best you can...

The "detached" group has not necessarily lost its
"conscience," but all feel a great deal of tension
with what they perceive as a left social service view
of work, credentials, unions, and political action. In
this study, occupancy of high administrative
positions occurred after a disillusionment with other
types of social service work. After entering the
managerial positions, subjects felt increasingly
isolated from both the culture of the Left and from
the symbols and identifications of their profession of
training, which all of them criticized.

The previous lack of strong ideological
attachment of these subjects to Marxism, Feminism or
other well elaborated political ideologies suggests
not that the "detached" group was less completely
socialized to left politics and culture, but that
their radicalization (which occurred in the 1960s) was
primarily framed by the New Left experience. Subjects
displayed a propensity towards activism, and were
categorized as "activist only" in Chapter 3 (as

opposed to intellectual or intellectual/activist radicalization). The decline of 1960s social movements and the New Left community particularly impacted upon these subjects. Unlike other subjects, the "detached" appear to have less fully integrated an intellectual interpretation of political events. This combined with the difficulties they experienced in the occupational structure detached them from previous political and professional associations, and reinforced a degree of cynicism and distance from both the profession and radical politics.

A Fourth Category?

As noted earlier, it would appear logical that a fourth alternative pattern would be available to radical professionals. Subjects could conceivably move over the years towards increased loyalty and association with professional norms, symbols, and paradigms while displaying a diminution of radical ideology. This orientation, which could be described as a "professionalist" stance, was not found among the subjects studied.

Since our study was a small one, no definitive statement can be made as to the prevalence of this orientation among the general population of (ex) radical social workers or professionals. However, I would suggest this orientation would be far less common than the three discussed above. First, increased mobility and commitment to professional paradigms and symbols were not associated with diminished radicalism in our study. While the question of militancy is a very different one (see Part II), even those subjects who were most identified with the mainstream organizations and theories of social work (like Court) did not feel great tension in mediating the two orientations. On the other hand, it appears that movement into managerial positions tends to hold the strongest association with diminished ideological commitment. As will be commented on further below, both the elasticity of professional norms in the social services as well as the function of the social services as a mediating institution which absorbs oppositional elements in society help professionals retain radical ideology. That is, increased professionalization for the "line" social worker, organizer or planner or supervisor would not appear to correlate with increased conservatism. It might be suggested that more of the administrative personnel in social services (and those who have the left the field) have become detached from left ideology than those engaged in direct practice or supervisory work. This would be a good area for further inquiry.

Summary and Conclusions of Part I

In the preceding chapters, we have examined the development of a group of radical social work professionals through reviewing their individual careers both as radicals and professionals. The majority of subjects were influenced by the New Left, and many began defining themselves as radicals in the context of the social movements of the 1960s. In Chapter 4, we noted the strong association between radical values and social service work that most subjects came to while in professional school. The possibility of combining "missionary zeal" with the normative career goals of upward mobility was optimistically anticipated at that point in their lives.

In contrast, the career experiences of many subjects, as noted in Chapters 5 and 6, led to a diminished optimism about radical professionalism. A majority of subjects felt considerable tension in social service positions and many suffered "negative career events." The combination of problems at social service jobs and the allure of other careers caused many subjects to either leave the social services or interpret their work roles in a more critical way. While some subjects did continue to identify strongly with social work, and continue in the tradition of Bertha Reynolds and other figures, there was a noticeable decline in "missionary zeal" over the years. Moreover, the "critics," who were more divorced from social service professionalism, outnumbered those who felt social work was very compatible with radicalism. Prior to moving to Part II, where we examine whether radical professionalism as a social movement has been successful, we suggest several conclusions from Part I of this book.

No "Big Chill"

While we have examined only a small group, the strong consistency of radical ideology over a long period of time (an average of 17 years for our subjects) argues against the popular conception of a "Big Chill" among radicals. Many subjects felt just as strongly about radicalism as they did in 1968 or 1972, and, in a number of cases, subjects intentionally limited their upward mobility strivings to defer higher rewards to remain working for unions, alternative organizations or low paying social service agencies. While a small number came to be "detached" from aspects of radical ideology, only one person actually repudiated much of his past ideology.

The 1970 study by Maidenberg and Meyer that suggested careers in teaching and social work "helped sustain radical sentiments" is certainly supported by this study. This contrasts sharply with the Durkheimian tradition in sociology as well as the radical critiques of the 1960s, which saw professionalization as a conservatizing process. In fact, in contrast to the relative consistency of radical political ideology, "professionalism" as both an identity and an ideology seems relatively shallower.

The Shallowness of Professionalism

Although all our subjects were trained as social service professionals and were exposed to much socialization about the norms, values, and traditions of their profession, after a number of years as professionals a majority of the subjects do not strongly identify as social service professionals. Professionalism seems a highly *contingent* ideology, subject to particular worksite and occupational role, and particular interpretation of work role.

One compelling reason for this, is the important sociological analysis of the professions themselves as being composed of "segments" which while maintaining a fictional unity to the public actually are fragmented by roles, paradigms, different core skills, and symbols[8]. It is not surprising that in our study, those closest to the dominant 'core skill' in social work--clinical social work-- had the strongest association with professionalism, while those whose job functions are more in community organizing, administration, fundraising or teaching feel more removed from professional identification. A second example of this split is evident in looking at workplaces: those who work closer to the 'core' missions of social work, in agencies serving families or individuals, feel more strongly identified with social work professionalism than those working for research and academic institutions, unions, community groups or alternative agencies.

Beyond the segmentation of the professions, the classical definitions of professionalism which center on colleagueality, the service ethic, and functional specificity, fails to account for alternative mediating ideologies existent in the professional labor market. For high level administrators, a "techno bureaucratic" orientation[9] would seem to better capture the nature of work. Such an orientation replaces the colleaguial group with a specific enterprise (Ann's publishing company, George's state agency) which is then viewed as the embodiment of positive good. Achievements at the workplace are seen as personalistic rather than linked to the mission of a profession. At its extreme (as in the case of George), the "service ethic" and client obligations are transferred to a complete identification with self and with one's own firm or organization.

An intellectual approach to worklife which focuses not on professional colleague reference groups or the service ethic or bureaucratic identifications, has rarely been commented on in the professional literature. Nevertheless, a majority of our subjects (the "critics") would be more adequately described as "organizational intellectuals"[10] than classical professionals. The intellectual sees his or her reference group as outside social forces and movements which links their work with social change or with knowledge production. It is surprising, perhaps, to find this orientation in a field that is rarely considered intellectual (social service work), and, interestingly, few subjects entered the profession with this goal nor would many of our subjects take well to this label. Nevertheless, their orientations seem best described this way.

Occupational Ideologies

While beliefs and identifications about work are quite abstract and ideal during professional training (greatly accounting for the stronger identification with social service professionalism in a school environment), after years in the workplace, radicals, like others, come to be strongly wedded to the particular occupational choices they have made. No matter how happenstance employment choices were, the subjects revealed strong psychic needs to justify their work and make such work consistent with their political ideals. That is, after a number of years in a work role, subjects had a strong vested interest in their subject matters, technique, and the philosophies they associated with their work roles.

In other words, particular occupational attachments do serve to mold particular political ideologies and behaviors. Those who have sacrificed mobility to enter "movement work" like Barbara have strengthened their political commitments at a time when others have weakened, and they take some pride in this. They are critical of people who are "merely" social workers, teachers or administrators, rather than being paid to do organizing. At the opposing extreme, those like Ann and George, who have entered positions of some power, have become less identified with the Left, which they see as potentially critical of their career choices. While, we cannot argue, based on such a small number of people, that all administrators feel this way, this does suggest a need for more research into the political implications of career mobility and particular job locations. Often social work, like many professions, urges its members on to bigger and higher positions such as management, without concern for how the values of the profession change as people assume such high positions[11].

Positions in counseling, supervising or teaching can be highly consistent with radicalism, but specific attitudes towards radical politics are also shaped along lines of self-interest. While counselors and faculty split to some degree between the "mediated" and "critics," when highly specific work information is obtained, their positions relative to their work and ideology are often highly consonant. Those, for example, who were involved in teaching direct social work practice as well as practitioners in dominant segments of social work emphasized the efficacy of 'micro level' change. Those who were faculty, researchers or consultants more wedded to sociology, academic psychology, social policy, or who were community organizers, naturally stressed the importance of 'macro' level change and the influence of political economy. Some counselors who were "critics," like Richard, were more occupationally wedded to connecting therapy to political organizing and theory, than in the day-to-day issues of counseling.

Some of these differences in interpretation are clearly influenced by gender, religious/ethnic family background, and the activist/intellectual split noted earlier. Certainly, the "mediated" group seems to reflect a certain tradition which is more female than male, more Catholic than Jewish, and more activist and "missionary" than the intellectual orientation of the "critics." While these generalizations have some validity, our study also suggests that specific career movement can supersede these stereotypes. Bea and Barbara, for example, entered social work as "missionaries" and activists to eventually become more allied with intellectual and Marxist paradigms of change. Court, who can quote Marx and Gramsci verbatim, and is an intellectual of the first order, has come to associate himself primarily with the micro level and with social work as an agency of change.

There is evidence of some historical tension between the two orientations. Years ago, Paul Halmos attacked his own field, sociology, for its tendency to criticize the human service professions, and praised "the faith of the counselors"[12] as something beyond the ability of critical sociologists to understand. More recently, Ann Withorn, criticized a 'hard left' approach which looks unkindly towards social services, favoring a more 'soft left' view favoring micro level change[13]. However, it would seem that both orientations are open to criticism since they are greatly based on vested occupational interests.

As we will note in Part II, radical counselors, teachers, and others working with people in the human services have very little proof that their 'micro' level efforts at empowerment ever move from 'conscious raising' to more collective activity. They often have trouble even verbalizing how their therapy, classroom teaching or planning efforts, differ tremendously from that of effective humanistic, but non-radical, practitioners. Those who operate on the more 'macro' level of intellectual thought have a similar problem in demonstrating how their writings, speeches or leaflets actually move people to act collectively or influence political events. In short, while not minimizing the ability of subjects to maintain their political ideologies over the years, there is considerable question as to whether these radical counselors, teachers, organizers and researchers, actually engage in political behavior which advances radical change in any measurable way.

Careerism and Professionalism

To return to the highly charged rhetoric of the 1960s and 1970s about 'professional power' and 'professional dominance,' it would appear that the New Left's critique of careerism carries stronger weight than its critique of professionalism. Indeed, in this study, those who chose upward mobility as a key goal, did appear to be most willing to surrender political values, and became detached from their idealism. In this sense, a strong commitment to occupational advancement, whether in social work, medicine, law, or in farming or carpentry, would appear subversive of radicalism. Careerism would suggest a higher premium is placed on personal gain or reward than on political or social values. In contrast, positions as professionals, can be consistent with radical goals. It is, of course, not the mere acquisition of professional education or skills which distances people from radical ideologies, but rather, the gradual development of a position consciousness, such as George displays, which sees clients, employees, or social movements as potential threats to personal power.

Perhaps the discussion of careerism and professionalism is most confused by the tendency of observers, including much of the New Left, to fail to distinguish 'deradicalization' or 'conservatization,' on the one hand, and 'co-optation' on the other hand (i.e. separating political ideology from political behavior as we have suggested). Despite the possibility of maintaining radical political ideologies in the professions, militant political action is highly constrained by the professional occupational structure, as we shall explore in Part II. In this sense the critique of professionalization may have more validity.

Notes

1. Haber and Haber,"Getting By...," p. 302.

2. see especially, Keniston, Radicals and Militants..., p. xi for a review of the studies of the 1960s.

3. Freire,Pedagogy of the Oppressed...

4. The term "segment" as used for a particular competing methodological, paradigmatic, and even ideological center of a profession was developed by Bucher and Strauss,"Professions in Process..." For a specific analysis of social work as a profession of segments, see Thomas Carleton, "Social Work as a Profession in Process,"Journal of Social Welfare, 4 (1977), pp. 15-25.

5. Ibid.

6. The works of Irwin Epstein have been most clear in suggesting social work does not constitute a unified profession. See "Organizational Careers, Professionalization, and Social Worker Radicalism,"Social Service Review, 41:2 (1970), pp. 123-131; "Professionalization, Professionalism, and Social Worker Radicalism,"Journal of Health and Social Behavior, 11 :1 (1970), pp. 67-77; and Epstein and Kayla Conrad,"The Empirical Limits of Social Work Professionalism," in Y. Hasenfeld and R. Sarri,The Management of Human Services, New York: Columbia University Press, 1978.

7. When Larson (see Rise of Professionalism...) and Toren (Social Work: The Case of a Semi-Profession...) analyzed the profession of social work in the 1970s, they saw social casework as the "core nuclear skill" which dominated the field. Because "casework" has expanded as a modality to often include family

157

treatment, I prefer the term "clinical practice" to indicate the dominant segment in the social work profession in the 1980s.

8. see Bucher and Strauss, Epstein, Carleton, Larson above.

9. see Larson.

10. see Meyer Zald and John McCarthy,"Organizational Intellectuals and the Criticism of Society,"<u>Social Service Review</u>, 46 (1975), pp. 344-362.

11. I have argued this point in "The Fate of Idealism in Social Work: Alternative Experiences of Professional Careers,"<u>Social Work</u>, 34 (1989), pp. 389-398.

12. see Paul Halmos,<u>The Faith of the Counsellors</u>, New York: Schoken, 1966; <u>The Personal Service Society</u>, New York: Schoken, 1970; and "Sociology and the Human Service Professions,"in Freidson, Elliot (ed.),<u>The Professions and Their Prospects,</u> Beverly Hills: Sage, 1973.

13. see Ann Withorn,"Beyond Realism: Fighting for Human Services in the Eighties,"<u>Catalyst,</u> 4 (2), 1982, pp. 21-38; also see <u>Serving the People...</u>, Chapter 1.

Part II:

Radicalism, Social Action,
and Social Service Careers

Introduction

Part I of this book focused on the individual subjects' experience of their careers as they confronted the dilemma of obtaining professional training and employment in an occupational structure which they viewed as contradictory to their political values. In this section, we will return to the objectives of radical professional movements, and develop some theoretical conclusions about the possibilities and constraints on political action posed by social service careers and the occupational structure.

This section will analyze the subjects' experience in reference to the shared goals these subjects embraced as members of *Catalyst* and other groups of radical professionals. For although the experience of work life, the meanings and interpretations of such experience, and the mediation of political values with a career, are, in many senses, highly personal phenomena, they also are highly bounded in shared meanings and objectives which the subjects held as part of a social movement of radicals. They also are deeply bound in historical processes and a political economy which is both shaped by the general contours of other social movements, and by the particular stages in radical professional movements.

Catalyst and other radical groups strongly held to a belief in the relevancy of radical political ideology for daily social service work. While radical social service groups recognized that activism at work would vary and that personal employment situations would affect the ability of group members to openly implement radical tactics or overtly espouse certain ideas, *Catalyst* nevertheless viewed its mission as assisting social service workers in promoting radical change. While radical theory and analysis of the social service system was a key tool in this struggle, theory was seen primarily as adjunctive to struggle rather than as an end in its itself.

Three clear activist goals can be gleaned from an analysis of *Catalyst*'s own pages as well as from the collective's internal documents. First, *Catalyst* sought to encourage social service workers to fight their employers *in their own interests as workers*:

> ...social service workers (should be engaged in) efforts toward unionization, better working conditions, and increased pay and benefits. We reject the appeal to the worker's guilt which equates material improvements for workers with reductions in client services. [1]

A second goal for *Catalyst* was to encourage radicals to provide assistance to "client struggles":

> ... supporting struggles by clients for increases in social service benefits and for increased control in delivery of those benefits. [2]

Finally, *Catalyst* saw a role for its members and readers in engaging in a "radical practice" in which all methods of social service work could be stripped of repressive functions, and be made emancipatory:

> ...we will encourage practice that emphasizes our helping functions while struggling against our function of social control...(help promote understanding of) the ways mainstream practice reinforces conformist attitudes towards class, racism, and sexism...[3]

This section will explore how the shared goals of *Catalyst* members: organizing as workers, supporting "client struggles," and practicing in a helping and "non-mainstream" way, were put into action by the study subjects in their own careers. An in-depth review of the biographies[4] of the subjects over the course of two decades provides the opportunity to analyze the actual experience of social actors who were key participants in a social movement. Their successes and failures, and the perceptions and interpretations of actions and strategies engaged in at work which flowed from the common goals of this group, provides valuable data about this social movement, and also provides important sociological insight into similar efforts to impart radical ideas and practice at the workplace.

Over the years almost all subjects had moved away from overt oppositional political action at the workplace or in the professions. This finding, particularly in reference to the 'professional as worker' orientation and the support of 'client struggles' is discussed in Chapter 7. As oppositional political action has decreased, these radical professionals have continued some focus on what early social work theorist Mary Richmond called the "retail" level of their work: the politics of individual transformations through one-to-one work. To the extent that these radicals do use their occupational positions as springboards for a type of radicalism it is best described as a 'prefigurative politics' which attempts to raise personal consciousness through psychosocial methods or through education of students and clients. These findings are summarized in Chapter 8.

The relationship between the decline of militancy in this small group and the macro level events structuring the 1970s and 1980s is developed in Chapter 9. The structural constraints of certain occupational positions, and, paradoxically, the increasing identification of radicals with their own employers as "labor market shelters" limits the possibility of oppositional political action on the job, and to an extent *off* the job as well. The social conditions that produced a movement of radical professions, beginning in the 1960s, are analyzed and compared with the history of the radical social service movements of the 1930s-1940s, as well as the reasons for their declines.

Notes:

1. "Why Catalyst?" in Catalyst, 1 (1), 1978, p. 3.

2. Ibid.

3. Ibid, pp. 2-3.

4. The methodology in this part of the book is somewhat different than in Part I. In the first part, since we were interested in describing, in a roughly chronological fashion, subjects' experiences with career choice, professional training, careers, etc., we followed a fairly straight forward content analysis and selection from interviewees' responses. In this section, I was interested in *inferring* from the subjects' accounts of their activities during the 1970s and 1980s, the degree to which they implemented radical precepts at their workplaces and elsewhere. Therefore, the material in this Part is taken from subjects' accounts of their careers and their answers to my questions about what constituted being a radical in the social services in the late 1980s. I intentionally did not prompt the subjects by asking them about organizing or radical practice, but rather analyzed the material after the fact. While, of course, there is the danger of not being comprehensive (there may be particular activities that were not discussed), the methodology has the advantage of reducing ideological or abstract answers which subjects may have given if the author presented them with a list of all the goals of *Catalyst*.

163

7

THE DECLINE OF
OPPOSITIONAL ACTIVISM

This chapter will compare the prescriptions of
Catalyst to organize at the workplace and within the
community with the efforts of subjects to actually
undertake such activity. I define oppositional
activity, as opposed to an ideological commitment to
radicalism, as public efforts at implementing radical
objectives through challenges to established
institutions including conflicts with employers,
professional associations, or schools, which are not
sanctioned by the individual's own employer (except in
the case of paid community or labor organizers, where
"employer sanction" while often ambivalent, is
ostensibly present to confront institutional
structures).

The Professional-as-Worker

As noted earlier, *Catalyst* arouse at a time
when the entrance of many New Leftists into the
professions, along with the fiscal crisis of the state
and cutbacks in many public sector professional jobs,
provided saliency to the view that professionals were
part of the "working class." From the first issue on,
most *Catalyst* articles addressing professional
employment and unionization, subscribed to the view
that professional work was becoming increasingly
"proletarianized." While the exact meaning of this
term varied, for the most part, authors projected an
increased immiseration of professional workers through
a decline in job security, income and benefits,
advancement and promotion, and reduced status, as work
became more "routinized" and subject to
"Taylorization"[1]. The journal, as well as other organs
of the Left in the 1970s, predicted that the fiscal
crisis of the state and the trends of "de-skilling"
would lead to increasingly militant employee actions
by public sector and professional workers.

164

The Decline of Oppositional Activism

There was a broad consensus among the authors of articles published in *Catalyst* and among members of the collective itself that: (1) Professionals should identify as part of the working class, and not with an elitist professionalism (2) Professionals should unionize and fight for improved pay, working conditions, and job control (3) Unions were often run by conservative bureaucrats who identified with capitalist ideology and, once unionized, radicals needed to fight for union democracy, more militant tactics, and more radical political programs and (4) Human service workers and their unions had an obligation, and were perhaps in an unique position, to form alliances with client groups so that the demands of the poor and other benefit recipients would be the joint demands of a worker/client alliance.

Radicals and Employee Organizing

Did the members of the *Catalyst* collective heed their own dictates about organizing at the workplace? In recounting their political and career histories, subjects frequently did refer to past union organizing efforts, attempts at unifying staffs against employers (even without a union), and internal union struggles around various issues. Not only does our study include a number of individuals who themselves contributed to the literature on the "proletarianization of professionals" (in *Catalyst* and other publications) and who urged unionization and client alliances, but five subjects were at one point officials or employees of unions, and an analysis of the interviews indicates that the vast majority of subjects had attempted to organize employees at their own workplaces.

While a complete inventory of the subjects' experience in union organizing and oppositional actions as employees is beyond our scope, several trends can be noted: (1) a strong militancy was expressed by the subjects about previous organizing efforts with a general sense of pride in their efforts, whether or not they were ultimately successful, (2) with several exceptions, the strongest employee activism occurred while these radicals were relatively young in age and relatively low in status in their organizations, and ceased or tapered off with age and mobility, (3) as has been the experience of the labor movement generally, successful efforts at organizing as well as overall adherence to the professional-as-worker view corresponds most strongly with public sector employment and with lower paid and lower status professional work.

When describing their previous jobs and organizing efforts, subjects were quite militant about their past work. This is particularly interesting in light of the tone of the latter parts of the interviews in which the subjects rarely displayed these sentiments about their current jobs and often did not even mention employee concerns. Rosalind and Howard's descriptions of employee struggles at early career junctures are indicative of our subjects' activities in the 1960s and 1970s:

> (Howard, on an organizing effort at a state mental institution): It wasn't only that we were paid poorly and treated like shit, but the kids were oppressed and brutalized. We were morally outraged that this was how the State was responding to mental retardation. We fought hard alongside the parents to prevent another Willowbrook, and, in great measure, we succeeded. Of course, most of us were harassed or forced to quit. When I resigned, I wrote in my resignation letter something about how the management were jailkeepers and should be transferred to Attica. You know, it wasn't that long after (Attica). Boy they hated me, and (I) certainly didn't think I'd ever get a state job again...

> (Rosalind, on a successful union organizing effort among teaching assistants at a university): The issue was professionalism. People wanted to think of themselves as young, upwardly mobile professionals and a lot of people didn't want to think of themselves as lackeys who were doing 30% of the university's undergraduate teaching. We didn't want to think of ourselves as exploited workers. We wanted to think of ourselves as starving intellectuals who were going to become genius academics and no way would we bite the hand that feeds us because

we knew academic politics and we knew if we
became rabblerousers in our departments, we
could sabotage our careers. So there was a
lot of debate about this union, should it
exist at all. But I knew! The Union was key,
it was the only way conditions would improve.
And I was self-supporting and poor, I didn't
buy this crap that I was privileged...

Such militancy and organizing activity
corresponded to subjects' early careers which
clustered in the late 1960s-early 1970s, and in the
1976-1980 period. For those over forty, the locus of
employment during the late 1960s in areas such as
public welfare departments and other state agencies
provided a context of militant strikes (such as the
S.S.E.U. strikes in N.Y.C. in 1966 and 1967), of
colonization by numerous left-wing groups into some
unions, and of solidarity between public workers and
recipient groups (such as the National Welfare Rights
Organization). For most subjects who are now under
forty, however, the mid-1970s period was their most
active period. This period corresponds to subjects'
average age of 25-30 and followed shortly after
professional training when subjects held positions as
caseworkers, planners or organizers. Significantly,
the years in which *Catalyst* was forming (1976-77) were
extremely active[2].

Indeed at one point (1976-78), at least nine
subjects were involved in some sort of organizing:
Bea, in one of the most successful of the organizing
drives (organizing a major settlement house); Howard,
Renee, and Alan, were all employed at a large hospital
where they sought to organize health care
professionals; Barbara was involved at her settlement
house in efforts to form a union; Rosalind was
involved in the teaching assistants union; Rita, was
active as a hospital social worker struggling with
other staff to get their union to take action; and
Court and Sam were both public employees at the time
and extremely active in their unions, serving as union
delegates.

As noted above, certain types of employment
correspond with greater consistency of activity and
success of unionization. Overwhelmingly those involved
in the public sector (welfare, corrections, city

planning, etc.) were more consistently involved in union activity and more successful in gaining the support of other employees. Among the small number of subjects who mentioned activity in recent years, almost all are employed in the public sector. Within the private sector, activity appears to correlate inversely with income and status. Bea and Richard were involved in unusual successes (for the labor movement in general) at a settlement house and a moderately sized social agency on contract with the public sector. While such success is not to be minimized, these workplaces contrast with higher pay and status agencies such as hospitals, psychiatric clinics, and family agencies where labor organizing efforts have been less successful.

The Detachment from Employee Militance

In contrast to these accounts of past union organizing, efforts to unify staff against managerial or state policies, and activity within unions, when subjects were asked about what constituted being a radical in the late 1980s, there was a surprising lack of mention of either unions, anti-management perspectives or on-the-job militancy.

At the time of the study, only a few subjects either commented on the professional-as-worker orientation or explicitly or implicitly saw their employment as related to a labor perspective. This small number included Sam, an official of a public sector union, and Jacqueline, employed as a union staff member. Other than Sam and Jacqueline, only three people (Agnes, Richard, and Barbara) suggested a key role for radicals organizing at the workplace. Significantly this represents the three people classified earlier as 'movement' employed, and two people (Agnes and Richard) who are in the small percentage of the population still engaged in counseling and still potentially eligible for collective bargaining unit membership (see below).

Agnes' strong commitment to union activity provides a good example of what one might have anticipated to be the common outlook of our subjects. When asked about her current job as a counselor in a public sector correctional agency, Agnes moves back and forth between client need and worker organizing, seeing both as critical tasks:

> This is a crazy place and sometimes I wonder
> what I'm doing here. I mean these people lock
> up poor oppressed people in jail, and the
> system stinks, its rotten, its disgusting. I
> see horrible things happen all the time. I
> guess this is all in answering how I ended up
> here and why I stay here. I think radicals
> need a commitment to people nobody else cares
> about, and second to (the) public
> institutions which everybody thinks are
> raggedy and terrible and thinks you can't do
> any social work in.(Pause) And above all, I
> wanted a union job! No, this is a whole other
> piece. It was crucial to me. (The) people I
> work with are as important to me, if not
> more, than those (clients)...yeh, I came to
> see myself more as a worker. Also my personal
> life had a lot to do with this. I had a lot
> of problems, I had no money. I was on the
> verge of eviction, and I wanted to
> know(pause) all of a sudden, the nobility of
> social work, the liberal kinds of notions,
> bull! They're not paying the rent! I'm a poor
> exploited person here, at least my (clients)
> have enough sense to go hit someone on the
> head to get money...

Agnes was recently elected a union delegate, and
seeks, in the tradition of *Catalyst*, to link efforts
for better pay with lower caseloads and higher quality
supervision to improve conditions for clients. Agnes
was quite pleased when a large number of workers had
protested at a manager's office and blocked the doors
as a protest against the doubling and tripling up of
office space, which affects client privacy as well as
worker comfort.

Agnes provides a contrast to other subjects in
several ways. Unlike others, she is working in the
public sector which, as noted, appears associated with
union and other oppositional sentiment. Also, while
Agnes is not young in age, she is among the most
recent professional school graduates (3 1/2 years
before the interview took place), and hence her
relative militancy and low level position corresponds
to where other subjects were in the late 1960s or mid-

1970s. However, if Agnes' sentiments do hold constant over time, it may not be her relative newness to the profession, but her negative view of mobility which separates her from other subjects. When I asked if she hoped to move on and do better, Agnes noted she had taken another job for four months at a psychiatric hospital which offered better pay and higher status, yet she hated it. She now feels:

> ...For me the goal is to stay in this agency until I retire, for me to retain a progressive attitude towards things, stay as a line worker, and a union member... I don't like this moving up in the organization stuff...Everything in this society teaches you to be competitive and to stomp on whoever you have to stomp on to move up in whatever you're moving up in....It's a real struggle for me, because every one in my family is like that, its inbred, like oxygen, the mobility stuff. So the fight is to keep a cap on it...

In contrast, most subjects have moved out of lower level positions in the social services. While as we have seen, it is not that subjects ideologically opposed unionism or worker opposition, but these radicals have become detached from on the job activism for three reasons: (1) Upward mobility which separates these radicals from major roles in employee opposition, often even excluding them from potential eligibility to be in a union (2) Strong evidence that union organizing and oppositional activity, while emotionally fulfilling at the time, did not satisfy their personal career needs and (3) The increasing movement of many subjects into an identification with their employers as they move into "labor market shelters" in which they feel their work (and hence their workplace) is 'progressive' or 'movement like' or is simply not very 'oppressive.'

Upward and Away from the Rank-and-File

Rick Spano's[3] study of radical social workers in the 1930s implies that it was not merely a change in politics (the Popular Front period), but the increased opportunities for employment mobility which led to a decline in militant, oppositional sentiment among

radical social workers. It is equally true in this
study that while professional career mobility may not
necessarily alter ideological commitment, it does
affect militancy and oppositional activism. Most of
our group, at some point, felt they wanted to take
advantage of the opportunities for increased pay,
autonomy, and control that higher level positions
allow. Rita is typical in describing why she left a
position as a hospital social worker after two years
to become an administrator:

> I had hated all authority. I always thought
> the superiors were incompetent assholes. So I
> struggled with this whole idea of being a
> supervisor. Part of it felt political. You
> know, if I become a supervisor, does it mean
> I identify with those authoritarian assholes?
> I was suspicious, the possibility of
> cooptation is there. *But I think you can
> assume authority without being authoritarian.*
> I had to ask myself, was I going to do
> something about the fact that lots of people
> who are in charge are such creeps?...And I
> thought I might be able to influence people
> more in some ways than working one on one,
> and I was sick and tired of being the 'low
> person' all my life...

Subjects interviewed in all work areas, from
faculty members to those who had held positions in
'movement like' organizations, described painfully
the "contradictions" of these work roles. Rosalind
found she was able to secure a faculty position due to
her radicalism. By re-formulating her previous
experience, she could present herself as a candidate
for a faculty job teaching Community Organization and
Social Policy. In fact, a leftist faculty member on
the search committee advised her on how to make her
political work relevant to the position. But she
speaks of the dilemmas of mobility:

> So (at first) to be a radical was a
> professional asset...I was hired and all the
> professional opportunities I have had is
> because I'm a progressive social worker.
> Maybe I'm making my upward mobility within
> the progressive social work side of
> professionalism. I'm just mimicking the

whole process, except I'm doing it within the Left...But (now) I can't take chances. I'm low on the totem pole at (university). The milieu wears you down. *And I'm not out to change them (the other faculty). If I pick a fight, I'm very vulnerable. Plus I need their cooperation*...(I) could only take the soapbox when things are less risky. There are these horrible decisions. I often have to let them slide. (And) the nights before faculty meetings, I have nightmares...

High level 'movement like' jobs, in a similar fashion, thwart subjects' ability to be militant and may place the occupant in an antagonistic role to other staff. Howard, after entering a labor relations career as a union staff person, was later elected to the union's executive office, which made him "management" over his staff:

It was really strange. I never imagined I would have to bargain *as management* with my staff, they had their own Union. And they were my friends. I had hired them. But when we got into negotiations, of course, the roles changed. They got angry at me. Of course I knew the union's budget, which was close to nothing, and although I wanted them to get more pay, and eventually we resolved a lot, I kept returning to our low budget. I felt just like these damn employers we bargained with...

The small number of subjects mentioning current union activity or employee activism is partly a reflection of the mass move into management, supervision, and small alternative settings. I analyzed the eligibility of each subject to be a potential union member over the ten year period between January 1, 1977 and January 1, 1987. Following the standards of the National Labor Relations Board (NLRB), the number of subjects eligible fell from nearly 100% in 1977 to less than one-third in 1987[4].

While eligibility for union membership is likely to fluctuate some in the future and is subject to continuing political and labor struggles[5], the small number of subjects eligible for unionization is

172

significant for a group which placed such a major emphasis on their role as employees. The trend towards management and supervisory positions contradicts the view of *Catalyst* collective members who predicted professionals would undergo continued proletarianization. At the time of the massive fiscal crisis in the mid-1970s it appeared as if human service jobs would shrink, fields such as social work and psychology would be subject to long term unemployment and lack of job security, a diminution in salaries and benefits, and that unionization and militant job actions would increase[6]. Surprisingly, it appears that the social service job market has remained relatively healthy and expansionist even in the face of economic stagnation and severe federal budget cutbacks by the Reagan Administration[7].

There was a strong tendency on the part of many subjects to describe their earlier occupational positions as "proletarianized," yet this word rarely came up when they discussed their current or recent positions. Further, in describing recent jobs, subjects were concerned not about their working conditions as employees, but about how to be a "radical" program administrator, supervisor, faculty member, therapist, etc. This trend affects both the groups labelled "mediated" and "critics," and both those subjects who are not eligible for unionization and those who are in union eligible positions. Of those who were union eligible, only three are actually union members, and, only Agnes was currently actively involved with her union.

Employee Militancy and Its Inability to Satisfy Personal Career Needs

There is strong evidence, particularly salient in the cases of subjects who were once extremely active in on-the-job oppositional activism, that organizing efforts do not ultimately satisfy the social psychological needs of subjects for intrinsic job satisfaction. I suggest that not only have job mobility opportunities been greater than anticipated by this group, but that many radical groups failed to anticipate the contradiction between radical activism *extrinsic* to job duties with the desire for job locations in which activism and overall job satisfaction ("labor market shelter") was *intrinsic* to

173

daily job duties.

This fascinating contradiction is illustrated in the cases of Bea and Howard, both of whom were trained as organizers, were committed to social activism on the job, and who had been consistently involved in oppositional activity. Bea was involved in a highly successful union organizing campaign at a major settlement house. Yet the success of the union drive and its emotional satisfaction bore no impact on Bea's ultimate decision to leave the organization:

> (I) wasn't doing it for anything personal. I was planning to leave, the only reason I stayed there was that I felt they needed a union and I could help with that. Once the election was over, I started to look for another job. I was tired of it(the job)...

Despite her ideological commitment to unionization, Bea apparently did not find the gains of unionizing personally satisfying. Bea found her staff organizing job limited and unfulfilling. She also sought more autonomy and higher status:

> (I) always had (the) idea of running (my) own agency and (I) was working for a supervisor that I detested, and being held back. I wanted a position that (I) could develop my own work rather than work for someone...

So ironically, the hard won victory of the union did not induce Bea to remain and "continue the struggle" as *Catalyst* or other radical organizations might have advocated, but served only to keep Bea employed at the agency a little longer than she perhaps had anticipated. She then moved into a position as executive director and has not since returned to a position which would be eligible for unionization.

Howard's career provides a similar example. Strongly committed to the professional-as-worker philosophy, he quickly became involved in initiating employee activism at a hospital, his first professional position. Shortly after his probationary period ended, he was involved in organizing staff to complain to management about higher caseloads which were creating pressure for workers and hurting patient service by reducing workers' ability to fully serve them. This organizing led to an effort to unionize the professional staff of the hospital. Howard found the organizing exciting, in contrast to his actual job duties as a social worker:

> It was great doing this organizing, and also being openly political there (at the hospital). And they (administration) were liberal about it. They really successfully outmaneuvered us, but they weren't going to fire any of us. But the work wasn't interesting enough to me (pause) I mean the union organizing was, but the job wasn't, not the day-to-day stuff which I was paid to do...

Since the organizing eventually failed, Howard was asked whether a union success would have made a difference in his decision to leave the hospital after a year and a half to enter a career in labor relations:

> To be honest, I don't think it would have mattered too much. Sure I would have loved it(if the union had won), and maybe I'd be a delegate or steward for awhile, but no, it wouldn't have changed my job that much. And also the more I got interested in union stuff, the more I wanted to enter it as a career. Now, even if we had won (the union campaign), (the Union) was not going to come in and say, hey we're giving you this job on our staff...

Bea and Howard's experiences suggest that not only does the opportunity for mobility fragment radical goals, but the desire to make day-to-day work intrinsically meaningful suggests a move away from the 'shop floor' of professional work to positions which appear more consonant with radical goals. Paradoxically, this entails leaving the very arenas of struggle that radical professionals had previously asserted were so critical.

Increased Identification with the Employer

One of the paradoxes of the drive for a "radical labor market shelter" is that previously militant radicals no longer feel hostile to their employers, but tend to identify their interests with those of their agencies. The majority of the subjects interviewed made laudatory comments about their places of employment; certainly an orientation which makes union organizing or other on-the-job militancy unlikely. While such an orientation is least surprising in agencies we have labelled as "movement like," a very large number of other jobs were described as being "good" jobs with little grounds for complaint. I found the comments of Alan, now employed as a counselor in a drug program, particularly striking. Alan had been a member of a Marxist party for eleven years and still describes himself as a "revolutionary socialist." He is employed as a counselor and remains eligible for union membership (though his agency is not unionized). His description of the agency shows his strong positive identification with his organization:

> This is my best job. The administrator is the best guy I've seen. You know, morale is high, it is well organized. There's a lot of autonomy, and the opportunity to do a lot of groups, which I like...Everybody considers the place great. The administration is benign. The non-economic benefits are great. There's a lot of time off which is important to me because of my daughter. Its informal, not straight laced. Certainly its not a place where there would be a union organizing drive...

Given the increased identification with and commitment of 'hard core' Marxists, like Alan, to their employers, it is less surprising that some of the younger subjects interviewed who were less affected by Marxism, the fiscal crisis, and the "proletarianization" argument show less consciousness of labor-management conflict. For example, when Josie was musing about her new job as an administrator of a community center, she was surprised to find people were treating her differently. When I volunteered that being an administrator might entail tensions with employees, she responded:

> I don't know. The agencies I (have) worked in, there wasn't much distinction between management and staff. Not a lot of flaunting of authority. (The) staff is very self-sufficient. (There's) not much of a hierarchical structure though titles are definitely there. People make distinctions, but I don't. People ascribe things to this position, like 'I'm associate director,' but I don't...

In some cases, subjects were able to reconcile their political values with positions which they found personally rewarding, but which they described as being hostile to their politics. For example, Rosa served as a program director for a private agency delivering services to battered women. She worked under a director who she described as being hostile to staff and connected to political powers which included the right wing:

> This was an excellent job! I quickly got in with (name of Director). She was known for firing people at her whim. She was very politically connected with the Mayor, she was head of the agency...all these political deals were fascinating to me. It was interesting. At first I found it repelling, but I learned to work the system. It was interesting to be that close to power...At first I was afraid of her. But I got in real good with her...It was strange though. I mean she had some bizarre ideas. One day I was working with (city union) to get funds, but the next day she sent me to the Heritage Foundation and the Junior League. Can you imagine to the Heritage Foundation, which is right wing, to get funds for victims of abuse? But it was all very interesting...

The increased identification with both the goals of the organization (whether drug counseling or service to battered women) and the increased perception of organizations as "non-hierarchical" and "non-oppressive" makes the professional-as-worker orientation less salient in the late 1980s than in earlier years. It has also led to a diminution even in the discussion of on-the-job militancy.

Client Organizing

Just as *Catalyst* consistently stressed the role of professionals in organizing their workplaces and struggling within their unions, the journal also stressed an obligation to help clients organize or to "support and assist client struggles." However, client or community organizing is a more difficult role to define for several reasons, and often, the precept of organizing and support of clients remained at a more abstract level than the prescriptions about workplace organizing.

First, professionals cannot create client unrest without indigenous movements on the part of low income or other mobilized groups. By the mid-1970s, many of the most dramatic instances of community organizing, such as the welfare rights and poor people's campaigns, the community control movement, and the civil rights movements had receded. Unquestionably, human service professionals lack the organic connection with mobilized client groups that existed in the days of the anti-poverty wars and welfare rights. Secondly, professionals work within a wide array of contexts some of which are more conducive than others to the possibility of organizing. For example, while a large degree of consensus exists within the radical community about the need for welfare clients, the homeless and low income tenants to engage in organizing, other populations such as the mentally ill, the retarded, children or substance abusers present, at a minimum, difficult "challenges" to organizing or may even arouse controversy as to their suitability for organizing.

Most importantly, community and client organizing has always meant different things to different people. Much of the theory about Community Organization in social work suggests that organizing or "change efforts" can range from the "collaboration" model in which the "change agents" confront a sympathetic target system (and therefore can rely on joint planning, moral persuasion and education to achieve desired ends) to "contest strategies" in which an all

out struggle is necessary[8]. While "contest" strategies
are most associated with the political Left in the
U.S. and with the Alinsky School of organizing, there
is considerable ambiguity as to what constitutes
support for clients, and under what circumstances
'contest' strategies are most appropriate. For
example, the articles in *Catalyst* itself present very
different organizing examples, some of which are
closer to collaborative strategies than to traditional
contest strategies. While the rhetoric of conflict
frequently filled the journal's pages, some examples
of actions described were collaborative such as
planning a display of gay culture in a library or
using sports as an vehicle for community development[9].
Increasingly, as the Reagan years proceeded, more
attention was focused on political legislation, the
need to combat the Right electorally, and other
strategies which might be more closely linked to
advocacy or campaign strategies, rather than grass
roots conflict tactics. Indeed, I will suggest that
over the years, grass roots organizing has been
replaced by less conflictual models.

The Lack of Client Organizing in Subjects' Accounts

To an even greater degree than the decline in the
professional-as-worker orientation, the self-reporting
of organizing or significant involvement in client
organizing was absent among the subjects interviewed
except for those few whose employment was
institutionalized in a leadership position within a
union or radical organization. Even those who might
arguably be involved in some client organization of a
collaborative nature did not cite this work as a key
role for radicals nor did they conceptualize their
advocacy along these lines. No subject was employed as
a grass roots organizer at the time of the study.

Some of the reasons for this are embedded in the
social context. The major movements of the 1960s/early
1970s provided direct employment in community
organizing for several subjects (Jacqueline in VISTA;
Martin with welfare rights organizing; George in a
community mental health center) which had now
evaporated. By the mid-1970s, even those who graduated
with professional degrees as community organizers had
difficulty finding jobs, with the possible exception

of positions in labor unions.

While this context is critical to understanding organizing history, there is also a tendency to overdetermine the decline of oppositional activism by reference to "the conservative times." There are still social movements and there are still those who are either paid organizers or who actively use their work roles to support client efforts. Secondly, the decline of oppositional organizing, in this study, corresponds *not* so much to the end of the 1960s movements, but (like the union efforts) to the period several years into employment (including the 1970s and 1980s) with the apparent decline corresponding to advancing age, status, and accumulated work experience.

As with our discussion of employee organizing, militant client organizing is limited both by structural constraints on those who serve as paid organizers, by alternative opportunities for employment available to subjects, and by an increased identification of subjects with their employing institutions.

The Crisis for Professional Organizers

In contrast to the counselors studied, most organizers found that a particular event or series of events led to a "crisis point" in which they felt "caught between" the employing agency and the clients and (at times) other staff. In most cases, the conflict was resolved by the subject departing from the organization, and, often, departing completely from a career as an organizer. These incidents are experienced with a great deal of trauma, and, in several cases, led to feelings of great bitterness.

Joseph's experience is illustrative of the struggles faced by organizers (and administrators of 'movement like' organizations such as neighborhood coalitions) when they engage in "contest strategies" which are highly visible. Joseph, as noted earlier, went to social work school in order to "organize the white working class." He had a very positive experience in one of his field placements, as a community organizer at a small neighborhood service center in a white, ethnic neighborhood. Upon graduating from school, Joseph was offered the position of director of the Center. Interestingly, Joseph told me "I really wanted to be an organizer, not a director, but there was no choice, if I wanted to work there, it was just that one paid (job)." But Joseph's interest in organizing and activism would not be wasted. Shortly after he began, some neighborhood residents informed him that a local firehouse was going to be closed by the city. Concerned with the issue of arson and redlining in the old residential working class neighborhood of wooden frame houses, as well as with cuts in city services which were discriminatory to this section of the city, Joseph and a small number of neighborhood residents began a series of protests which quickly escalated to a human chain blocking the firehouse. The organizing of rallies and a sit-in that followed began a two year neighborhood struggle in which the firehouse occupation was perhaps one of the most visible fights against municipal budget cutbacks. Joseph talks with pride about his role, and at the same time, notes the attitude of his employer to these actions:

> We started it (the occupation) ourselves. We orchestrated the whole thing! And yeh it was very exciting, the rallies with hundreds of people, being on TV. (We) had people ready to come in and mobilize at anytime, but when we started there was no identified leadership yet from the community, mostly it was me, my staff, and the students. (My) Board President was scared shit, at first he just wasn't there at all. Then he began to undermine me, he became a link to the police and the politicians to work out a quick way to get these people (protesters) out...

As the protest continued, an indigenous leadership of local community people did arise, aided by outside activists drawn to the fray. On the other side were the local political "ward heelers," including some of Joseph's own Board, who regarded the conflict with great suspicion. While publicly siding with the need for fire protection, they were fearful that things were getting 'out of hand,' and that the local political machine would be harmed by such conflict and by an emerging new leadership. As the months of the occupation continued on, Joseph's role became more problematic:

For a long time I was in the lead, and our agency continued all the time to funnel money to the protesters, you know, everything from food provisions, to the xerox machine to free phones. I had to start backing off though. Partly it was, I lost control over it. The students and other activists were going their own way. And also my Director opposed what I was doing. He felt I wasn't his boy and he wasn't controlling me...

Finally, because of the confrontative tactics of a militant organizer hired by Joseph, the Board began to confront Joseph, blaming him for the actions of his staff. As Joseph described being attacked and continually threatened with firing, he spoke in saddened tones about the lack of support he received from his own staff and from the community activists he was personally close to:

There was incredible conflicts between the Board of Directors, the Firehouse, and me. I guess I was the fence between the radicals on one side and the conservative neighborhood folks including my bosses. (I) was heavily red-baited and provoked...The battles were constant. But I got no support (from occupiers) at all. They started to feel I was against them. I was there by myself. It was real lonely... When I quit I (felt) hated by Board, hated by (people organized)... (I) was really beaten by it...

Joseph's description of this episode and his tone of bitterness are also reflective of his detachment from his early career goal of organizing. His subsequent career thusfar (ten years) would not be in organizing. When Joseph left the neighborhood center after two and a half years, he accepted a position as director of a coalition of settlement houses. When I asked him why he took this career route, Joseph replied:

I decided (that) I didn't want to work with lay people. I wanted to work with professionals. I figured they would be better, saner. And working with the service

182

providers did feel better...

Joseph's career development reflected a move from "contest" style "grass roots" organizing which had been his career goal to a series of administrative positions which can be characterized as "collaborative" organizational tasks in nature. He served as a fundraiser and planner at the settlement coalition, securing money for job training, the provision of home health care, and funds for the homeless. In later positions, he also worked on developing housing programs, services for the homeless, and low cost rehabilitation programs. But in each case, the work was conducted in a "top down" manner typical of large private and public agencies who determine a community's needs and seek funding from corporate and public sources to develop programs. Joseph, in the course of his career to date, came to identify more and more with his fellow professionals, and view community groups as unrealistic and hostile.

While some of Joseph's interpretation of his job experience contrasts with other former organizers, Joseph's *experience* itself is mirrored by other subjects who were organizers. As noted earlier, Bea was "caught between (the) Board, (her) staff and (the) community" when she tried to defend militant organizing among new immigrants to the neighborhood; Barbara's work as a planner/researcher put her in conflict with her agency directors. Howard, in several union positions, was able to secure the support of union leadership only as long as the goal was to organize new employees or to defend an incumbent union against outside threats. When Howard moved into "contest" strategies within the Union itself, in an attempt to have rank-and-filers control the structure of the Union, he was attacked by the leadership. Like Joseph and Bea's situation, Howard found himself isolated as certain staff and rank-and-filers, who were previously strong supporters, were influenced by conservative unionists and outside political leaders to either stay neutral or dissociate themselves from Howard.

The constraints on community organizers and planners, have been well documented and debated elsewhere. The dangers of "contest strategies" have been a subject of much interest to social service thinkers some of whom imply that these strategies are ineffective[10]. Despite the gulf between leftist thinking on organizing and professional views of organizing, there is some consensus that lacking a broadly based organic support from an entire client group or community, paid organizers or administrators are quite limited in confronting their own employers or funding sources. Virtually all the subjects interviewed expressed strong disappointment, not only with their funders and employers, but with their constituents (community residents, union members, etc.) who failed to view the professional organizer as worthy of support or who failed to mobilize sufficiently on their behalf.

Clearly, paid organizing suffers considerable constraint as contest strategies are limited by the objectives of unions, social service agencies, neighborhood groups, and other institutions. As long as the organizer carries out the functions of increasing funding for an agency or securing more members for a union, conflict can generally be avoided. But when aspects of a political agenda are brought in, and conflict ensues, few institutions are prepared to back the organizer. Most interesting in noting the structural constraints on organizers "assisting client struggles," is the rather self-conscious effort by the subjects in avoiding such problems by either departing the field (like Joseph and Bea) or by trying to find a job shelter which hopefully is more akin to their political views. Howard, for example, switched union positions several times, hoping to find positions in more "progressive" unions where a militant agenda could be reflected by his employer; after six years he left this field, finding himself critical of unions and skeptical of the possibility of institutional support for militant actions.

The very mobility structure of the economy allows these radicals to ultimately leave behind the crisis of organizing, and accept positions in different areas (Howard and Bea moved to academia and Joseph and Josie to administration). As with the decline of the professional-as-worker orientation, organizers have generally moved up and out of staff positions where their previous focus was on militant organizing activity.

Organizing by Other Social Service Workers

Despite the broad 'call to arms' in the journal about 'client struggles,' and the tradition of social action in social work, subjects who were employed as therapists or educators or supervisors *did not* mention organizing nor did they conceptualize their work with clients or students or consumers in these terms. With the exception of the late 1960s/early 1970s, when older subjects were able to support N.W.R.O. and other organized groups, it appears that both the diminished organization of clients as an interest group in the last decade and the constraining structure of employment positions has precluded major professional support for clients at the workplace.

If collaborative tactics or social advocacy are defined broadly as a type of organizing, then client support can be identified by analyzing our interviews. The most common orientation is suggested by an advocacy approach to professional work in which many subjects attempted to interpret client need which often comes to the practitioner in individual cases ("private troubles") into broader concerns which they demand their employers respond to ("public issues"). A second type of organizing has occurred sporadically when the interest of clients, professionals, and social agencies coalesce enough to allow for a unified action against another target (such as a funding source).

The first orientation typifies many subjects who conceptualize a radical professionalism as moving from "case" to "cause" to demand that the collective problems of clients/consumers be heard rather than simply individualizing them into "cases"[11]. For the most part, however, subjects were unable to use their positions in counseling or education or administration to catalyze their clients into action, but were reduced to appealing to the employing organization for new funds, a different orientation to service or new program initiatives.

Brenda, for example, stressed in her interview, the necessity of all social workers seeing problems in broad terms, linking up individual problems with broader issues, and demanding agencies live up to

185

their missions. Indeed, in Brenda's accounts of her
jobs, casework with children, hospital patients and
union members, she did just that; frequently "opening
her big mouth" to complain about client issues or urge
others to do so. In her position as a social worker
with a union, for example, Brenda viewed the low pay
scales of clients, the lack of affordable housing and
constant displacement of clients, and the lack of
available child care for clients as issues the union
should address at the macro-level through political
action, collective bargaining or organizing. But her
advocacy, as well as that of her colleagues, was not
successful:

> I saw it as a failure of vision. A failure of
> commitment...It's not progressive if there
> isn't any attempt to organize things. I think
> caseworkers can be a part of that and use
> their experience and gather information that
> should then be fed up the line and management
> and supervisory (staff) then have the burden
> to do something with that. But that
> commitment was not there. They were content
> to kind of limp along and continue to put
> bandaids on...
>
> Interviewer: What would happen when you
> brought up these issues, that the union
> should address these issues in a militant
> way...?
>
> Brenda: Oh, we kept raising it, but (it) was
> frustrating. People there were around forever
> and some got into (their) positions and just
> sat. But the commitment was not there on the
> part of the Administration because of the
> power structure there, you couldn't go very
> far. Continually you brought it up (and) got
> superficial responses. It would be 'Yes,
> but...' 'What after all, can we do about
> housing in the City? What can we do about
> poverty? We are doing the best we can'....

Difficulties emerge with the social advocacy
approach for two reasons. In Brenda's case, and many
similar situations described by subjects, employers
will not radically change their agendas without
massive pressure. But social workers like Brenda do

not feel they are in sufficiently powerful positions
to be able to mobilize clients. As she notes:

> (The social service Unit of Union) is very
> compartmentalized. We're isolated from the
> power in the Union. We each see some
> individuals out of the thousands of members
> (of the union)...we just didn't feel it could
> be our place to organize the union's
> members...

Secondly, advocacy without client mobilization
usually succeeds, at best, in the development of new
programs or new funding which subjects were able to
achieve from their employers or by permission to write
grants. In some cases, such as Rosa's efforts on
behalf of battered women and Rita's program
development for adolescents, this can be seen in broad
terms as being advancements in social services.
However, since actual mobilization of clients is not
involved, it is difficult to ascertain the degree to
which clients actually viewed new services as a
victory or whether they even viewed services as
necessary. Since clients are atomized as population
groups, rather than mobilized, the sense of
"empowerment" that radical organizers seek does not
occur with the funding of a new program by
professional grantsmanship. Essentially, the advocacy
planning approach, while in a broad way presumably
responsive to some client need, represents a
collaborative strategy of seeking agency/institutional
response to client problem without resorting to actual
engagement of clients in their own affairs. Although
again fashionable in the social service literature
today, the advocacy planner was often attacked in the
late 1960s[12].

Of course, one can argue that in the absence of
client unrest, these subjects are not located in
structural positions in which they can do otherwise.
Since individualized professional services isolates
clients from each other (as well as workers who may
sit in private offices all day with their individual
clients, separated from their colleagues) organizing
at the juncture of service provision is quite
difficult. Moreover, the critique of 'experts' and
'professionals' as imposing their values and agendas
on people has historically been shared by Left and

Right. These critiques, to a great degree, led to rise of the self-help movement of the 1970s. While much of this movement has remained at the level of service delivery (self-help groups for cancer victims, drug users, battered women, etc.), one can argue that the majority of successful community organizing in the last decade has flowed from indigenous local sources (such as local environmental and tenant protests). Ironically the critique of the 'expert' doubly restricts the caseworker or educator. They are perceived as experts lacking the local community legitimacy to lead struggles around issues. Unlike paid organizers, however, they do not have a structural link with an organization that can mediate between them, client groups, and macro-level issues, providing a legitimate credential to engage in organizing.

A second type of organizing is possible, at times, in which organizational needs are threatened by outside sources. Here, the militancy and involvement of clients provides a taste of 'contest' tactics, but importantly, the social service professional is exercising a strong degree of *collaboration* with their own employing institution. For example, Monica provided an example of "radical practice" which developed around the City's decision to stop funding for her agency which provided group home services to adolescents. In response to the City's decision to cut funds (and therefore depriving the children of their only homes, forcing them back into either foster care or new homes elsewhere), "the kids went wild." Monica decided "the time was right for a demonstration." In this instance, Monica was able to do successful strategic organizing by suggesting the idea to the teenagers, rather than imposing her own idea. Moreover, the idea aroused no opposition from agency executives who promptly helped with the organization which culminated in a spirited march by the children on City Hall. Because the agency's funding and existence were at stake, contest strategy (at least for this brief time period) was embraced by employer, workers, and clients.

In a similar vein, Renee also described a recent effort at her program for homeless mentally ill women in which she and her staff assisted the clients in taking over a tenants council. Renee's program, an on-

188

site mental health team, could ally with clients, since the primary target was the management of the hotel which had co-opted the rather moribund tenants meetings. The agency's (Renee's) goal of empowering the formerly homeless clients conflicted with the key goal of control held by hotel management. While the clients succeeded in taking greater control of their own meetings (as opposed to the unsuccessful results of Monica's demonstration), the implications for client organizing are unclear. To Renee, the tenants meetings:

> ...have a radical flavor to them. A hell of a lot of programs would not have enabled this. The tenants empowered (them) selves. (They) knew the program could help them take over...

Yet there are considerable ambiguities to the situation. Renee strongly identifies with her own employer (a social agency) which assisted the clients against the hotel staff, who are employed by another non-profit social service agency. Structurally, since Renee's agency does not have to worry about rent collection or other instrumental issues in the hotel, it can have a freer role in organizing clients. But the clients' "empowerment" is greatly symbolic, since neither clients nor social workers placed emphasis on specific issues of hotel control, material benefits or conditions. Rather the idea that the tenants groups should be self-led is embraced as a goal in itself, which while commendable, runs the risk of remaining at the level of "sociotherapy"[13] if not broadened out to attack the structural issues of concern to the low income tenants.

At best, there is considerable ambiguity in the small amount of "client organizing" and efforts at advocacy planning that have been undertaken by subjects. While the late 1960s/early 1970s saw some very strong client groups emerge which occasionally received organized support from professionals, in the last decade both community organization, as practiced by paid organizers, and assistance to client organizing, as attempted at times by professionals not paid to organize, has suffered disarray. Paid organizers, in this group, were quite successful in some efforts at organizing community residents and workers, but eventually felt caught between the competing demands of their employing organizations and elements in the community/worksite that may have wanted to go further than the organizer or who did not support or understand the professionals' limitations. Nor can it be asserted, that client or union groups are always the more militant of the organizer/client dyad. As many accounts indicate, it is often the conservatism of the community or union members that is the eventual downfall of the organizer. In any case, this study shows a strong trend away from paid organizing positions and into administrative or faculty positions where the pressures are evidently fewer.

For those employed in non-organizing positions, there is little evidence of an oppositional strategy or even an inclination to challenge the agencies in which subjects are employed in order to change policies, benefit provisions or other aspects of client treatment. In some cases, subjects have raised their voices about client needs, and sometimes have been able to achieve success only in so far as they themselves were allowed to plan or develop new programs. In other cases, agencies allow employees some autonomy in challenging other organizations where it is in the agency's own vested interest. However, a consistent strategy of client organizing was not developed or integrated into the workplace by these subjects. Indeed *Catalyst* itself, in an introduction to an issue, publicly shared the frustration felt by its members:

> As human service workers, we have consistently tried to integrate our work and our politics... we have found that our jobs are not always the best places for political organizing. Human service agencies often subordinate the political issues of service delivery to the technical problems of program development and implementation. As a result, workers who have tried to politicize their work often find themselves caught between the contradictory demands of their agencies and those of communities in which their agencies are located...[14]

Notes

1. The most influential work in terms of 'deskilling' and professional work, was Braverman, Harry, <u>Labor and Monopoly Capital</u>; for its specific applications to social service work, see William Patry,"Taylorism Comes to the Social Services,"<u>Monthly Review</u>, 12 (1978), pp. 9-23; Wagner and Cohen,"Social Workers, Class, and Professionalism"; Adams and Freeman,"On the Political Character of Social Service Work"; and Webber,"Abandoning Illusions: the State and Social Change."

2. Since these years were the beginning of the *Catalyst* collective itself, there may have been some force to the new reference group which encouraged organizing. However, the primary reason for this clustering of activity beyond the age, status, and position of subjects, was the widespread cuts in public spending (particularly the N.Y.C. fiscal crisis) which led to a number of union struggles against service cuts, caseload rises, pay and benefit freezes in the 1976-78 period.

3. Spano's work is commented on and expanded upon, particularly in reference to his discussion of the decline of the Rank and File Movement in David Wagner,"Radical Movements in the Social Services: A Theoretical Framework,"<u>Social Service Review</u>, 63 (2), 1989, pp. 264-284.

4. The author's many years of work in labor relations allow for an informed guesstimate of the eligibility of subjects for union membership. Generally, national labor law precludes those with substantial, meaningful input into hiring and firing of employees, and substantial control over agency policy to be union members (see NLRA, as amended). As interpreted, almost all managers and supervisors in the population would not be eligible for unionization. Further, the NLRA also excludes very small agencies (usually less than five employees) from coverage. Despite the very political nature of the NLRB (see below), the fact that the labor law has a great degree of legitimacy (it feels like "common sense") is reflected in the degree to which most subjects regarded themselves as

administrators/supervisors rather than employees.

5. The labor laws are not fixed and are subject to highly political decisions reflective of national political policy and the relationship of the classes. An important example for this study is the recent *Yeshiva* decision (1980) which ruled many collective bargaining contracts at private universities to be invalid because, at least at certain universities, faculty allegedly were managers within the "meaning of the law"(NLRB). Since many of our study subjects are now in academe or preparing to enter this area, this highly political, anti-union move has a strong effect. Nevertheless, despite the highly contingent nature of any summary of the bargaining unit eligibility of this group (subject to change as subjects switch jobs and as the sociopolitical context changes), it would seem highly unlikely that the trend discussed will reverse itself in the future. Most subjects who were now in administrative/supervisory positions noted that economically it would be impossible for them to return to "line" positions. For the faculty members, a change in employee orientation would require not only a seachange in the political, economic, and legal environment (including the reversal of decisions like *Yeshiva*), but a major change in the self-consciousness of faculty as employees. Neither faculty as a whole (particularly in private universities in the United States) nor the subjects who were faculty members tended to stress employee militancy or trade unionism.

6. see in particular, O'Connor,Fiscal Crisis of the State. For a very optimistic account of social service workers and other employees becoming both militant and radical, see Paul Johnston,"The Promise of Public Sector Unionism,"Monthly Review, 30:4 (1978), pp. 1-17.

7. See Sheldon Siegal, "The Social Service Labor Force: 2000," Draft Manuscript, Silver Spring, Md.: NASW, dated 9/23/86,pp.5-6. Siegal reports growth in the number of social service employees continued unabated in the eighties, increasing at a rate of 14.4% in 1980-1985 compared to an increase of only 7.9% in the overall growth of the total employees in the U.S. Since Siegal's data combines all levels of social service employment, it may underrate growth at

the highest levels in this profession. In a phone interview with Miles Johnson, senior staff associate at the National Association of Social Workers, he noted that employment of M.S.W social workers has increased at a much higher rate in recent years than these figures (Siegal's) would indicate (phone interview, June 8, 1987). Statistics available from Columbia U. School of Social Work (employment summary, 1980-1986, CUSSW Job Development Information Services) indicate that their graduating M.S.W.s have steadily done better in the employment market from 1980 to 1986. For example, in 1980, 23% of graduates were unemployed (including some voluntarily) nine months after graduating; this figure dropped to 13% by 1982, and to 6% by 1986.

In addition to the actual number of jobs, importantly, there is a cohort effect as social workers trained in the 1960s and 1970s are able to move upward, as not only jobs increase, but a smaller number of new recruits enter the social services by the 1980s for a variety of reasons. We believe these factors left more "room at the top" for those committed to obtaining managerial or supervisory positions in the human services than might have been anticipated.

8. The range of strategies in community organization was originally developed by Roland Warren. See Jack Rothman, "The Three Models of Community Organization Practice: Their Mixing and Phasing," in Cox et. al.,Strategies of Community Organization, pp. 25-44.

9. I don't mean to suggest that *Catalyst* members would not continue to support "contest" strategies nor did articles in the journal always represent the thinking of the actual collective. However, in the 1980s, most articles and reports which are about conflict tend to be about non-social service issues (the Miami, Fla. ghetto riots, the women's march on the Pentagon, etc.), while it appears that conceptualizations of social work practice printed in the journal tended to be more collaborative. For a more in-depth review of articles in the journal on organizing, see Wagner, Political Ideology..., pp. 402-405.

10. This is my reading of many of the comments in the widely used book by George Brager and Stephen

Holloway,<u>Changing Human Service Organizations</u>, New York: The Free Press, 1978 which tends to 'bracket' contest strategies. See particularly pages 14-15 on their disdain for the 'David versus Goliath approach' and p.133 for their comments on the irrelevancy of contest strategies for organizational change.

11. This view contrasts sharply with C. Wright Mills famous critique of social science and other experts as turning all social problems into cases. See Mills,"The Professional Ideology of Social Pathologists,"<u>American Journal of Sociology</u>, 49 (1943), pp. 165-180.

12. Frances Fox Piven's "Whom does the Advocate Planner Serve?,"<u>Social Policy</u>, 1 (1), 1970, pp. 32-37 offers a strong critique of planners as essentially substituting their expertise for political mobilization.

13. See Martin Rein,"Social Work in Search of a Radical Profession"...

14. Introduction,<u>Catalyst</u>, 4:1 (1982), p. 3.

8

POLITICS AT THE RETAIL LEVEL: "RADICAL PRACTICE"

The third goal of *Catalyst* suggested radicals engage in a "radical practice" within the social service professions. Because the very definition of "radical practice" was the focus of much debate in the pages of the journal and elsewhere in radical social work, as well as in a variety of related disciplines, this is the most difficult of *Catalyst*'s goals to measure. Clearly, there were strong feelings that radicalism must be made relevant to the daily transactions of counselors, group workers, organizers, educators and administrators, but little consensus emerged as to how to do this. In this chapter, we will review the "radical practice" debate as reflected in the journal, analyze the experience of the study's subjects in implementing "radical practice," and assess what political meanings and social impact can be attributed to subjects' engaging in such practice.

"Radical Practice"?

A large number of articles over the years appeared in *Catalyst* (as well as in other radical human service journals) on the relationship of radical politics and therapy. While there are occasional articles on radical planning, research, education, and organizing, these are fewer in number. Perhaps this is because most social workers are engaged in direct practice work or perhaps this is due to an assumption that organizing and planning were already being utilized for radical ends.

A review of the journal's many practice articles suggests only one point of consensus; in comparison to some of the most anti-professional tracts of the late 1960s in mental health (such as the early issues of the *Radical Therapist*), there is little tendency on the part of authors to disparage social workers or

mental health workers as being solely social control
agents or instruments of repression. While elements of
the earlier radical mental health movement sought
abolition of professionals and their replacement with
a self-help methodology, in recent years there has
been a wide acceptance of the role of social service
professionals, and a legitimation of their presence on
the Left.

Secondly, there is little evidence of what
Maglin[1] describes as an "aggressive therapy" aimed at
overt political conversion of clients to leftist
politics through therapy. Maglin suggests this
approach primarily operates as a self-selection
process in which clients who are already radical tend
to see alternative counselors who are politically
leftist[2]. Presumably, both the authors of journal
articles and the subjects themselves found this mode
of counseling unrealistic or inappropriate in their
positions in social agencies, working generally with
non-radical clients.

The majority of articles in the journal, as well
as letters and comments, support the notion that
counseling (and other forms of practice) can have a
liberating effect as people come to feel less personal
alienation and hence feel more empowered to challenge
the "system." The practice of clinical work by
radicals could link oppression at the personal level
with the experience of alienation under capitalism.
The separation of the "personal" from the "political"
was argued to be an arbitrary artifact of capitalism
which the therapist/practitioner could help bridge by
helping individuals, groups, and communities discover
the roots of their own oppression. Ann Sparks in
arguing for the use of Gestalt therapy, for example,
suggests this link:

> How is restoring our best human potential
> politically relevant? Our social structure
> can only be changed by people who will not
> tolerate exploitation, compete
> individualistically or ignore the fact that
> individual well-being depends on the general
> well-being. People who experience themselves
> and their lives vividly, who feel secure in
> their capacity to assimilate experience and
> grow, do not need to compete. They can

196

recognize their frustrations and they can take risks. People who are not aware of their alienation, who hold back their anger or isolate themselves intellectually, cannot take a stand...[3]

A difficulty, as we shall see, with the broad assertion that therapy can lead to activism is the problem of how the caseworker or therapist bridges the personal gains of counseling to any overt link to political activism or radicalism. David Weingord in a letter to *Catalyst* about a conference of radical therapists[4] makes several common criticisms of the radical therapy movement. Weingord saw radical therapists as increasingly operating on an interpersonal level detached from any active movement for socialism:

> At the conference I attended...*radical therapy was a personal experience and there was almost no discussion of organized politics.* I found...the tendency...was for interpersonal relations to dominate the larger notions of politics...(there was) no particular theory as to how socialism arises and radical therapists' role in it. The closest thing I could surmise (in their theory) was a 'socialism in family by family' approach. In other words, they approach socialism by creating egalitarian families and non-sexist, non-racist, and non-anti-working class children. Or as Carl Boofs has described it, as a complete prefiguration of socialist interpersonal relations...Another problem of radical therapy is that its values can be extracted from its ideological content or long range strategy. One can like the mode of therapy but have little interest in the formation of a socialist society where the material basis for sexism, racism, and non-egalitarianism no longer exists. Radical therapists do not have to see socialism as part of their purpose. *In other words, working at egalitarian relations and becoming powerful persons (the technique of radical therapy) is developed outside the context of confronting capitalism in its institutional, political, and economic spheres...* (author's

emphasis)

Generally critics like Weingord tended to see the "radical practice" concerns as a diversion for radical social service workers from more political and strategic questions of organizing as employees and among client groups.

A few articles, while supporting the positive influence of therapy or other practice, suggested that the context of service delivery or the political environment were critically important to its success and distinguished among the different types of "radical practice." Both Maglin and William Caspery [5] warned that the overall political environment was a key variable in what practitioners could achieve:

> ...As powerful as therapy can be, it is seldom enough to offset the weight of the culture. If the political environment of the nation and the immediate subculture of the client is moving rightward, then the radical therapist's job will be a tough one indeed...

> All of this (radical therapy) presumes a long gradual building of a larger movement...

Maglin described a frequent type of "radical therapy" as a "defensive" radical therapy [6]. "Defensive" radical therapy is aimed at helping clients survive the oppressive system and at helping them cope with alienation; it does not aim at specific changes in individual's political consciousness so that clients become socialist or radical. Maglin identifies "defensive" practice as the practice which is usually used with "non-radical" clients and in social agency settings. Presumably, a middle level of "radical practice" might exist in between "defensive" and "aggressive" therapy (Maglin calls it "social therapy"). That is, counselors could see non-radical clients, but assist them in some transitional way to become more politically active.

Neither the journal articles, other professional literature, nor our subjects have any one view on these questions. The study confirmed that there was a great deal of ambivalence about how "radical" the practice of human service could be, and, to the extent subjects felt there was a "radical practice," it tended to be in a prefigurative sense or in the "defensive therapy" mold of Maglin.

The Self-Conscious Ambivalence of Subjects about Radical Practice

There were many contradictions in the subjects' own expressed views of 'radical practice,' and in the extent they feel their daily work was "political." On the one hand, as compared with employee organizing and client organizing, virtually all subjects felt there were ways in which they tried to integrate their radicalism into their jobs as therapists, counselors, supervisors, administrators or teachers. Yet all subjects, including those previously identified as "mediated," mused that they were not sure there really was a "radical practice" per se, and that perhaps this formulation was bounded in the headier days of youth and the New Left:

> (Rita, identified as "mediated"): I don't know. (pause) Earlier on, I would have said 'yes, there is a radical practice.' (The) older I get, the more experienced I get, I'm not jaded, but the sense of what's possible and not possible, I suspect its like working outside the system (pause) What can you do that's not inside the system?...

> (James, identified as a "critic"): (I) used to think there was something called radical practice, more recently I've been much more dubious about the possibility of it...being an administrator it's extremely difficult...

Generally all subjects were self-conscious that their daily practice, even when described in radical terms, was not exactly what they thought of as "revolutionary." The majority of the subjects used the phrases below to distinguish their daily actions as social service workers from other radical activity:

> This isn't exactly bringing the revolution, but I try to...

> I don't know how *radical* this is, but...

Politics at the Retail Level

It's no revolution, but within limits, I...

Subjects, were well aware that their roles were limited and that "radical practice," as compared with militant organizing or political action would not bring about great social changes. Further, the difficulty in measuring any political outcome at all in counseling was noted by Rita:

> I feel like this (her private practice therapy) is radical. But what is radical? It's the question of judging the outcome, how do you do that? How can we measure at all whether these people have become active after therapy or whatever.Or if they're more conscious, is that radical? Or vote differently? I don't think we really know...

Indeed, Rita's point is a critical one. Since few conceptualizations of "radical practice" have a method of accountability to them to establish how patients or clients were radicalized, there is little opportunity to say that this or that has worked. Although there is vagueness about "radical practice," the subjects studied did share a positive vision which can be described as 'prefigurative.'

Radical Practice as Prefigurative Politics

Rather than characterizing these radicals as performing only "defensive therapy," I would argue that they do indeed share a vision. Wini Breines'[7] study of the New Left and Women's movement captures some of the ingredients of the "personal is political" view of politics of the generation of radicals from the 1960s on:

> The New Left sought community as it sought to unite the *public and private spheres of life*. By community I mean a network of relationships *more direct, more total and more personal than the formal, abstract and instrumental relationships characterizing state and society*...In saying the new left sought community I refer not only to the desire to create a sense of wholeness and communication in social relationships, but to the effort to *create non-capitalist and*

200

communitarian institutions that embodied such relationships, for example counter-institutions. In this sense, prefigurative politics, by attempting to *develop the seeds of liberation and the new society prior to and in the process of revolution through notions of participatory democracy*, often grounded in counter-institutions, meant community building...[8] (author's emphasis)

Although our subjects could not succeed in building counter-institutions or total participatory democracy in light of the overall failure of larger social movements to do so, the strong impulses towards egalitarian relationships, non-oppressive institutions, consensual and collective decision-making, and the "Great Refusal" to take part in 'immoral' or 'elitist' acts characterize the subjects approach to counseling, administration, supervision, and teaching.

Through a content analysis of the interviews with radical counselors and other practitioners, we can develop a concrete list of the attributes of a "radical practice." Our subjects' practice was characterized by: (1) A desire on the part of subjects to minimize formality and social distance between counselor and client, teacher and student, and administrator and employee, to make these relationships more egalitarian and less oppressive (2) A vision, particularly striking on the part of supervisors and administrators, of non-hierarchical leadership with a desire for consensual decision making among small staff groups (3) An approach to practice, most notable in the counselors, which seeks to combat sexism, racism, classism, ageism, and heterosexism and overcome oppressive family relationships (4) A sympathy with and preferential treatment for oppressed and excluded groups as clients or employees (5) A refusal, usually undramatic, to implement some policies or directives which are contrary to humanitarian and democratic procedures (6) A vision of family, work, and other institutions which, for some subjects, transcends normative societal notions allowing for encouragement of clients to break away from prescribed aspects of the work ethic and typified family patterns (7) An attempt, not always successful, to network among those leftists in

201

the professions for assistance to clients or to
students (8) An attempt, often surreptitious, to
support unions or progressive groups in various
efforts.

Missing Linkages

The difficulty with such "radical practice" on
the micro level, as Weingord noted, is its tendency to
operate in isolation from broader social movements and
to not make a connection between improved client
functioning and visible political action. The radicals
interviewed had trouble enunciating how their work
actually carried clients forward to radical activity.
For example, Monica came to clinical social work with
an interpretation drawn from Left experience. She
provided a clear defense of radical work on the
personal level:

> (I) saw that certain groups didn't get
> involved in the Left. I mean working class
> people, others, they were so busy struggling
> with the day-to-day life stuff. You know,
> single mothers with three kids. That gave me
> the realization that if someone is feeling
> abused and exploited by a pathological,
> symbiotic relationship with a mother, they're
> not going to go out and fight back and get
> involved in (the) real world. It became clear
> to me that empowering people in the
> interpersonal (realm) gave them the ability
> to take the next step...

Monica is now employed at a fairly traditional
mental health agency working with children and
families. The examples she gives of "radical practice"
tend to remain at level of reducing social distance
(she gives out toys and gifts at Christmas to her
clients, a practice which her agency frowns on), and
at undoing oppressive family relationships. In the
discussion, Monica becomes frustrated, wondering if
these actions are "political":

> I guess I'm not giving a good answer as to
> what radical social work is...I would like to
> see a different political and economic system
> in (this) country, but I guess I don't get to
> play that out in my actual work. (I) do that

202

by working with *Catalyst* and other kinds of things...

Brenda, in her role as a supervisor and director of a small program within a child welfare agency, feels her role with the agency allows her to have a radical impact through equalizing pay differentials, buffering her staff from government controls (such as statistical forms required by government), and promoting more equal decision making:

> I'm a much more effective advocate for workers and clients in this position. That's the way I've organized the program...as an administrator I've been able to re-structure the salaries. We have juggled the budgets to move up the pay of the lower workers. So I feel very much a worker-advocate in relation to the agency. (I) make sure the staff understands that the forms and statistics and all this, while necessary for funding, are not key, but client treatment (is). And we operate as a team, we share the decisions. And we've led the agency away from this narrow intrapsychic stuff... I think this is much more useful in working with poor families...

Like Monica, Brenda does not link the treatment of staff, client practice philosophy, and cooperative work arrangements with a broader macro-level leftwing politics. When asked if somehow clients or workers become radicalized in a political sense or if she identified with leftist groups, Brenda returns to the realm of personal transformations:

> I guess I'm not interested in organized groups. Its more a way I organize my own thinking. In some ways, I'm a radical leftist, particularly in the way (I) continue to deal with people personally and in my work experience...but no, there isn't a direct connection between our work and organized politics, and I'm not sure there should be...

Some might argue that the context of working with children and families under stress, as Monica and Brenda do, may limit any overt political thrust to counseling. Agnes, working in a public correctional system, seems to have clients (adult offenders) who are dealing with more overt political issues as they face the criminal justice system. Because of her employment location (and possibly her "critical" rather than "mediated" approach), Agnes sees her role as validating to poor and working people that the 'system' does not work:

> They come to court, you know, they plead, see how the evidence is misused, how the lawyers don't help. They are amazed, 'They couldn't have found me guilty!'they say. Or 'that's not right, that's not fair!' Or they say 'This court system is not fair...why isn't it?' The kind of progressive work I can do in the system is very simplistic. You need to validate their experience. Help them fine-tune the perception. Deal with issues of class and race. Yes, the world is out to fuck you. Speaking the truth is powerful. Because they still want to think the system is fair. They still, no matter if they're poor or Black or Hispanic think things will be fair. And if I don't say it, I don't know who else in the system will. The correction officer won't, the judge isn't, the police officer isn't. You have to say its a horrible classist, racist, sexist, nasty system. It doesn't give a shit. It's a game...

Such a counseling approach certainly could promote more discussion of certain elements of the social system--the courts, race, class, gender--than the previous examples discussed. But Agnes also notes frustration. There are no clear cut links between the comments she may make in briefly seeing her clients and their political ideology or behavior. She feels limited by the lack of a context that includes active political groups or movements she believes in or any active organizing among victims of the criminal justice system:

> You do what you can, but, of course, its limited...Some (clients) are going to be back in prison...because they blew someone's brains out. Some (clients) do real well, and they come to see the system in a political

way...(but) there are too many of them, too
little time, and too many barriers to say
you're going to radicalize many...

In contrast to counselors, educators
(particularly those teaching subjects which include
social science or other overtly political topics) are
able to comment on political events and provide
students with a context for radicalism. For example,
Naomi, in teaching about health policy, provides a
political perspective to her students:

The perspective I give students is political.
(One) can't talk about (the) health care
industry, I mean, the basic issue of
organizing health care, is equity, financing,
access, quality of care, a national health
insurance. And it's...every course it comes
back to politics...

But teaching as a occupational role, at least in
the 1980s, does not sharply differ from counseling in
actually creating radicals or linking people to
political action. Naomi states she feels constrained
to a middle range analysis with her students:

I have a political perspective (pause) but
it's not the most heavy duty kind of stuff.
(I'm) not going to stand up and say, 'hey,
I'm a socialist and this is what should be
done.' Even in the labor policy (course), you
can't get up and say,'Let's talk about
workplace democracy.' I wouldn't bring it up
that way. It's built into the course...

When asked about the avoidance of the "heavy duty
stuff," Naomi cites the conservatism of her students
who she describes as "apolitical" or "conservative."
She believes her students would be needlessly
alienated by radical labels and explicit analyses.
Moreover, the functional role established for faculty
can be as limiting as the counselor's functional role
over only health or mental health:

You have to remember your role...teaching
health care or labor, whatever, you can't get
off on such tangents that you're not
following a syllabus or covering what they

need to graduate...it's kind of a limited
thing, except once in awhile, when you get
someone (in class) who is already radical or
open to it...

Movement Work as "Radical Practice"

Perhaps it is not surprising that the few
subjects who seemed to practice more "aggressive"
approaches to "clients" were located in movement or
movement type work and had training, if not
functional roles, as community organizers. Much of
Jacqueline's work as a union representative involves
handling the grievances and arbitrations of public
employees. But a number of years ago, Jacqueline
became involved with active solidarity work with
Central America. She was able to organize a union
committee on Central America and on peace and women's
issues. When workers come to talk with her about
grievances or other problems, she can sometimes move
them into aspects of union activity which are overtly
political.

What appears to distinguish Jacqueline's role
from other subjects seeking a radical practice is both
her organizational auspices and her particular
employers. Unlike social service agencies or
universities, many union members now accept that their
organizations will take political positions and
advocate for certain causes. More significantly, the
leftist orientation of her immediate supervisors,
including the chief local officers of the union,
permit her to spend a large amount of time on issues
many other unions would dismiss as irrelevant to day-
to-day business. In this sense, they have given her
permission (within limits) to proselytize for anti-
intervention and peace causes.

While the few subjects like Jacqueline who worked
for more radical employers, were most able to connect
their work with overt political causes, they too were
skeptical about "radical practice" and often
frustrated. Jacqueline notes the union's need to be
primarily a contract enforcer and the overwhelming
accent on the "day-to-day" makes the relevancy of
radical politics difficult:

Sure, I can do some of this (political work),

but no one's reducing my grievance work or
all the other stuff that takes 8 or more
hours a day...And then we have to be
concerned, and mostly the members are
concerned, about the day-to-day grievances.
That's the bread and butter. If you forget to
do these things, (her superiors) they'll be
voted out...These political things, the
members, if they're not opposed to them
totally, they see this as a side thing, an
extra...Labor work...is really pretty
conservative. They're afraid alot...They'll
say, 'oh this, Central America, whatever,
it's too controversial.' ...I don't totally
identify (my) whole self with this. I mean
with being a professional labor person...

Evaluating "Radical Practice"

Assessing the impact and social/political meaning
of the subjects' practice is extremely difficult. Like
Catalyst's call to support "client struggles," the
support of "radical practice" was at a high level of
abstraction and lacked clear agreement on what social
service professionals should actually do with their
clients, patients or students. If the prescription of
"practicing radical" is seen as a refusal to
participate in elitist, racist, sexist, and classist
practice, then, like "the Great Refusal" that
characterized the New Left, the subjects have strongly
followed their principles. If "radical practice" is
defined as "defensive therapy" or as a prefigurative
politics which provides a humane, egalitarian
professional relationship to clients in need of
service or students seeking education, again the
subjects have admirably carried out radical
prescriptions.

However, if "radical practice" is thought to
relate to influencing the political ideology or
behavior of client, student or even union groups,
there is less evidence of success. Most subjects, like
Monica, Brenda, and Naomi, whether working as
counselors, teachers, researchers or supervisors no
longer thought of 'radical practice' in this fashion.
While they may have chosen human service work because
of a desire to "change the world" and to radicalize
people, they no longer saw having a specific

ideological influence on people as a major part of their work roles.

Those subjects, classified earlier as "critics," who still held to a more "aggressive therapy" standard of practice in which they hoped to have some measurable influence on clients, expressed more frustration and skepticism about radical practice. Agnes and Jacqueline, for example, were keenly aware of the lack of overt politicization among their clients/members, of the lack of existing outside movements, and the strong limits of their functional roles. Since we have less comparative data about radical practice in the past decades than about workplace or community organizing, it is unclear whether "radical practice" in its more ambitious form was ever a very realizable objective, or, whether the dominant conservative political context of the 1980s has made it impossible.

Another important aspect for evaluation is to what extent these subjects, and *Catalyst* as a journal, succeeded in the goal of "developing alternative...practice models" or of transforming the practice of the profession. The difficulty here is that while many subjects had integrated into their daily work a sense of egalitarian relationships with clients/students, a non-hierarchical approach to supervision and organizations, a consciousness of race, class, and sex, these changes were also being simultaneously integrated into the established curricula of the professions themselves by the mid-1970s, particularly within Social Work. It would be theoretically unsound to compare the practice of these subjects with the "straw man" of the distant psychoanalyst or an authoritarian teacher which would be only a caricature of reality. While indeed there may be plenty of authoritarian teachers, supervisors, and therapists, and, certainly, many who are classist or racist or sexist, the general training within the social service professions changed significantly in the 1970s and 1980s.

Radicals, in other words, were dealing with a "moving target." There is much evidence that the profession of social work, if not other professions, has moved leftward in the last two decades. Social Work has moved from a primarily intrapsychic expert-client paradigm of social casework in the early 1960s to a focus on mutual "contracting" between client and worker by the 1970s, with a great deal of curriculum emphasis on the social environment including social class, race, and sex. Additionally, many professional agencies, in theory at least, also adopted (or co-opted) elements of alternative organizations to the social services. In the 1970s and 1980s, there has been a proliferation of new devolved, de-bureaucratized social agencies, which are at least stylistically more informal and non-hierarchial. This has dramatically changed the delivery of social services since the 1960s. Professional conferences are sometimes dominated by discussion of gender and women's oppression, political action strategies on behalf of the poor, strong rhetoric about oppressed minorities, and strong attacks on the New Right.

While some of the changes in the theory of social service provision and the practice of social work can be criticized for their incompleteness and even cynicism at times, the key point is that, like the coalescence of the Rank and File Movement with the Functionalist School in the late 1930s[9], *Catalyst* and individual subjects appear to have reached political maturity at the very time that social service and even mental health practice were significantly changing. Radicals in Social Work had a strong impact on these changes, particularly the criticisms made by major academic figures in the 1960s and 1970s attacking earlier paradigms of social service work[10]. In dialectical fashion, protest and social movements had by the 1970s dramatically changed the professions. Paradoxically, by the 1980s, the radical critique no longer appears very marginal in the professions since it has been somewhat integrated into current practice and curricula.

Similar changes have occurred in other professions. For example, the student movement's attacks on education, the issue of "relevancy," and the critique of "cold, distant" bureaucrats and educators has certainly led to profound changes in teaching, particularly at the university level. Within administration and supervision, the liberal disciplines like Social Work, Education, Public Health, and Nursing, for example, have developed specialties in management and administration which seek to *distinguish themselves* from M.B.A.s and other managers on the very grounds of their humanitarian tradition, sensitivity to values, and to clients' rights. Because of these important changes, it is extremely difficult to argue that the subjects actual practice strategies as counselors, administrators or educators vary so much from mainstream human service professionals as to constitute a deviant subculture or an alternative model of practice.

Many analysts of radicals in the professions fail to note the major changes in the liberal professions in the 1960s-1980s. If we look only at the activities of radicals, we leave out the other side of the equation, the professions themselves. Radicals helped change the professions, but those who remain radical now confront a somewhat more sophisticated body of knowledge and leadership.

It would appear that only at the borders of the continuum of practice do these subjects vary markedly from other sincere, humanistic social service professionals. The political imperative to support the causes of unionism, institutional reform, and social movements sometimes cause the subjects to address such issues in their practice with clients. For some subjects, the professional autonomy of the classroom or interview room allows them to raise some political issues and focus discussion on structural societal issues that impact on individual needs. However, such practice tends to be detached from overt radicalization and any overt efforts to link clients or students to leftwing groups. In the absence of this connection, the remainder of the radical practice style would appear to be insufficient to dramatically distinguish it from good social work values as they are currently defined in the most progressive of professional schools.

Notes

1.   Arthur   Maglin,"Social   Values   and Psychotherapy,"<u>Catalyst</u>, 1:3 (1979), p. 75.

2. <u>Ibid.</u>

3.   Anne   Sparks,"Radical   Therapy: A   Gestalt Perspective,"<u>Catalyst</u>, 1:1 (1978), p. 96.

4. Catalyst, 1:4 (1979), pp. 146-147 ("Letters").

5. William Caspery,"Psychotherapy and Radical Politics,"Catalyst, 2:3 (1980), pp. 27-36.

6. Maglin,"Social Values...," pp. 69-79.

7. Breines,Community Organization...

8. Ibid, pp. 6-7.

9. see Spano,Rank and File..., and Wagner,"Collective Mobility..."

10. The paradigm conflicts and resulting changes are the subject of Wagner,Ibid in which I develop the idea that leftist thinkers in social work serve as a major bridge in paradigm shifts. In the 1960s, the critical works of people connected with Mobilization for Youth in New York City including Richard Cloward, Frances Fox Piven, George Brager, and Charles Grosser, and many left-leaning groupworkers like William Schwartz had a major impact on both the psychiatric focus of the field and the development of new community organization, generalist practice, advocacy, and planning paradigms. Examples of other major changes involving radicals include the change in Social Work's Code of Ethics in 1969 to place client need above agency/employer loyalty; the forced acceptance of BSWs into the professional association in 1970 led by many on the Left; and the development of new theoretical practice models such as ecological and systems theory approaches (see Germain & Gitterman, The Life Model...; Meyer, Social Work Practice). While none of the demands of radicals or the social movements of the 1960s were, of course, ever fully met, the history of social work suggests that leftist and left-leaning segments of the profession serve as a bridge between client (poor and working class) unrest and the legitimacy of the profession. Many theorists who surfaced as important figures in the 1960s, were not always explicitly identified as leftists, but often had a history of prior association. For example, some were victims of McCarthyism in the 1940s and 1950s.

9

THE ABSORPTION OF RADICALISM

The Decline in Subjects' Militancy

This chapter will seek to analyze theoretically the apparent failure of the subjects to apply the prescriptions of *Catalyst* in their work as social service professionals, at least by the 1980s. The change in the nature of "radical professionalism" from a highly oppositional, anti-authoritarian movement in the 1960s to a somewhat more "loyal opposition" within the social services in the 1980s will be suggested to represent a "professionalization of radicalism" which allows subjects to become paid experts, occupying or seeking to occupy, "radical labor market shelters" in which radical political ideology can be maintained by employment in liberal social service (or other) settings. I will situate the apparent contradiction of the strong ideological consistency among the subjects of this study with the apparent weakening of militant activism, in terms of economic, social structural,and ideological changes which influence the possibility of radical professionalism as a social movement.

Our discussion in Chapter 7 suggested that two major goals of *Catalyst*, employee militancy, and client organizing, suffered serious declines in the last decade. At best, in recent years, subjects experienced radical prescriptions as enormously difficult to apply in their own careers as social service professionals. In general, most subjects were no longer actively engaged in employee organizing or in supporting such efforts nor were they involved with client organizing, and few expressed much recent interest in these activities when asked to describe their current lives. Our review of 'radical practice' in Chapter 8 had more ambiguities, but there was a widespread feeling of failure among many subjects about actually practicing professional work very differently from non-radicals. My own evaluation suggests that, indeed, the differences between 'radical' and 'non-radical' work on the micro-level of "practice" are at best subtle. I believe that the occupational constraints of social service careers have been greatly subversive of the political objectives of *Catalyst*, and that the difficulties subjects had in applying these objectives has probably been a major factor in the decline of *Catalyst* and other radical groups in the social services by the 1980s.

When our subjects' own comments are analyzed in conjunction with the organizational declines in the 1980s (the declining fortunes of *Catalyst* itself beginning in the 1980-81 period; the decline and disappearance of many radical professional groups in the social services like R.A.S.S.W., U.R.S.H.W., and H.S.A.N.; and the apparently similar decline in organizations among other radical professionals)[1] and the changed relationship of radical professional groups to the "mainstream" professional community (a "Popular Front" type alliance in the 1980s which primarily was aimed at combating Reaganism), it is clear that the 1980s represent a downturn in 'militant' radical professionalism as a social movement.

"Overdetermined" Views of Social Change

One sweeping conclusion made by many study participants, political activists, and many social scientists, is to simply associate the decline in militancy with the "change in the times" caused by the conservative political domination of the 1980s by Reaganism. Many also would argue that middle class or professional radicalism is reliant on social unrest and social movements extant at the lower end of the social structure for its existence. Without denying the political changes in the last two decades, it seems to me the key question is how do micro-level events (such as the movements and careers of radical social service workers) relate to macro-level events (such as the triumph of Reaganism). To simply cite the triumph of conservatism as explanatory is overly deterministic, and tells us little.

213

First, this 'explanation' fails to answer the question of how "the times" get to be "conservative" to begin with. Moreover, there are many constraints and limitations on radical professionals, but similarly there are major social constraints on the poor, the working class, Blacks and Third World populations, women, ad infinitum. We could conclude in circular fashion that in a time of political conservatism and repression, no group can afford to take militant action, therefore, blocking any possibility for social change.

Thirdly, the complete reliance on the link between social unrest by the poor and working class and professional radicalism is problematic. It denies the possibility of treating professionals (or radical students) as social actors in their own right, seeing them only as "acted upon" rather than as self-conscious actors. Further as so called 'middle class' radicalism played such a prominent role in the social movements of the 1960s and 1970s, particularly the New Left, the student movement, and women's movement, and in the original leadership of the civil rights movement, the argument fails to account for millions of participants in social movements. As we shall see, while there are strong links between social unrest at the base of society and middle class radicalism (e.g. the activism of the Depression, the civil rights movement and ghetto riots of the 1960s), there are also differences. For example, it can be argued that radical social service movements became more radical in the 1970s, at a time when militancy among the lower classes was certainly fading.

Finally, if sociological theory proposes special constraints on professionals or 'middle strata' radicals, than these constraints need to be clearly studied and specified. Otherwise, no analytic understanding is possible of how radical professionals differ from autoworkers, truckers, welfare recipients or salespeople in the manner in which the occupational structure and social movements affect their potential for radical social action.

Rather than simply consign radical professional movements to the 'conservatism of the times,' I will compare the post 1960s radical movements with the previous movement of radical professionals in the

1930s. The similarities of these two movements will suggest several key sociological variables in the rise and fall of radical social movements which this book concludes with.

The Historical Consistency of Radical Social Service Movements

Among many radicals, movements of the 1930s have often been glamourized. Obviously, great gains were made in the 1930s and several moments within the 1930s appear almost pre-revolutionary in nature. But a study of the Rank and File Movement in social work, the center of social service trade unionism and radicalism in the 1930s and early 1940s, and its associated journal *Social Work Today*, suggests far more similarities to the 1960s-1980s than differences. Jacob Fisher's conclusions about the radicalism of the 1930s in social work show similarities with the 1960s-1980s both in the relatively small numbers claimed to be "radicalized" and the difficult distinction in social work between radicals and liberals:

> Measures of the level of political consciousness, and the number of adherents each level attracted...still await development. There is some reason to believe that several hundred social workers were politically radicalized in the early 1930s. It is difficult to determine the relative contribution...of the Rank and File Movement...and...the broad influence of the swing to the left among liberal writers...[2]

It is possible that far more social service workers were radicalized in the 1960s and 1970s than Fisher's estimates of the 1930s. But more importantly, the militant period of the Rank and File Movement, despite its critical contributions to the union movement and other achievements, was quite brief.

Rick Spano's[3] history of the Rank and File Movement in social work divides its history into three periods. While indeed radicalism in social work was closely linked to the overall rise in radicalism in the early 1930s, particularly the Communist Party U.S.A., it also followed some unique and autonomous historical vectors. In the early period of a beginning radicalism, identified by Spano as 1926-1934 (the "incipient period"), considerable anger and militancy grew among social workers (as well as other professionals, such as teachers, librarians, pharmacists) who were beginning to experience widespread pay cuts and unemployment. Additionally, of course, social workers were among the first exposed to the massive immiseration caused by the Depression. In areas like N.Y.C., the relative sophistication of the workers, their Jewish ethnicity, and the beginning influence of the C.P.U.S.A. are cited by Spano as leading many social workers to Marxism. However, a review of Spano's material indicates that in this period, the radicalism of these professionals *was not aimed* at the profession. Rather social workers fought to unionize, fought along with "clients" as tenants or demonstrators themselves, and were not distinguishable as their own "social movement."

The founding of *Social Work Today* in 1934, as well as a consolidating convention that year of the many discussion groups and radical unions in social service, led to a distinguishable radical professional movement in social work. Spano locates the highpoint of this movement in the period 1934-1936. In these years, *Social Work Today* and its leaders attacked the professional leadership as failures, preached a "white collar proletarian" line, and attempted to draw the social work field to the left.

In reviewing the content as *Social Work Today*, as well as the actions of its leaders and associated unions and other groups, Spano detects a major change in the post 1936 period. The journal and its leaders began cooperating with the professional associations and established leaders in Social Work. The journal and many RFM leaders began to ally with a particular practice technique of social casework, the Functionalist School. The journal began to pay increased attention to social work practice, no longer suspecting it was merely reformist or only applying "bandaids." Strong support for the public services was a cornerstone of the groups, with a decreased criticism of social welfare as an institution. Spano attributes the major changes in the RFM as follows:

By 1936, some of the conditions that led to the emergence of the Rank and File Movement

216

were altered. Social Insurance, however meager, became a reality with the passage of the Social Security Act. The Wagner Act guaranteed labor's right to organize which was especially significant for the Rank and File Movement. Public social services, in which most rank and filers worked, were now firmly entrenched in the federal government. Thus, most rank and filers were no longer outsiders who had no investment in current social institutions, but rather an integral part of the emerging governmental response to poverty. Further, where they saw themselves as 'temporary' recruits in social work during the early 1930s, they now (saw) themselves as permanent members of social work, thus they were concerned with developing their professional skills. These factors, along with the rise of Fascism on the international level, contributed to the transformation of the Movement from a radical to a reform 'cause' model...[4]

As I have noted elsewhere[5], the movement of radical social service professionals followed a similar ebb and flow between the 1960s and 1980s. The three periods of "client centered unrest" (1965-1974 corresponding to 1926-1934); "militant professionalism" (1974-1979 corresponding to 1934-1936 for the RFM); and "absorbed radical professionalism" (1980 on corresponding to the post 1937 period of the RFM) are illustrated in Table III.

TABLE III:

STAGES OF RADICAL SOCIAL MOVEMENTS IN
THE SOCIAL SERVICES

I. Client Centered Social Unrest (Professionals as adjunctive to other Social Movements):

Time Periods: 1926-1934; 1965-1974

"Membership": Pre-professionals and clients; not organized within an actual professional structure

Ideology: Militant attacks on the profession from *outside*; struggle in the interest of *clients* is key (e.g. the early Depression battles over eviction and relief; the 1960s battles for welfare rights, community control);minimal degree of self-interest and self-consciousness as professionals; minimal concern re: "practice" as an issue; period of highest "negative class consciousness."

II. Militant Radical Professionalism:

Time Periods: 1934-1936; 1974-1980

"Membership": Young professionals (and pre-professionals) organized at the workplace and within the profession to challenge the dominant segments of the profession

Ideology: Professionals develop 'self-consciousness' of importance of professional leadership and hegemony; self-interest as workers; the critique of 'proletarianization' is key; beginning interest in 'practice' concerns; increased energy placed upon changing professional paradigms.

III. Absorbed Radical Professionalism:

Time Periods: post 1937; post 1980

"Membership": Increasing professionalized membership

in radical groups; Loss of some radicals to other professions and occupations.

Ideology: Less critical of professional leadership; open to alliances with liberals; foreign policy, defense against the right-wing and "radical practice" as key issues; decline in critique of proletarianization and decline in client organizing; radicals move toward intrinsic job satisfaction through achievement of labor market shelters and increased identification with employers.

Beginning in the mid-1960s, student and young "middle class" activists first became drawn to "new working class" theories as a political concept. But while the European theorists (Gorz, Mallet, etc.) firmly located their analysis of the white collar/professional proletariat along Marxist lines, the dominant New Left perspective used the "new working class" theory to justify viewing students as a agency for change. Since the working class appeared to many young leftists as "having sold out," new agencies for change were primary. So while the radicals-in-the-professions movement can be dated to as early as 1965 (and certainly to 1967 when S.D.S. held the first Radicals-in-the-Professions Conference), the strong militancy of the late 1960s and early 1970s were analogous to the 1926-34 period discussed above. New Left and other radical social workers strongly involved in the civil rights movement, the anti-war movement, and welfare rights organizing, mounted what was, perhaps, their most militant attacks on "professionalism." However, it was generally an attack from *outside* of the professions. That is, both the subjects interviewed in this study, and, as far as can be determined, other social work activists of the late 1960s, acted primarily in concert with and on behalf of oppressed client groups and external causes (e.g. the Vietnam War). They did not identify as professional social workers, did not join associations or read journals, and did not attempt to strategically "bore from within" the professions in an attempt to change them.

There is little indication of well-organized left opposition in social work until the 1973-74 period. It was these years that saw the development of a beginning literature on radical social work, a beginning organization of leftist groups (like RASSW in N.Y.C.) and an increase in other oppositional efforts. Like the Rank and File Movement in the 1934-1936 period, radical professionalism could not be identified as a separate social movement until it, on the one hand, associated some importance to the role of the professions in society and the importance of professionals-as-workers, and, on the other, developed its own critique, particularly linked to Marxism, which was hostile to the established professional leadership. The 1973-74 period not only represented the "growing up" of many New Left students, but most importantly included a severe economic recession followed by a severe budget crisis in state services. The subjects studied, as well as other radical social workers, began for the first time to see their own futures as threatened and their own work "proletarianized." At the same time, they saw an opportunity for increased radicalism within their own profession.

It would appear from our limited evidence: the rise and fall of many small groups of radical social workers (RASSW, URSHW, Chicago Alliance of SSW, Philadelphia Radical Human Service Workers, etc.); the decline in *Catalyst*'s membership and subscriptions; and the major change suggested in this study in the group's own oppositional activities; that this period may have ended around 1980-81. Like the post-1936 period, the Eighties has seen a continuation of some radical groups in social work and related professions, but with less of an oppositional focus. Both individual radicals and their organizations have been far more amenable to alliances with the liberal leadership in the social services; have focused on diverse areas such as practice and foreign affairs rather than on militant oppositional activity in the workplace or with clients; and, like the post-1936 *Social Work Today* leaders, many individual radical social workers have achieved significant status mobility into academia and administration.

While both movements were intimately related to societal unrest, the specific nature of the radicalism within the social service professions were dictated by the following: the youth of the movement's members, the relative low income, status, and hierarchical positions held by its members, the reality and the perception of blocked mobility of radicals, and the response of the professions' own leadership to radical demands.

The cadre of both the RFM in Social Work and the many radical social work groups of the 1960s/1970s were overwhelming young (20-30) new entrants to the field. As Spano indicates, the social workers of the early RFM had little or no conception of themselves as professionals or even as necessarily permanent employees within the welfare state. Similarly, our interviews have indicated, and they seem consistent with studies of the New Left, that the young entrants to social service type jobs were hardly careerists in the 1960s-1970s periods, were unsure of their vocational interests, but rather viewed themselves simply as "doing good." For many young leftists of the 1960s and 1970s, jobs as organizers or caseworkers were to have been a way station to other careers; while to others the lack of commitment represented an ambivalence about partaking in the "system" altogether.

In addition to youth, the RFM and the late 1960s/1970s radical social workers shared a low status, income, and power position. As Spano notes, the RFM were overwhelmingly welfare caseworkers and other low level public employees, many of whom were not even eligible for membership in the professional associations in social work at the time. While the radical social workers of the 1965-80 period were not quite as clustered in the very bottom of the income levels of social work, they again were primarily line social workers without administrative or supervisory authority and without faculty, private practice or other high status positions. Primarily they occupied jobs as public sector caseworkers or as low status child welfare, hospital, community action, or settlement house workers.

The low status position of these social workers in the 1926-1936 and 1965-1980 periods significantly confronted realities of blocked mobility. Most obviously, the Great Depression led to the first widespread left analysis of at least some professionals as "proletarian." To young social caseworkers who faced low pay, poor working conditions, and a future of little apparent advancement, self-conscious working class status was not mere rhetoric. While the economic situation of the 1960s and 1970s was quite different, at first blush for young professionals, there were similar interpretations. Even in the prosperous 1960s, there was a beginning awareness that the elite free standing professional and managerial positions which many college educated youth had trained for were both declining in number and being reduced in status. Much of the student revolt can be interpreted in this context. For example, a close reading of Kenneth

The Absorption of Radicalism

Keniston's interviews with New Left youth in 1967 indicates that these so-called "privileged" youth were well aware they faced a future in the "bureaucracy" in which a regimented 9-to-5 day awaited them[6]. Somehow unrecognized in the much of the analysis of the New Left was the fact that most of these youth would not be businesspeople or even doctors or lawyers, but relatively low level white collar, professional, and technical workers.

The oppositional militancy within the professions as expressed through unionization and specific challenges to the leadership of the professions gained particular salience after the 1973 Recession and the ensuing fiscal cutbacks in the social services. That is, the mid 1970s radicalism in social work was greatly stimulated by the economic crisis which affected the public and private social services. The interview data which suggests that subjects felt "proletarianized" in low paid positions with little future reflected to some degree an accurate assessment of the conditions for social work in the 1970s. The self-consciousness of "proletarianization" suggested the widespread feelings of blocked mobility that the "baby boom generation" confronted in their mid 20s and early 30s faced with tremendous competition in fields such as social work and teaching. For while there were jobs, those with high autonomy and prestige were highly fought over, and jobs such as low level casework or public school and community college teaching hardly fit the "baby boom" generation's image of "professional" labor.

While it is not argued that radicalism in the professions can be solely ascribed to economic conditions, I suggest that there has been a significant lack of attention to the state of professional employment markets when analyzing the radical social movements among the non-industrial working class in the U.S. While a great deal of sociological analysis utilizes data on market fluctuations to explain the trajectories of working class radicalism and trade unionism, there has been far less research in this area among professionals. Clearly one chief cause for the diminution in oppositional radical activity in the 1980s among social workers has been a revival in the ability of 'baby boom generation' professionals to advance within

223

the social services. This, of course, interacts with a process whereby frustrated and blocked professionals leave to other fields; therefore leaving behind the more professionally secure and successful, as the radicals' leadership. As indicated throughout this study, despite their own predictions, the subjects studied have achieved significant mobility, both in terms of income, and, perhaps more importantly, in terms of status, as many enter administrative, supervisory, and faculty positions as well as more autonomous clinical positions. In a similar fashion, the leadership of the RFM and *Social Work Today* achieved a fair degree of mobility as well by the late 1930s. Many of the leaders themselves became faculty members and administrators. The permanent construction of a public social service system provided increased social service positions, not only for "line" caseworkers, but for administrators and supervisors, and a significant growth in educational programs and grants to obtain degrees followed as well.

Of course, I do not argue that the mass of social workers follow the *exact* career course of the small number of subjects in our study or of the numerically small leadership of *Social Work Today* and the R.F.M. The mobility of these individuals is only indicative of improved economic conditions which did affect the followers of radical leadership. That is, while most readers of *Social Work Today* could not become academics or administrators, the general economic trends were upward for social workers in the post-1936 period. Similarly, while the readers of *Catalyst* may not follow the exact career trajectory of our subjects, the recent employment trends have been in the same direction. Moreover, in both cases, the most militant and radical leaders in the profession, would also by their mobility have had some influence on other social workers.

The radical movements described were clearly not isolated from the general direction of the 1930s movements (the Communist Party and other left-wing organizations and the activities of labor militants and unemployed councils) or the 1960s movements (civil rights, the student and anti-war movement, etc.). However, despite their boundedness by the broader social movements, there are autonomous directions which emerge in movements of professionals in the social services.

One important difference was the effect of the Popular Front on the Rank and File Movement and other radical social workers. In other social strata, such as the blue collar workforce, the Popular Front did not correspond to a downturn in militancy. While Communists and others cooperated in union organizing with established leaders, the direction of these social movements were still towards increased militancy and politicization. In the professions, or at least in social work, the movement of the 'mainstream' leaders to support some of the left agenda as well as the upward mobility of the constituency of the movements, made militancy rarer after 1936. A further reason for decreased militancy was the intent of many radicals to use their organizational positions (such as social service) as a base to do what was regarded as more important movement work (e.g. foreign affairs such as the Spanish Civil War effort).

In the 1970s, economic conditions were primarily responsible for the movement of radical professionals taking a different turn than the social movements of students, minorities, and the poor. While the early to mid-1970s saw a general decline in militant activism among significant sectors of the population (the decline of the Black movement and other Third World organizing, the virtual end of student protest, etc.) the Recession of 1973 and the state budget crises that followed, along with the growth of Marxist and other radical influences, led to increased militancy in the social services and among other radical professionals for a period of years. Obviously such militancy could not be sustained under the constraints of the occupational structure discussed throughout this study or with the decline of other social movements with which radical professionals shared commonalities (student movement, New Left, Black militancy, etc.).

These important divergences in radical professional movements in the social services are important in framing future studies of radical movements. Rather than reduce radical professionalism to only a reflection of other social movements, such movements should be treated as developing an important life of their own. The key variables limiting radical professionalism are suggested to be the political economy of the profession itself, i.e. the possible mobility available within the professional job structure; the limitations of organizational attachment; and the dominance and re-emergence of liberal paradigmatic basis for the professions.

Economic and Cohort Factors in Radicalism

I have indicated throughout this study that the perceived economic and status mobility within the professions strongly shapes the militancy of radical movements. As noted, the early 1930s caseworkers suffered deprivation, therefore having a strong self-interest, as well as an altruistic interest, in protest movements. We have noted above, that while the post 1960s period appears quite different, there were considerable fears among the large "baby boom" cohort approaching the job market in the late 1960s and early 1970s that they would not achieve the mobility they had been socialized to expect. When with the recessions of the 1970s and the fiscal crisis of public governments, their fears appeared confirmed, at least a segment of social service professionals re-developed the "proletarianization" argument of the 1930s and adopted militant anti-professional rhetoric, and sometimes engaged in militant action.

Unlike the dramatic employment gains for social workers by the late 1930s due to the growth of public welfare (and then the end of the Depression with the World War), economic changes have occurred more subtly in the 1980s. The social service cutbacks of Reagan and some economic contraction have obscured several countervailing trends. First, social service jobs have increased despite federal cutbacks. Partly, this represents state and local governments making up for federal cuts. But, as importantly, the growth of a middle class market for services (particularly the private psychotherapy market, but also the growth of employee assistance and wellness programs, the attention to drugs and alcohol and other popular services not confined to the poor) has provided new and higher status roles for social workers.

Moreover, the professional market for services is affected not only by purely economic factors, but by cohort and competitive factors. As the "baby boomers" aged, those who remained in social service acquired further human capital to advance. Our study has shown the tremendous frustration of subjects in the 1970s with low level jobs in hospitals, clinics, child welfare agencies and the like. But many of these subjects had by the 1980s become managers, supervisors, therapists or faculty members. The cohort was also aided by the departure of many people from the social service field and by a sharp drop in new entrants to social work in the early 1980s.

Hence, I suggest that while there has been no dramatic depression and recovery in the 1970-80s, important downturns in the job market have sparked militancy, while the combined effects of aging and increased acquisition of higher status positions in the 1980s has helped diminish militancy.

The Constraints of Organizational Attachment: 'Not in My Backyard' Radicalism

But in both the 1930s-1940s and 1970s-1980s, there was a further important dynamic occurring. As we have suggested throughout this book, radicals seek intrinsic job satisfaction through a "radical labor market shelter" which can meet their career needs while conforming to their idealistic views. In this effort, we find a major condition which separates radical professionals from their counterparts who are autoworkers, businesspeople or welfare recipients. As radical professionals come to locate the nature of political action in terms of a professionalized radicalism in particular organizations, certain forms of activity or advocacy are *paid for* and *sanctioned* by their employer. This professionalized radicalism produces only a certain type of limited radicalism, encouraging certain activities, but strongly discouraging others, both on and off the job.

Positions as faculty members, as therapists or supervisors in social agencies or as administrators of movement organizations, provide both a high degree of perceived autonomy *and* a forum for these subjects to become experts in functionally specific areas of radical politics. For example, James, Rosalind, and Renee, are becoming experts in homelessness; Josie identifies much of her work with the 'housing movement'; Sam and Howard have become experts in the

227

'labor movement·; Rita's current position allows her expertise in a chronic disease; Richard is becoming expert on drug abuse; and Martin on the use of self-help groups and professional models. This professionalization of radicalism does have dramatic implications for how "radicalism" is expressed and what meanings "radicalism" or even "activism" comes to have for subjects.

On the one hand, being an academic expert on homelessness or a labor movement official provides a forum for radicals to legitimately address a broad audience, often filtering in radical or even Marxist critiques of the issues at hand, and often changing the discourse within academic, labor or even public arenas of debate. However, these roles carry severe limitations which affect both on-the-job activity and off-the-job activism. These limitations often serve as only a subtext of the interviews. That is, because the subjects were generally socialized enough to their occupational roles and the expectations of what a professional career could offer, the constraints of their jobs were primarily a "seen-but-not-noticed" background for the interviews.

One key sacrifice of these positions as "program professionals" as Harold Wilensky referred to them[7] is a diminution of militancy. For example, Richard, working as a counselor and administrator at first in his interview saw no limits to his job politically:

> I haven't felt restrictions on (my) political activity from work. I still can be active, there isn't repression...

But thinking further Richard distinguishes between his ideological adherence to certain political views and his micro-level efforts to discuss radical ideas with clients or staff, and actual militant action or political behavior:

> But I suppose, yeh, if I was organizing (in employer's) backyard that would be different. Or if I was raising the banner of an overtly Marxist group. Or if I was challenging their authority directly...But, yeh, I guess as long as I hold to my radical views myself or just talk with other (staff) about them or

228

even the clients, that's Ok, as long as I'm
not challenging them (the organization)...

I suggest there is an important distinction in
the ability of radical professionals to influence
clients in the interview room, students in a class or
public audiences on a subject of major interest, and
the type of oppositional activity which *Catalyst*
suggested to its readers. The latter activity which
would "rock the boat" of the employing agencies
include direct challenges to employer authority, major
challenges to professional associations and other
bodies, the incitement of client activity in
opposition to agency policy or the association with
certain leftist political groups which would be viewed
with discomfort (or worse) by employers or even the
profession. In this sense, the liberal organizations
such as social service agencies, trade unions or
universities which employ these subjects have a strong
"not in my backyard" syndrome.

This NIMBY syndrome also affects activism outside
of work because evidence of membership in ultra-left
groups or participation in militant behavior which are
highly visible would reflect poorly on the employers.
Indeed, subjects had dissociated themselves from these
activities. Because of the self-conscious elimination
from consideration of certain militant tactics and
radical actions by our subjects, the unnoticed context
is one of a "goodness of fit" between most expressions
of radicalism on the part of the subjects and the
general political environment of the most liberal
elements of the social service community (as well as
the trade union movement). That is, professionalized
radicalism of the 1980s tends to mirror on a micro
level the Popular Front attitudes and strategies of
the 1930s and early 1940s.

For example, Sam's union can permit public calls
for different policies on Central America or on
racism, but Sam's union would not suffer open
challenges to the authority of its leadership in
contract talks. Nor if Sam publicly adhered to Marxist
or anarchist precepts (even outside of work) would
this be wise; his union does not have a good record of
tolerating overt Marxists or militant troublemakers.
Renee's position with an agency for the homeless
permits radical statements on particular issues as

well as some innovative practice and policy ventures, but the agency responds hostilely to employees who challenge the authority of its leadership, and it is unclear whether radicalism that was not functionally related to its mission would be tolerated. Rosalind's university permits autonomy in the classroom and even membership in outside groups which identify with a social work left, however, it would be clearly hostile to an implementation of left politics which challenged the school's authority over its students or employees or which challenged the basic paradigms of its teaching. Moreover, to the extent Rosalind publicly identified with a controversial ideological position, even away from the university, this also might also invite trouble.

Zald and McCarthy[8] comment on the capability of organizations, including movement based and social service organizations, to allow for a high degree of dissent and liberal to radical beliefs. Zald and McCarthy distinguish, however, between intellectual dissent and liberalism and revolutionary action:

> But dissent is not revolutionary activity and rhetoric. At the same time that modern institutions provide the opportunity for dissent, they shape and narrow the dissent. Both inside and outside the university, reform rhetoric and activity are an accepted mode. Revolutionary rhetoric rarely finds wide acceptance. Organizational attachment requires the moderation of dissent, and those intellectuals who violate this norm find themselves at odds with the very institution which allows widespread reform dissent. In this sense (C. Wright) Mills is correct: radical dissent is unlikely among organizationally attached intellectuals...[9]

I suggest that high mobility and the increased availability of movement positions as well as "mediating organizations" positions in the social services which grew out of the 1960s movements, creates an occupational culture of a markedly different kind from the early positions held by most subjects in welfare departments, psychiatric institutions or child welfare agencies. The very achievement of a modicum of ideological complementarity between employee and employer constrains militant activity. Subjects survive as radicals in the professions by tempering oppositional activities at the workplace and by avoiding external political activism which would endanger their legitimacy. It is suggested that it is not a mere fear of retaliation, though this is an important factor, but also the high absorption of time and energy by the "expert" radical roles of this population which serves to limit outside activism that is not functionally related to the subjects' area of expertise and that is not within certain bounds of political discourse permissible within the left-liberal boundary of social service work. This movement from the 1960s to 1980s is quite similar to encapsulation of militant leftists in the 1930s in the bureaucratic offices of the New Deal (T.V.A., N.L.R.A., etc.) as well as in the trade unions, social services, and academy. In a sense the conditions for an alliance with liberalism which existed for the Communist Party and other left organizations in the 1930s returned once again by the 1980s. Part of the historical decline of the conditions for an anti-professional, anti-authoritarian movement in the professions, is the successful employment of leftists in positions within the legitimating organizations of society.

The Dominance of Liberalism

The growth of the welfare state apparatus in the 1930s and again in the 1960s, along with the major paradigm shifts and structural changes within the professions accomplished in the 1930s-1940s and 1960s-1980s, are paradoxically victories for radicals and an absorption of their militancy.

Radicals criticizing social welfare and social work in 1932 would find a far different constellation of existing services and professional philosophies by 1937; similarly the attacks by radicals like Cloward and Epstein[10] in 1965 noting "social work's disengagement from the poor" would also find a different environment and structure of service ten years later. While we have stressed throughout this book the existence of mediating institutions of social welfare which absorb militancy and the changing professional curricula and paradigms which absorb radical ideas, we need to clearly locate these trends

231

in social welfare in the continued domination of liberalism as an ideology within American society.

In the 1932-1936 period and in the late 1960s and early 1970s many radicals saw liberalism as an ideology whose time had run out. Yet the drama and charisma of FDR and the New Deal changed the equation and ultimately, radicals, led by the Communist Party, saw liberals as their allies against "economic royalists" and fascists. To the Popular Front radicals (and by extension the Rank and File Movement), the welfare state and social work as a profession were allies against reactionary forces.

Because the movements of the 1960s and 1970s were less centralized and more multi-faceted than the 1930s, the political absorption has been more gradual. No one group declared or affected a "popular front." However, in retrospect liberalism's weakness seems most apparent only during the height of the Vietnam War (1967-1971) when it appeared that the legitimacy of the Democratic Party (*and* other elements of society including the professions and the social welfare apparatus) were in danger. The McGovern campaign (1972) brought many protesters back to the liberal fold albeit in defeat. While a more Marxist left emerged in the 1970s, by the time Ronald Reagan was elected in 1980, it was not only conservatism that had been triumphant, but in a sense liberalism as well. Major electoral alternatives to the New Right were severely circumscribed and gradually little independent leftist thinking came to exist apart from liberalism. The newspapers and rhetoric of not only radical professionals, but major leftwing papers such as *The Guardian*, *In These Times* or *The Militant* became focused on an anti-Reagan alliance with liberals or support for the welfare state now under considerable attack.

Like the 1930s, the conservative attack on the welfare state raised what for many of the left was the necessity of a defense of the gains of liberalism, including the services of the welfare state. Of course, in this sense, it is not surprising that radical professionals would mute their rhetoric and weaken their critique of the problems inherent in the welfare state. Moreover, radical social workers, by this time, found a profession dominated by liberals or left-liberals whose organizations were not only militantly opposed to Reaganism, but who generally had adopted some of the rhetoric of the 1960s.

While there is room for much debate as to whether either the official Popular Front strategy of the 1930s or the more implicit popular front strategies of the 1980s were wise, the net effect was the continued domination of leftwing movements by liberal visions and organizations.

Importantly the decline in oppositional militancy suggested in this book and the continued domination of liberalism over radical thinking is *not a process of co-optation* as was so bandied about by radicals in the 1960s. Co-optation implies conscious acquiescence by radicals or conscious manipulation by the system to vitiate radical movements. "Co-optation" has always been a rhetorical charge which centers on a private guilt, as if this or that person or organization 'sold out' its members.

While co-optation does occurs, what I am suggesting on a broader basis is different. As long as the economy functions and is able to absorb major cohorts (such as 'baby boom' professionals) and as long as the social welfare state in its broadest sense (including education, health, and other state apparatuses) is considered legitimate, radical militancy will be weak. There is simply no reason for disorder when the structure of capitalism is functioning. This notion is frequently applied and supported by leftists to *all classes except the middle classes*. For example, organizers and advocates all know of militant welfare recipients or poor tenants or homeless people who as they advance themselves, depart from militant or radical organizations. Frequently militant unionists or shop stewards secure promotion to management or other jobs, and leave their unions. Rather than cast about for personal guilt, the analytic observer expects these changes, as long as the social system can maintain economic and status mobility and ideological domination.

In the same vein, the radical social service professionals studied are a small example of the ability of the social system to provide a degree of mobility primarily through the organizations of the state and with it, to weaken militant attacks and postures. Radical social service activists then need not feel guilt, but should re-examine the possibilities and bases of radical professionalism and strategic prescriptions. Perhaps those who urged the emerging radicals of the late 1960s or early 1970s to "colonize" the blue collar workforce or to leave the system had some valid points[11] in that a self-conscious denial of upward mobility seemed in our study to relate to a maintenance of militancy. In any event, an honest strategic and political assessment of the conditions for radical professionalism is again in order as we approach the 1990s.

Notes:

1. Lily Hoffman's recent book, The Politics of Knowledge, Albany: SUNY Press, 1989, notes throughout her study of radical planning and medical movements, the decline of most of these groups (with the exception of trade unions) right around the 1980-1981 period, though she does not specifically analyze the decline herself.

2. Jacob Fisher, The Response of Social Work to the Depression, Boston: C.K.Hall and Company, 1980, p. 238.

3. Rick Spano, Rank and File Movement...

4. Ibid, p. 258.

5. Wagner, "Radical Movements in the Social Services..."

6. A close reading of the interviews conducted by Keniston, Young Radicals..., in 1967, suggests a relationship between the recognition of blocked mobility (careers within the bureaucratic system) and radicalism.

7. Harold Wilensky's 1956 work Intellectuals in Labor Unions, Glencoe: Ill: The Free Press, 1956, was extremely helpful to the author. It is among the few books to probe a similar problem. For 'program professionalism,' in particular, see pp. 138-140.

8. Zald and McCarthy, "Organizational Intellectuals..."

9. Ibid, p. 359.

10. Richard Cloward and Irwin Epstein,"Private Social Welfare's Disengagement from the Poor: The Case of Family Adjustment Agencies," in Meyer Zald (ed.),Social Welfare Institutions, New York: John Wiley and Sons, 1965.

11. A recent article in the *Guardian* newspaper on the group *Labor Notes*, and my own observations, suggest that leftists who "bored from within" the factories and offices to radicalize the labor movement have had somewhat more success than many other left groups since the 1960s (notably dominating some major opposition caucuses in the unions). Despite the scorn frequently lavished on those on the left in the late 1960s who advocated "joining the working class" rather than entering higher status work, a large number of prominent dissident caucuses have been developed in the labor movement, some with considerable radical influence.

However, labor radicals who have come to have an influence over the years are probably susceptible to similar critiques as radical professionals: as a general rule, they come to shed their more militant behavior the closer they have come to having actual power within the union movement.

BIBLIOGRAPHY

Ad Hoc Committee of NASW,"The Social Worker as
Advocate:Champion   of Social Victims," Social Work,
14:2 (April 1969), pp.16-22.

Adams, Paul and Freeman, Gary, "On the Political
Character of Social Service Work" Catalyst, 2:3
(1980), pp. 71-82.

Agel, Jerome, The Radical: The Radical Therapist
Collective (New York: Ballatine Books, 1971).

_____, Rough Times,(New York: Ballatine Books,
1973).

Alternative View, Radical Alliance of Social Service
Workers, Volumes 1-6, 1975-1980.

Aries, Nancy, "Small Changes, Big Changes:
Restructuring   Political Organizations for the
Eighties," Catalyst, 4:4 (1984), pp. 59-68.

Aronowitz, Stanley, False Promises, (New York: McGraw-
Hill, 1973).

_____, "Strategies for Radical Social
Change: A Symposium," Social Policy (Nov-Dec. 1970),
pp. 9-23.

Astin, Alexander, "Personal and Environmental
Determinants of Student Activism," Measurement and
Evaluation in Guidance, 1 (Fall, 1968), pp. 149-162.

Astin, Helen, "Themes and Events of Campus Unrest in
Twenty-Two Colleges and Universities,"(Bureau of
Social Science Research, Washington, D.C., 1969).

Auger, Camilla et. al., "The Nature of the Student
Movement and Radical Proposals for Change at Columbia
University," The Human Factor, 9:1 (Fall, 1969), pp.

Bibliography

18-40.

Bailey, Roy and Brake, Mike(eds)., Radical Social Work, (New York: Pantheon Books,1975).

Bell, Daniel,The Coming of Post Industrial Society,(New York: Basic Books, 1973).

Berlant,Jeffrey,Professions and Monopoly(Los Angeles: University of California, 1975).

Billingsley, Andrew,"Bureaucratic and Professional Role Orientations in Social Casework," Social Service Review, 38 (Dec. 1964), pp. 400-407.

Bisno, Herbert,"How Social Will Social Work Be?" Social Work, 1(April 1956), pp. 12-18.

Blakenship, Ralph(ed.),Colleagues in Organization: The Social Construction of Professional Work, (New York: Wiley, 1977).

Bledstein, Burton,The Culture of Professionalism, (New York: W.W.Norton, 1976).

Brager, George, and Holloway, Stephen, Changing Human Service Organizations, (New York: The Free Press, 1978).

Braungart, Richard,"Family Status, Socialization, and Student Politics: a Multivariate Analysis," American Journal of Sociology, 77:1 (July 1969), pp. 108-130.

Braverman, Harry, Labor and Monopoly Capital, (New York: Monthly Review Press, 1974).

Breines, Wini,Community and Organization in the New Left, 1962- 1968: The Great Refusal, (New York: Praeger, 1982).

Bruno, Frank,Trends in Social Work 1874-1956, (New York: Columbia University Press,1957).

Brym, Robert J.,Intellectuals and Politics, (London: George Allen and Unwin, 1980).

Bucher, Rue and Strauss,Anselm,"The Professions in Process,"American Journal of Sociology, 66(Jan. 1961),

Bibliography

pp.325-334.

Business Week, Special Issue, "Capital Crisis: The 4.5 Trillion America Needs to Grow,"September 22, 1975.

Caplow, Theodore, The Sociology of Work, (Minneapolis: University of Minnesota Press, 1954).

Carleton, Thomas,"Social Work as a Profession in Process,"The Journal of Social Welfare, 4(Spring 1977), pp. 15-25.

Carr-Saunders, A.M. and Wilson,P.A.,The Professions, (Oxford: Clarendon Press, 1933).

Caspary, William, "Psychotherapy and Radical Politics," Catalyst, 2:3 (1980), pp. 27-36.

Catalyst: A Socialist Journal of Social Services, Volumes 1-19: 1978-1986 (New York: Institute for Social Service Alternatives).

Chambers, Clarke A., Seedtime of Reform, (Minneapolis: University of Minnesota, 1963).

Clarke, J.W. and Egan, J.,"Social and Political Dimensions of Campus Political Activity,"Paper read at Florida Academy of Sciences, March, 1971, Melbourne, Florida.

Cloward, Richard, and Epstein, Irwin,"Private Social Welfare's Disengagement from the Poor: The Case of Family Adjustment Agencies,"in Meyer Zald (ed.), Social Welfare Institutions, (New York: John Wiley and Sons, 1965).

Cloward, Richard and Piven, Frances Fox,The Politics of Turmoil,(Pantheon: New York, 1974).

_____ ,"The Acquiescence of Social Work,"Society, Jan-Feb. 1977, pp. 55-65.

Cohen, Marcia & Wagner, David, "Social Work Professionalism: Myth or Reality?"in Derber, Charles,Professionals as Workers, (Boston: G.K. Hall & Co., 1982).

Corey, Lewis,The Crisis of the Middle Class, (New

Bibliography

York: Covici, Friede, 1935).

Cox, Fred, Ehrlich, John, Rothman, Jack, and Tropman, John, Strategies of Community Organization, (Itsaca, Ill.: F.E.Peacock, 1974).

Cullen, Yvonne Taylor, "An Alternative Tradition in Social Work: Bertha Capen Reynolds, 1885-1978" Catalyst, 4:3 (1983), pp. 55-74.

Derber, Charles,Professionals as Workers, (Boston:G.K. Hall & Co.: 1982).

Deutsch, Steven and Howard, John, Where it's at:Radical Perspectives in Sociology,(New York: Harper and Row, 1970).

Doress, Irvin, "A Study of a Sampling of Boston University Student Activists," Ed. D. thesis, Boston University, 1968.

Dumont, Matthew,"The Changing Face of Professionalism," Social Policy 1:1 (May-June 1970), pp. 26-31.

Durkheim, Emile,Professional Ethics and Civic Morals,(New York: Free Press, 1958).

Dykema, Christopher, "Toward a New Age of Social Services: Lessons to be Learned from our History," Catalyst, 1:1(1978), pp. 57- 75.

Edwards, Richard, M. Reich, and T. Weisskopf (eds.), The Capitalist System, (Englewood Cliffs, N.J: Prentice-Hall,1972)

Ehrenreich, Barbara and John, The American Health Empire(New York: Vintage Books, 1971).

_____,"The Professional Managerial Class," Radical America, 11:2 (March-April 1977), pp. 7-32; and "The New Left and the Professional-Managerial Class," Radical America, 11:3 (May-June 1977), pp. 7-24.

Ehrenreich, John, The Altruistic Imagination: A History of Social Work and Social Policy in the U.S, (Ithaca: Cornell University Press,1985).

Bibliography

Epstein, Irwin,"Organizational Careers, Professionalization, and Social Worker Radicalism," Social Service Review, 41:2(June 1970) pp. 123-131.

_____,Professionalization and Social-Work Activism, Ph.D. Dissertation. Columbia University. 1969.

_____"Professionalization, Professionalism, and Social Worker Radicalism," Journal of Health & Social Behavior, 11:1(March 1970),pp.67-77.

_____"Professional Role Orientation and Conflict Strategies" Social Work, 15:4(Oct.1970), pp. 87-92.

Epstein, Irwin and Conrad, Kayla,"The Empirical Limits of Social Work Professionalism,"in Hasenfeld,Y.& Sarri,R.,The Management of Human Services, (New York: Columbia University Press, 1978).

Erlich, John,"The 'Turned On' Generation: New Anti-Establishment Action Roles," Social Work, 16:5 (October 1971), pp. 22-27.

Etzioni, Amatai,The Semi-Professions and Their Organization, (New York: The Free Press, 1969).

Everson, David, "The Background of Student Support for Student Protest Activities in the University," Public Affairs Bulletin, 3:2 (Mar-April 1970), pp. 1-7.

Feldman, Kenneth and Newcomb, Theodore, The Impact of College on Students, (San Francisco: Jossey-Bass, 1969).

Fisher, Jacob, The Rank and File Movement in Social Work 1931- 1936, (New York: New York School of Social Work, 1936).

_____, The Response of Social Work to the Depression, (Boston: G.K. Hall and Company, 1980).

Flacks, Richard,"Strategies for Radical Social Change," Social Policy, 2:2(March-April 1971), pp. 7-15.

Bibliography

_____, "The Liberated Generation: An Exploration of the Roots of Student Protest," _The Journal of Social Issues_, 23:3 (July 1967), pp. 52-75.

_____, "The New Working Class and Strategies for Social Change," in Cox, Fred _et. al._,_Strategies of Community Organization_, (Itasca, Illinois: F.E.Peacock Publishers, 1974).

_____,_Youth and Social Change_, (Chicago: Rand McNally, 1971).

Flacks, Richard and Neugarten, Bernice, "The Liberated Generation: An Exploration of the Roots of Student Protest," Youth and Social Change Project, University of Chicago, 1966.

Flexner, Abraham, "Is Social Work a Profession?,"_Proceedings of the National Conference of Charities and Corrections, 1915_ (Chicago: Hildmann Printing Co., 1915), pp. 576-90.

Freedman, Marcia,_Labor Market Segments and Shelters_, (Montclair,NJ: Allanheld, Osmun, 1976).

Freidson, Elliot,"Occupational Autonomy and Labor Market Shelters"(unpublished manuscript, 1985).

_____,_The Profession of Medicine_,(New York: Harper and Row, 1970).

_____,_Professional Dominance_,(Chicago: Atherton, 1972).

_____,_The Professions and Their Prospects_,(Beverly Hills:Sage, 1973).

Freire, Paulo, _The Pedagogy of the Oppressed_, (New York: Continuum Publishing, 1984).

Freudenberg, Nick and Kohn, Sally, "The Washington Heights Health Action Project: A New Role for Social Service Workers in Community Organizing," _Catalyst_, 4:1 (1982), pp. 7-24.

Galper, Jeffrey,_The Politics of Social Services_,(Englewood Cliffs:Prentice- Hall, 1975).

Bibliography

_____ ,Social Work Practice: A Radical
Perspective, (Englewood Cliffs: Prentice-Hall, 1980).

Gamson, Z.F., Goodman, J., and Gurin, G.,"Radicals,
Moderates,   and Bystanders during a University
Protest," Paper read at the   American Sociological
Association, August, 1967, San Francisco.

Gaylin, Willard, Glasser, Ira, Marcus, Steven, and
Rothman, David,Doing Good: The Limits of Benevolence,
(New York: Pantheon, 1981).

Geller, Jesse and Howard, Gary, "Some
Sociopsychological Characteristics of Student
Political Activists," Journal of Applied Social
Psychology, 2:2 (Apr-June 1972), pp. 114-137.

Gelineau, Victor and Kantor, David, "Prosocial
Commitment among College Students," Journal of Social
Issues, 20 (October 1964), pp. 112-130.

Germain, Carel, and Gitterman, Alex, The Life Model of
Social Work Practice, (New York: Columbia University
Press, 1980).

Gerstl, Joel and Jacobs, Glenn,Professions for the
People: The   Politics of Skill,(New York:
Schenkman,1976).

Gilb, Corinne L., Hidden Hierarchies: The Professions
and Government, (New York: Harper & Row, 1967).

Gilbert, Neal and Specht, Harry,The Emergence of
Social Welfare and Social Work, (Itasca, Ill: F.E.
Peacock, 1976).

Goffman, Erving,Asylums, (New York: Anchor, 1961).

Goode, William,"Community Within a Community: The
Professions," American Sociological Review,
22(1957),pp.194- 200.

_____ ,"Encroachment,Charlatanism, and the
Emerging Professions:Psychology, Sociology and
Medicine," American Sociological Review, 25 (December
1960),pp.902-914.

Gorz,Andre, A Strategy for Labor: A Radical Proposal,

Bibliography

(Boston: Beacon, 1964).

Gouldner, Alvin, <u>The Coming Crisis of Western Sociology</u>, (New York:Avon Books, 1970).

_____ <u>The Future of the Intellectuals and the Rise of the New Class</u>, (New York: Seabury Press, 1979).

_____"The New Class Project," <u>Theory and Society</u>, 6(2), (Sept.1978).

Gramsci, Antonio, <u>Selections from the Prison Notebooks</u>, (New York: International Publishers, 1971).

Greenwood, Ernest,"The Attributes of a Profession" <u>Social Work</u>, 2 (July,1957), pp.45-55.

Grosser, Charles, <u>New Directions in Community Organization</u>, (New York: Praeger, 1976).

Gurin, Gerald, "A Study of Students in a Multiversity," Office of Education, Project 5-0901, University of Michigan, 1971.

Haan, Norma, "Further Studies in the Relationship between Activism and Morality II: Analysis of Case Deviant with Respect to the Morality-Activism Relationship," Unpublished paper, Institute for Human Development, 1969.

Haan, Norma, et. al.,"Moral Reasoning of Young Adults: Political- Social Behavior, Family Backgrounds, and Personality Correlates," <u>Journal of Personality and Social Psychology</u>, 10, (1968), pp. 183-201.

Habermas, Jurgen,<u>Toward a Rational Society</u>,(Boston: Beacon Press, 1971).

Halmos,Paul,<u>The Faith of the Counsellors</u>,(Schoken: New York, 1966).

_____,<u>The Personal Service Society</u>, (New York: Schoken,1970).

_____ (ed.),<u>Professionalization and Social Change</u>, (Keele: University of Keele, 1973).

Bibliography

_____,"Sociology and the Human Service Professions," in Freidson, Elliot,The Professions and Their Prospects (Beverly Hills: Sage, 1973).

Haug, Marie and Sussman, Marvin, "Professional Autonomy and the Revolt of the Client," Social Problems, 17 (Fall 1969), pp.153- 160.

Heist, Paul, "Intellect and Commitment: The Faces of Discontent," in Knorr, Owen and Minter, W. John (eds.),Order and Freedom on the Campus, (Boulder, Colo: Western Interstate Commission for Higher Education, 1965), pp. 61-69.

Hoffman, Lily M.,The Politics of Knowledge: Activist Movements in Medicine and Planning, (Albany: SUNY Press, 1989).

Hughes, Everett, Men and Their Work, (New York: The Free Press, 1958).

_____,"The Professions," Daedlus, 92(Fall 1963), pp. 655-668.

Illich, Ivan et.al.,Disabling Professions, (Boston: Marion Boyars, 1977).

Jackson, J. A.(ed.),The Professions and Professionalization, (New York: Cambridge University Press, 1971).

Jacoby, Russell,The Last Intellectuals, (New York: Noonday Press, 1987).

Johnson, Dale (ed.).,Class and Social Development, (Beverly Hills: Sage, 1982).

Johnson,Terence,The Professions and Power, (London: Macmillan Press,1972).

_____,"Professions in the Class Structure,"in Scase,Richard,(ed.),Industrial Society: Class, Cleavage, and Control, (New York: St. Martins,1977).

Johnston, Paul,"The Promise of Public Sector Unionism," Monthly Review, 30:4 (Sept. 1978), pp. 1-

Bibliography

17.

Kadushin, Alfred, "Prestige of Social Work: Facts and Factors," Social Work, 3 (April 1958), pp. 37-43.

Keniston, Kenneth, Young Radicals: Notes on Committed Youth, (Harcourt, Brace & World: New York, 1968).

_____ ,Radicals and Militants: An Annotated Bibliography of Empirical Research on Campus Unrest, (Lexington, Ma:D.C. Heath & Co., 1973).

Knickmeyer, Robert "A Marxist Approach to Social Work," Social Work, 17:3 (July 1972), pp. 58-65.

Larson, Magali Seffreti, The Rise of Professionalism, (Berkeley: University of California, 1977).

Lee, Porter, "Social Work: Cause and Function," Proceedings of the National Conference of Social Work, 1929, (Chicago, 1930).

Liebert, Robert, Radical and Militant Youth: A Psychoanalytic Inquiry, (New York: Praeger, 1971).

Lipset, Seymour, Rebellion in the University, (Chicago: University of Chicago Press, 1976).

Lipset, Seymour and Schwartz, Mildred,"The Politics of Professionals," in Vollmer and Mills,Professionalization, (Englewood Cliffs: Prentice-Hall,1966),pp. 299-310.

Long, Priscilla (editor),The New Left: A Collection of Essays, (Boston: Extending Horizon Books, 1969).

Lubove, Roy, The Professional Altruist: The Emergence of Social Work as a Career,(Cambridge: Harvard University Press,1965).

Lyonns, Glenn, "The Police Car Demonstrations: A Survey of Participants," in Lipset, S.M and Wolin, S. S. (eds.), The Berkeley Student Revolt: Fact and Interpretations, (New York: Doubleday, 1965).

Lynn, Kenneth,The Professions in America, (Boston: Beacon Press, 1965).

Bibliography

Maidenberg, Michael, and Meyer, Philip,"The Berkeley Rebels Five Years Later: Has Age Mellowed the Pioneer Radicals?," _Detroit Free Press_, seven part series, February 1-7, 1970.

Maglin, Arthur,"Social Values and Psychotherapy," _Catalyst_, 1:3 (1979), pp. 69-79.

Mallet, Serge,_La Nouvelle Classe Ouvriere_, (Paris:Editions Soliele, 1969).

Mankoff, Milton, "The Political Socialization of Student Radicals and Militants in the Wisconsin Student Movement during the 1960s." Ph. D. dissertation, University of Wisconsin, 1970.

Mannheim, Karl,_Ideology and Utopia_, (New York: Harcourt, Brace, 1955).

Marshall, T.H.,"The Recent History of Professionalism in Relation to Social Structure and Social Policy," _Canadian Journal of Economic and Political Science_, Aug. 1939.

Maxmen, J.S., "Medical Student Radicals: Conflict and Resolution," _American Journal of Psychiatry_, 127:9, (March 1971), pp. 131-134.

McCormick, Andrew and Minkle, Beryl, "Organizing Workers in the Contracted Human Services," _Catalyst_, 4:2 (1982), pp. 59-72.

MacKinlay, John,"Towards a Proletarianization of Physicians," in Derber, Charles,_Professionals as Workers_ (Boston: G.K. Hall & Co, 1982).

Merton, Robert, _Social Theory and Social Structure_, (Glencoe: The Free Press, 1949).

_____,et. al.,The Student Physician_, (Cambridge: Harvard University Press, 1957).

Meyer, Carol, _Social Work Practice_, Second Edition, (New York: The Free Press, 1976).

Meyer, Marshall, "Harvard Students in the Midst of Crisis," _Sociology of Education_, 44:3 (Summer 1971), pp. 245-269.

246

Bibliography

Miller, James, Democracy is in the Streets, (New York: Simon and Schuster, 1987).

Miller, Paul R., "Social Activists and Social Change: The Chicago Demonstrators," The American Journal of Psychiatry, 126 (June 1970), pp. 1752-1759.

Mills, C. Wright, "The Professional Ideology of Social Pathologists," American Journal of Sociology 49,(1943), pp. 165- 180.

_____,White Collar, (New York: Oxford University Press, 1956).

Monchek, Mark, "Drawing the Lines: My Political Education in Social Work School," Catalyst, 1:4 (1979), pp. 19-34.

Montagna, Paul, Certified Public Accounting: A Sociological View of a Profession in Change, (Houston: Scholars Books, 1974).

_____,Occupations and Society: Towards a Sociology of the Labor Market,(New York: Wiley, 1977).

Morgan, Robin (ed.), Sisterhood is Powerful, (New York: Vintage, 1970).

Morgenbesser, Mel, et. al.,"The Evolution of Three Alternative Social Service Agencies," Catalyst, 3:3 (1981), pp. 71-84.

Moynihan, Daniel P., Maximum Feasible Misunderstanding, (New York: The Free Press, 1970).

Naison, Mark, "Sports and Community Organizing: Hope for the Eighties," Catalyst, 3:3 (1981), pp. 15-22.

National Association of Social Workers, NASW Data Bank, (Silver Spring, Maryland: NASW, 1985).

_____, 1983-1984 Supplement to the Encyclopedia of Social Work, 17th Edition, (Silver Spring: NASW, 1983).

_____, Social Work Code of Ethics,

247

Bibliography

(Silver Spring, Md: NASW, 1988).

O'Connor, James, <u>The Fiscal Crisis of the State,</u> (New York: St. Martin's Press, 1973).

Oppenheimer, Martin,"The Proletarianization of the Professional,"<u>Sociological Review Monograph £20</u>,(1973).

_____,"The Unionization of the Professional," <u>Social Policy</u>, 5:1 (Jan-Feb 1975), pp. 34-40.

_____,<u>White Collar Politics</u>, (New York: Monthly Review Press, 1985).

Parsons, Talcott,"The Professions and the Social Structure," in <u>Essays in Sociological Theory</u>, (New York: Free Press,1954).

_____,"Professions,"in <u>The International Encyclopedia of the Social Sciences</u>,(New York: Macmillan, 1968), pp. 536-46.

_____, <u>The Social System</u>, (Glencoe: The Free Press, 1951).

Patry, William,"Taylorism comes to the Social Services," <u>Monthly Review</u>, 12 (1978), pp.9-23.

Paulus, G., "A Multivariate Analysis Study of Student Activist Leaders, Student Government Leaders, and Nonactivists." Ph. D. dissertation, Michigan State University, 1967.

Perrucci, Robert, "In the Service of Man: Radical Movements in the Professions,"<u>Sociological Review Monograph £20</u> (1973).

Pincus, Fred and Ehrlich, Howard, "The New University Conference: An Empirical Analysis of Former Members of an Organization of Academic Radicals." Paper given at the American Sociological Association, August 1987, Chicago.

Piven, Frances Fox and Cloward, Richard, "A Strategy to End Poverty," <u>The Nation</u>, May 2, 1966, pp. 510-17.

Bibliography

_____,Poor People's Movements, (New York: Praeger, 1978).

_____,Regulating the Poor,(New York: Vintage, 1971).

Piven, Frances Fox "Whom Does the Advocate Planner Serve?" Social Policy, 1:1, 1970, pp.32-37.

Polansky, Norman et. al., "Social Workers in Society: Results of a Sampling Study," Social Work Journal, 34 (April 1953), pp. 74-80.

Porter, Jack, "Student Protest, University Decision-making, and the Technocratic Society: The Case of ROTC." Ph. D. dissertation, Northwestern University, 1971.

Poulantzas, Nicos,Classes in Contemporary Society (London: New Left Books, 1975).

Pritchard, Colin and Taylor, Richard, Social Work: Reform or Revolution?, (London: Routeledge,1978).

Rein, Martin,"Social Work in Search of a Radical Profession,"Social Work, 15:2, (April 1970), pp. 13-28.

Reisch, Michael and Wencour, Stanley, "The Future of Community Organization in Social Work: Social Activism and the Politics of Profession Building," Social Service Review, 60 (March 1986), pp. 70-93.

Resnick, Herman and Patti, Rino, Change From Within: Humanizing Social Welfare Organizations, (Philadelphia: Temple University Press, 1980).

Ressner, Linda C., Professionalization and Social Activism. Ph. D. dissertation, Bryn Mawr School of Social Work, May 1986.

Reynolds, Bertha, An Unchartered Journey, (New York: Citadel, 1963).

Richan, Wilard and Mendelsohn, Allen, Social Work: The Unloved Profession, (New York: New Viewpoints, 1973).

Rosengard, Bob, "Subjective and Ideological

Bibliography

Impediments to Activism," <u>Catalyst</u>, 4:2 (1982), pp. 73-80.

Ross, Robert,"The New Left and the Human Service Professions,"<u>The Journal of Sociology and Social Welfare</u>, 4:5 (May 1977), pp.694-706.

Roth, Julius,"Professionalism: The Sociologists' Decoy," <u>Work and Occupations</u>, I (February 1974), pp.6-23.

Ryan, Jake and Sackrey, Charles, <u>Strangers in Paradise: Academics from the Working Class</u>, (Boston: South End Press, 1984).

Sale, Kirkpatrick, <u>S.D.S.</u>, (New York: Vintage Books, 1974).

Schorr, Alvin,"The Retreat to the Technician," <u>Social Work</u>, 4(January 1959), pp.29-34.

Schwartz, William,"Public Issues and Private Troubles: One Job for Social Work or Two?" in R. Klenk and R. Ryan (eds.),<u>The Practice of Social Work</u>, 2nd Edition, (Belmont,Ca: Wadsworth, 1974, pp. 82-99).

_____, "Bertha Reynolds as Educator," <u>Catalyst</u>, 3:3 (1981), pp. 5-14.

Sennett, Richard, and Cobb, Jonathon, <u>The Hidden Injuries of Class</u>, (New York: Vintage, 1973).

Siegal, Sheldon, <u>The Social Service Labor Force: 2000</u> (Draft Manuscript), N.A.S.W., Silver Spring, Maryland, dated 9/23/86.

Smith, M. Brewster et. al.,"Social-Psychological Aspects of Student Activism," <u>Youth and Society</u>, 1 (March 1970), pp. 261- 288.

Solomon, Fredric, "Youth and Peace: a psycho-Social Study of Student Peace Demonstrators in Washington, D.C.," <u>Journal of Social Issues</u>, 20 (October 1964), pp. 54-73.

Sommers, Robert H., "The Mainsprings of the Rebellion: A Survey of Berkeley Students in November 1964," in Lipset, S.M. and Wolin, S.S. (eds.), <u>The Berkeley</u>

Bibliography

Student Revolt: Facts and Interpretations, (New York: Doubleday, 1965).

Spano, Rick,The Rank and File Movement in Social Work, (Washington,D.C.: University Press of America, 1982).

Sparks, Anne, "Radical Therapy: A Gestalt Perspective," Catalyst, 1:1 (1978), pp. 91-99.

Specht, Harry, "The Deprofessionalization of Social Work" Social Work, 17(March 1972),pp.3-15.

Stamm, Alfred,"NASW Membership: Characteristics, Deployment, and Salaries,"Personnel Information, (National Association of Social Workers, May 1969).

Sullivan, Gail, "Cooptation of Alternative Services: The Battered Women's Movement as a Case Study," Catalyst, 4:2 (1982), pp. 39-58.

Szasz, Thomas,The Manufacture of Madness, (New York: Delta, 1970).

Todres, Rubin, "The Radicalization of Social Work Students," Unpublished paper, January, 1978.

Toren, Nina, Social Work: The Case of a Semi-Profession,(Beverly Hills: Sage, 1971).

Touraine, Alan, The Post-Industrial Society, (New York: Random House, 1971).

Useem, Michael, "Involvement in a Radical Political Movement and Patterns of Friendship: The Draft Resistance Community." Ph. D. dissertation, Harvard University, 1970.

Vollmer, Howard and Mills, Daniel (eds.),Professionalization, (Englewood Cliffs: Prentice-Hall,1966)

Wagner, David,"Collective Mobility and Fragmentation: A Model of Social Work History,"Journal of Sociology and Social Welfare, 13: 3 (Sept. 1986), pp. 657-700.

_____,"The Fate of Idealism in Social Work: Alternative Experiences of Professional

Bibliography

Careers,"Social Work, 34:5 (Sept. 1989), pp. 389-398.

_____,"Political Ideology and Professional
Careers: A Study of Radical Social Service Workers."
Ph. D. dissertation, City University of New York,
1988.

_____," The Proletarianization of Nursing in
the U.S.   1932-1946," International Journal of Health
Services,10:2 (1980), pp.271-90.

_____," Radical Movements in the Social
Services: A Theoretical Framework,"Social Service
Review, 63:2, 1989, pp. 264-84.

Wagner, David & Cohen, Marcia B.,"Social Workers,
Class, and   Professionalism,"Catalyst,1:1 (1978), pp.
25-55.

Walker, Pat (ed.),Between Labor and Capital, (Black
Rose: Montreal, 1979).

Wasserman, Harry, "The Professional Social Worker in a
Bureaucracy," Social Work, 16: 1(Jan. 1971), pp. 89-
95.

Watts, William et. al.,"Alienation and Activism in
Today's   College-Age Youth:Socialization Patterns and
Current Family   Relationships," Journal of Counseling
Psychology, 16 (Jan.   1969), pp. 1-7.

Webber, Marlene,"Abandoning Illusions: the State and
Social   Change" Catalyst, 2:2 (1980), pp. 41-66.

Westby, David, "The Alienation of Generations and
Status   Politics: Alternative Explanations of Student
Political   Activism," in Sigel, Roberta(ed.), Learning
about Politics, (New   York: Random House, 1970).

Wilensky, Harold, Intellectuals   in   Labor
Unions,(Glencoe,   Ill.:The Free Press, 1956).

_____"The Professionalization of Everyone?"
American   Journal of Sociology, 70 (Sept. 1964),
pp.137-158.

Wineman, Steven, The Politics of Human Services,
(Boston: South End Press, 1984).

Bibliography

Withorn, Ann, "Beyond Realism: Fighting for Human Services in the Eighties," <u>Catalyst</u>, 4:2 (1982), pp. 21-38.

_____, <u>Serving the People: Social Services and Social Change</u>, (New York:Columbia University Press,1984).

_____,"Surviving as a Radical Service Worker: Lessons from the History of Movement Provided Services," <u>Radical America</u>, 12 (July/August 1978), pp. 9-23.

Wood, James, "The Role of Radical Political Consciousness in Student Political Activism: A Preliminary Analysis," Paper read at the American Sociological Association, September, 1971, Denver, Co.

Wright, Erik Olin,"Class and Occupation,"<u>Theory and Society</u>, 9 (1980), pp. 177-214.

_____,"Varieties of Marxist Conceptions of Class Structure,"<u>Politics and Society</u>, 9 (1980), pp. 323-370.

Zald, Meyer and McCarthy, John D., "Organizational Intellectuals and the Criticism of Society," <u>Social Service Review</u>, 46 (1975), pp. 344-362.

INDEX

Index

Index

ABOUT THE AUTHOR

DAVID WAGNER is an assistant professor of social welfare at the University of Southern Maine. He holds Masters degrees in Social Work (Columbia University), Labor Studies (University of Massachusetts) and a Ph. D. from the City University of New York in Sociology. Dr. Wagner has published articles in numerous journals including *Social Work*, *Social Service Review*, *The International Journal of Health Services*, *Contemporary Drug Problems*, *Catalyst*, and the *Journal of Sociology and Social Welfare*.